WORKING WITH PRAGMATICS

DEDICATION

We should like to dedicate this book to the memory of our friend and inspirational colleague, Jenny Eastwood, and to Wenda and Andy Andersen.

WORKING WITH PRAGMATICS

A PRACTICAL GUIDE TO PROMOTING COMMUNICATIVE CONFIDENCE

LUCIE ANDERSEN-WOOD
& BENITA RAE SMITH

Speechmark Publishing Ltd

Published by
Speechmark Publishing Ltd, 70 Alston Drive, Bradwell Abbey,
Milton Keynes MK13 9HG, United Kingdom
Tel: +44 (0)1908 326 944   Fax: +44 (0)1908 326 960
www.speechmark.net

© L Anderson-Wood & BR Smith, 1997
Reprinted 1999, 2000, 2001, 2005, 2008

All rights reserved. The whole of this work including all text and illustrations is protected by copyright. No part of it may be copied, altered, adapted or otherwise exploited in any way without express prior permission, unless in accordance with the provisions of the Copyright Designs and Patents Act 1988 or in order to photocopy or make duplicating masters of those pages so indicated, without alteration and including copyright notices, for the express purposes of instruction and examination. No parts of this work may otherwise be loaded, stored, manipulated, reproduced or transmitted in any form or by any means, electronic or mechanical, including photocopying and recording, or by any information, storage and retrieval system without prior written permission from the publisher, on behalf of the copyright owners.

002-1943/Printed in the United Kingdom/1030

British Library Cataloguing in Publication Data
Anderson-Wood, Lucie
Working with Pragmatics: A Practical Guide to Promoting Communicative Confidence
1. Pragmatics
I. Title   II. Smith, Benita, Rae, 1934-
306.4'4

ISBN 978 0 86388 401 6

Contents

FOREWORD
vii

PREFACE
ix

Chapter 1
INTRODUCTION TO PRAGMATICS
1

Chapter 2
THEORETICAL APPROACHES TO PRAGMATICS
5

Chapter 3
PRAGMATIC DEVELOPMENT
15

Chapter 4
PRAGMATIC DYSFUNCTION
27

Chapter 5
INTRODUCTION TO THE ASSESSMENT OF PRAGMATICS
37

Chapter 6
INFORMAL ASSESSMENT
47

Chapter 7
PRINCIPLES OF INTERVENTION
63

Chapter 8
BASIC INTERVENTION & TRAINING
75

Chapter 9
FACILITATION & TEACHING
91

Chapter 10
SPECIFIC CLIENT GROUPS & SPECIFIC PRAGMATIC DIFFICULTIES
125

Appendix I
ANNOTATED BIBLIOGRAPHY
135

Appendix II
CLIENT-CENTRED ASSESSMENT
141

Appendix III
CHILD INFORMATION SHEET
144

Appendix IV
CLIENT INFORMATION SHEET
145

BIBLIOGRAPHY
146

INDEX
160

Lucie Andersen-Wood qualified as a speech and language therapist in 1984. She is currently a researcher at the Institute of Psychiatry, University of London, England.

Benita Rae Smith has worked as a speech and language therapist since 1958 and from 1971 she has also taught student clinicians in Leicester, England.

Lucie and Rae have both worked as senior lecturers in speech pathology at De Montfort University, Leicester, England and have been tutors on the University of Birmingham, School of Education distance learning course in speech and language difficulties.

EDITOR'S NOTE
This text uses 'he' and 'she' for the sake of clarity alone.

FOREWORD

I am delighted that this book has been written; it fills a gap that has long needed filling and will give an excellent basis for us to move forward in working with pragmatics. In 1983 we heard about the 'pragmatics revolution' (**Lund & Duchan**), and thought that this would change our approach to therapy. In fact, it has proved more difficult than anticipated (**Gallagher**, 1991) to move towards working therapeutically in a way that involves everyday communication in real contexts. Working with pragmatics requires a total approach to clients and therapy which involves working via the relationship to make communication meaningful and effective — it is not simply a matter of providing games and exercises. Approaching therapy in this way overcomes some of the problems with generalization which can be encountered in other approaches to therapy.

This book is exciting in that it encourages therapists to work in situations that create the desire and need to communicate. It suggests the importance of sharing power in the therapeutic relationship to allow clients sometimes to take the lead, creating a more balanced relationship. I like the emphasis on the two-way process of communication, that both partners are responsible for making an interaction work and that it's not just the 'problem' of the client. It is refreshing to see discussion of the fact that it may be necessary to accept limitations and that finding ways of communicating in spite of these may be the challenge.

This book will give encouragement to therapists to work in new ways and for those who have already started there is guidance for developing practice and encouragement to do research.

What is needed is more research into the efficacy of pragmatic approaches to therapy and it is essential if we are to progress our work, to make a well argued case for working with pragmatics.

It makes such good sense to work in a way that enables people to communicate more effectively with therapy using real communication in natural contexts; we need to build a body of research that will help us to move forward with knowledge.

This book gives us an excellent basis for developing our skills and confidence in working with pragmatics.

Susie Summers, City University, UK
April 1997

ACKNOWLEDGEMENTS

We wish to thank firstly Eeva Leinonen for her generous support and earlier work, without which this would be a very different book. Helpful criticism and encouragement were also received from Francis Bowdery, Kay Coombes, Margaret Davison, Judy Dunn, the late Jenny Eastwood, Katrin Hahn, Anne Harding, Lisa Keaveney, Debbie Kerbel, Rebecca Lander, Wendy Philips, Mike Rutter and Kate Smith.

We should also like to thank Stephanie Martin and Sue Christelow of Winslow Press, for being extremely patient and encouraging during all stages of writing *Working with Pragmatics,* and the proofreader, Valerie Mendes. We take full responsibility for the content of *Working with Pragmatics*.

Lastly but most essentially to our partners Mike and Colin, who somehow managed to remain supportive throughout the years of preparation of *Working with Pragmatics*.

PREFACE

Working with Pragmatics was written for a combination of reasons. First, we have both felt frustration at not seeing theory becoming accepted and integrated within practice. In particular, research literature in the area of early development of social relationships (**Bruner**, 1975; **Kaye & Charney**, 1980; **Stern**, 1974 and 1981; **Stern** *et al* 1975; **Fogel**, 1977 and 1993; **Fogel & Thelen**, 1987; **Snow**, 1984; **Bates**, 1974, 1976a and 1976b) has influenced our thinking and our approach to clinical work. Our experience suggests that the naturalistic, enjoyable interactions that form the basis of early development of communication are something that should be incorporated into the speech and language therapist's or teacher's range of options when choosing intervention strategies to work with clients with a pragmatic impairment. We have been excited by research findings supporting a naturalistic approach (**Fey**, 1986; **Fey & Leonard**, 1983) and are hoping that this book will support therapists who use naturalistic approaches by helping them to feel confident that they have made an appropriate, scientifically sound decision. We are also hoping that our book will encourage students embarking on training and those therapists trained in a school emphasizing more traditional linguistic approaches to experiment with a wider range of intervention approaches.

Second, our experiences training and working in the USA allowed us to use a wide range of intervention approaches for clients with pragmatic impairments. Lucie's work as a speech pathologist in the USA has led to her belief in early intervention and the power of training those who know clients best and who spend most time with them: families and other caregivers. She has been particularly influenced by the work of **MacDonald & Gillette** (1986) and **Fey** (1986) who have highlighted the importance of empowering families and caregivers with the knowledge and skills necessary to help clients. Rae's work as a clinician in Essex and Derbyshire encouraged her to make use of clients' own personal resources, empowering them to become active learners. We feel that our approaches differ in some respects from current practice and would like to share what we have learnt with students and colleagues.

Third, *Working with Pragmatics* was written through our experiences as tutors on a speech and language therapy course where we felt frustrated with the lack of an accessible sourcebook for teachers and clinicians working with child and adult clients who had difficulties in interacting with others. When preparing courses on pragmatics, we could find no book written at an appropriate level for students and practitioners who needed to have a grounding or refresher in theory and ideas for the practice of working with a range of clients with pragmatic difficulties.

Finally, another factor that prompted us to write this book was the lack of attention paid to preventive intervention. In *Working with Pragmatics* we suggest several indirect intervention approaches, such as training teachers and parents, that could be used for all pupils in nursery classes and with children who are considered to be 'at risk' of developing communication or developmental disorders or delays.

In addition to these shared reasons that contributed to the impetus to write *Working with Pragmatics,* Rae found that, after writing *Clinical Pragmatics* with Eeva Leinonen, it became clear that the length of the book would not allow specific approaches and techniques to be dealt with adequately. It was felt that a separate volume on practical clinical intervention would allow many of the issues left untouched in *Clinical Pragmatics* to be investigated in more depth. This book is our attempt to cover some of these issues in a way that will be useful to students, clinicians and other professionals.

LUCIE ANDERSEN-WOOD & BENITA RAE SMITH

CHAPTER 1
INTRODUCTION TO PRAGMATICS

Introduction/2
What is Pragmatics?/2
Why is Pragmatics Important?/2
Summary/3
Recommended Reading/3

CHAPTER 1
INTRODUCTION TO PRAGMATICS

Introduction

This chapter will introduce the area of pragmatics and discuss its importance for developing an understanding of communication. The emergence of the field of pragmatics will be mentioned briefly and current approaches will be introduced in this chapter but expanded upon in Chapter 2.

What is Pragmatics?

Pragmatics is a topic that is given many different definitions by clinicians and researchers. They include the following:

> Among other things, it includes how speakers use utterances to make requests, promises and threats; how utterances differ in the degree to which they are polite; how the structure of utterances allows speakers to background some information while foregrounding other information. In fact it [pragmatics] covers all the ways in which the grammar serves the needs of speakers as social human beings. (**Foster**, 1990, pages 6–7)

> Language development in the context and environment in which it is generated. (**Nicolski, Harryman & Kresheck**, 1989, page 207)

> The study of how expressions of meaning by humans gain significance in context and use. (**Smith & Leinonen**, 1992, page 27)

> Rules governing the use of language in context. (**Bates**, 1976a)

> The relationship existing between signs and their human users. (**Morris**, 1946)

> The study of meaning in relation to speech situations. (**Leech**, 1982, page 6)

Why is Pragmatics Important?

There are many reasons why pragmatics is an important focus for communication and why neglect of pragmatics can be damaging for the communicative success of individuals with communicative difficulties.

1. **Pragmatics is important for successful social development.** The social penalties attached to pragmatic impairment restrict interaction and thus impede future development by restricting people's opportunities for experimentation and learning.

2. **Pragmatics is important because it develops early in the developmental progression**. There are strong arguments for the priority of pragmatics assessment over other areas of speech and language therapy assessment. Developmentally, pragmatics precedes the acquisition of speech and language, while in the adult and older child pragmatic knowledge, confidence and skill underpin the personal and communicative uses of language in all its forms (spoken, written and signed).

3. **Pragmatics is important in assisting generalization.** Generalization of skills in both children and adults cannot be taken for granted (**Hughes**, 1985; **Rosenbeck, LaPointe & Wertz**, 1989; **Leith**, 1984). Generalization may not occur or may be of limited range when intervention focuses exclusively on the form of language. Clients who are offered assessment and intervention only in the areas of grammar and phonology all too often restrict their use of newly acquired speech and language skill to the situation in which these were taught. (See **Leonard**, 1981, for a wide-ranging review of the research on this issue.) Since what clients actually need is improved communication in real life, there is a need to identify what assists generalization. Pragmatics-based, that is communication-based, therapy aims to improve the client's knowledge of speech

and language use and to teach skills within appropriate contexts. All types of speech and language difficulty can be treated in this way; however, it seems especially appropriate when the client's difficulties lie mainly within the area of semantics (word and sentence meanings that are 'fixed' in the native language) or pragmatics (real-life use and comprehension of flexible meanings). We suspect that further scientific investigation of the effectiveness of treatment approaches will reveal that combinations of skills-based and communication-based approaches will provide the optimum form of treatment for many types of communication difficulty. Our proposal is that treatment effectiveness should always be judged on the basis of how clients perform in non-clinical settings.

4 **Inclusion of a pragmatic approach in intervention is important as it may prevent problems with later educational performance.** Schools sometimes report that children with apparently resolved speech and language problems fail to develop as expected in later stages of education (**Klein,** 1985). This may possibly be due to the children's difficulty with using what they have learnt or because underlying pragmatically based difficulties were not diagnosed early on and remained undetected and untreated.

5 **A pragmatic approach is important in intervention as it provides opportunities to work on building communicative confidence.** People with a history of speech and language difficulties have been reported to be lacking in communicative confidence (**Steckol,** 1983; **Donahue,** 1987). Addressing communicative confidence may provide a buffer for those whose repeated failures have eroded self-esteem and reduced the enjoyment of interaction. Persisting lack of confidence is evident to many teachers and parents. **Baginsky** (1991) conducted a survey of the post-school education and employment of pupils from British special schools for those with speech and language disorders. Despite being invited to do so, all but one of the 87 ex-pupils involved failed to respond personally. Response was left to parents, employment officers and education staff. This must indicate either that parents did not inform their children that their views were being sought, or that the young people did not wish or feel able to contribute.

6 **Pragmatics is important for addressing the assertiveness of communicatively impaired children.** AFASIC (Association for All Speech Impaired Children, UK) has also become aware of the lack of assertiveness and self-esteem in communicatively impaired children (personal communication, AFASIC, 1995). The association suggests that these children expect to have little impact on events. It is therefore valuable to investigate clients' assertiveness and to consider in what situations they may feel that they can or cannot influence other people or events (see pages 121–2 on assertiveness).

Summary

This chapter has investigated the field of pragmatics and why it is such an important one. The range of definitions presented at the beginning of the chapter highlights the various perspectives of different writers on the field of pragmatics and underlines the fact that pragmatics is an area still in its infancy as far as theoretical models and applications for practice are concerned. The next chapter will expand on this introduction to pragmatics by examining a range of theoretical approaches to communication development and intervention including pragmatic approaches.

Recommended Reading

McTear M & Conti-Ramsden G, *Pragmatic Disability in Children,* (Whurr, London, 1992) and **Smith BR & Leinonen E,** *Clinical Pragmatics: Unravelling the Complexities of Communicative Failure* (Chapman & Hall, London, 1992) cover most of the topics in this book and are recommended to those seeking in-depth coverage.

An older text which is familiar to many clinicians and which will provide useful starting-points for readers new to the area is **Gallagher TM & Prutting CA** (eds), *Pragmatic Assessment and Intervention Issues in Language,* (College Hill Press, San Diego, 1983).

We recommend the following journals that

carry accessible articles on pragmatics and speech pathology:

Topics in Language Disorders, ASPEN, Swets Publishing Service, PO Box 825, 2160SZ Lisse, Netherlands.

Seminars in Speech and Language, Thieme Medical Publishers Inc, 381 Park Avenue South, New York, 10016, USA.

Child Language Teaching and Therapy, CLTT, Turpin Distribution Services Ltd, Blackhorse Road, Letchworth, Hertfordshire SG6 1HN, UK.

CHAPTER 2
THEORETICAL APPROACHES TO PRAGMATICS

Introduction/*6*
Social Learning and Interactional Approaches/*6*
Pragmatic Approaches/*7*
    Functional or Intentional Communication (Speech Acts)/*7*
    Conversational Management/*9*
    Presuppositional Knowledge/*12*
Summary/*13*
Recommended Reading/*13*

Chapter 2
Theoretical Approaches to Pragmatics

Introduction

Pragmatics as a theoretical area is in its infancy and has developed from the diverse fields of proxemics (the study of spatial positioning in communication), psychology, linguistics, sociology, philosophy, education and speech pathology. The theoretical ideas on which *Working with Pragmatics* is based come from these fields.

Social Learning and Interactional Approaches

Two approaches that have played a significant part in the evolution of pragmatic theory are approaches based on social learning theories (**Vygotsky**, 1962; **Halliday**, 1975) and interactional approaches (**Ainsworth,** 1974; **Bruner**, 1975, 1978, 1981, 1983, 1986; **Blurton-Jones**, 1972; **Brazelton**, 1982; **Kaye**, 1982; **Fogel & Thelen**, 1987; **Schaffer**, 1977).

Social learning theorists have suggested theories of child development that give centrality to the social and cultural environment of the child in acquiring meanings. Vygotsky has played a role in heightening awareness of the social, rather than the purely cognitive and syntactical, use of language. In social learning theory approaches, language is viewed as being acquired through the observation of modelled events and outcomes. The child observes, connects and then deduces the rules and implications for future social functioning.

With regard to intervention, the following points are emphasized:

▶ It is important for children to learn from someone with whom they have a motivating social relationship.
▶ The clinician's role is to model communication and to motivate the client to experiment with language forms.
▶ Goals should be chosen that are within the client's capabilities from the point of view of attention, retention and motor reproduction. Thus the child is able to become a creative user of the forms and rules that he has observed. **Vygotsky** (1962) described this as working at the 'zone of proximal development' (ZPD), that is, at the point where a child is just able to make further progress if assisted by an adult.

Researchers taking an *interactional* perspective suggest that children learn language through reciprocal interaction with their significant others. During the early stages of development, infants and their caregivers can be seen to alternate between bursts of non-verbal activity (such as kicking, arm waving and vocalizing) and pauses which provide an opportunity for the partner to be active. This apparently natural behaviour forms the basis for communicative interaction (**Schaffer**, 1977; **Kaye**, 1982; **Bruner**, 1983; **Brazelton**, 1982; **Stern**, 1981). During interactions one partner can be seen to ***initiate*** the exchange and the other to ***respond***. Ideally, there is a balance in the frequency with which partners make use of these two behaviours, though different circumstances alter this balance in acceptable ways. A third type of behaviour which can be observed during interactions is the ***response/initiation*** (R/I). This is a type of response which serves to carry the interaction forward by initiating further talk (**McTear**, 1984), such as 'No, I didn't. Did you?' or 'What do you mean?' Furthermore, interactional theorists suggest that the various areas of language, conceptual and social development interact with one another to turn the child into an effective communicator through experience.

The interactionist approach suggests some basic but easily overlooked ideas for intervention:

▶ Caregivers are important and should be involved in intervention.
▶ A conversational approach with enjoyable joint activities is the preferred medium for therapy with young children (and those who are developmentally delayed).
▶ In order to teach conversation, clinicians need to allow clients to take an active role in interaction for at least part of the time.
▶ As clients gain confidence, it is important to establish a reasonable ***balance of dominance*** in conversational situations. Clinicians may sometimes hold more power than clients, but need not use it to

dominate. Clients who themselves tend to dominate can be encouraged to share the responsibility for communication more equally.
▶ This approach highlights the importance of providing sufficiently varied communicative and social experiences for the child.

Pragmatic Approaches

Currently there is no single theory of pragmatics that is widely accepted within the scientific community. Pragmatics has sometimes been brushed aside as 'unscientific' because it deals with complex and subjective communicative experience. Indeed, it was at one time regarded simply as a 'dustbin' into which scientific investigators of language should sweep those matters which impeded proper investigation of linguistic phenomena. It is viewed here as **the study of the social use of language.** As such it places an emphasis on the ***functions*** of communication rather than the ***forms*** of language. Pragmatics is concerned with unpredictable utterances (for example, 'It had always been going to happen', 'The door is alarmed', 'Him go gee gee') and with real people in real situations applying rules that are sometimes difficult to identify.

Present-day pragmatics encompasses everything that goes on externally in the course of human communication, as well as much of what goes on in the minds of the participants. It concerns the outward behaviours which are used in the process of sharing thoughts and feelings and also the internal knowledge and processes involved in 'making sense'. Making sense can be a purely internal process, as when one muses to oneself about the meaning of life and experience. At other times, it is a two-way matter involving interpretation of the thoughts and intentions of others and using appropriate behaviours to fit both the circumstances and their intentions.

We discuss below pragmatics in three interrelated areas, based on **Roth & Spekman's** (1984a and 1984b) organizational framework: (1) Functional or Intentional Communication (Speech Acts) (2) Conversational Management and (3) Presuppositional Knowledge. We will present information relevant to each of these three areas in turn and indicate after each topic the relevance of the theoretical ideas presented for intervention with clients with pragmatic difficulties.

Functional or Intentional Communication (Speech Acts)

Being communicatively competent involves being able to achieve one's personal goals by means of expressing communicative intents and correctly interpreting the intents of others. This is known within pragmatics as successfully performing and comprehending 'speech acts'. **Searle** (1975a and 1975b) argues that a 'speech act' is the most basic unit of language. He suggests that the speech act, rather than a sentence or a word, should be viewed as the simplest unit. The philosophers **Austin** (1963) and **Searle** (1969) discuss the proposition that, when words are uttered, speakers and listeners, between them, create a meaning beyond that of the words themselves. This meaning ensures that ***something has been done*** by the utterance. 'Doing things with words' may be formal, as in 'marrying', 'sentencing' or 'introducing', or it may be informal. Informal speech acts, in which the participants have to guess, or decide between them, what has been ***done*** constitute the bulk of human exchanges. Some examples of the type of acts (communicative functions) that can be performed informally with words are greeting, requesting, informing, suggesting, persuading, explaining, denying, complaining and deceiving.

It is suggested (**Searle**, 1975a and 1975b) that every speech act consists of the following three components:

1 ***The speaker's intention,*** sometimes called the illocutionary force: for example, the wolf intends to ensnare Red Riding Hood by ingratiating himself and discovering where she is headed.

2 The ***utterance*** itself, called the locutionary aspect: for example, the wolf's actual words, "Hello, little girl. Where are you going this fine morning? Shall I carry your basket?"

3 The ***effect*** on the listener, or perlocutionary force: for example, Red Riding Hood is taken in, just as the wolf intended. She construes the utterance on a superficial level as a friendly greeting, thus completing the speech act to the wolf's satisfaction but to her own cost.

A different listener, Red Riding Hood's mother, for instance, who warned her daughter to speak to no-one, would have produced a different perlocutionary effect because she would have interpreted the wolf's meaning or intention differently. It can be seen, then, that it takes more than one person to complete a speech act, though of course an act may be originated or attempted by a single individual.

The success or failure of speech acts depend on the co-operativeness with which the parties involved play the 'communication guessing game'. It also depends on the ability of the act's originator to weigh up the suitability of the circumstances for the fulfilment of their intention. For instance, the conditions for the wolf's deceitful purposes would not have been present if mother, father and daughter had been walking together in the forest. Judging when so-called 'felicity conditions' (**Grice**, 1975 and 1978; **Searle**, 1975a and 1975b) exist, that is when circumstances are suitable for the fulfilment of intentions, is an important part of being a successful communicator. It is also something which children have to learn to do.

Another part of being a successful communicator is noticing what other people are attempting and then responding in a suitable way, for one's own purposes as well as, possibly, for their communicative partner. The *performance* and *interpretation* of speech acts is a pragmatic skill which depends on one's ability to pursue personal goals and to co-operate with others by *integrating* knowledge of the world, social knowledge and communicative knowledge (linguistic and non-verbal) with one's analysis of the context and one's relationship to the people present.

It should be noted that non-vocal behaviour can constitute a 'speech act' in the theoretical sense. For example, sign-language or a communication aid can be used to perform most types of act (communicative function) that can be accomplished by an utterance. Also most people make use of non-verbal means to perform 'speech acts' from time to time, for instance when they beckon (calling), shake their heads (refusing or denying) or raise a finger (threatening or warning).

Indirect speech acts

Speech acts are sometimes performed indirectly. For example: "I wonder who broke that cup?" (these words might represent simple 'self-questioning' or might serve as an indirect 'accusation'); or "Can you tell me the time?" (this is a request for information, but about the time, not about the ability of the listener to tell it). Performing and interpreting these indirect acts is partly a matter of knowing the words, idioms and conventions of one's own language and culture, and partly a matter of using other types of knowledge in order to guess what is intended.

In communication people need to be able to take on the roles of speaker and listener. These two roles could also be labelled 'originators'/'interpreters'. During dyadic (two-person) interaction, one person originates an initiation (directly this time): for example, "Who broke the cup?" (speech act = 'request information'). The second person originates a response, having interpreted the initiation: for example, "Me" (speech act = 'confess' or 'supply information').

As we hope to have shown, these behaviours involve the *integration* of a great deal of information in order to select the appropriate words and say them in the appropriate way at the appropriate moment. What is called for is not only linguistic and world knowledge (knowledge of aspects of the world such as relationships, customs, objects and events) but an appreciation of the 'felicity conditions' (suitable circumstances) in which a wide variety of speech acts might be successfully performed.

In order to design and perform one's own speech act successfully, one has to interpret the language, body language, proximity, prosody (rhythm, quality, volume, intonation, stress), facial expression and, if possible, the intention of one's partner. One has to analyse every aspect of the various contexts of the communication (linguistic, physical, personal) and to be aware of the social issues such as territory (one does not demand chocolate biscuits in someone else's house) and status (one does not interrupt the head teacher at school). All this has to happen before one's own contribution is even begun. Small wonder, then, that people who lack social experience make pragmatic errors and experience difficulty in negotiating successfully with their communicative partners.

The relevance to intervention of the foregoing may be summarized thus:

▶ All clients need to be able to contribute to the successful performance of speech acts, either as 'speakers' (including non-verbal contributors) or as 'listeners' (including watchers). They therefore need opportunities to practise doing so in supportive and stimulating circumstances. This can only happen spontaneously in relatively unstructured interactions where communication rather than language forms the focus of therapy.

▶ For the impaired or inexperienced person, the complexity of speech act interpretation and performance can be artificially reduced by clinicians providing communicative support. However, the eventual aim of treatment must be geared to reality, which is unavoidably complex.

▶ Clients can at times get into difficulties with personal relationships as a result of inadequate speech act performance. Misinterpretation of the speech acts and intentions of others can also cause problems. These misunderstandings are not limited to clinical populations. At an international level, politicians and diplomats can play a role in conflict resolution. In the workplace arbitration services can assist the negotiation of agreements between workers and management. On a more local level, marriage guidance counsellors can help couples to communicate more easily with each other.

Co-operative principle

Grice (1975) proposed that speakers co-operate with one another for the performance of speech acts. He also proposed four maxims for their successful completion:

1. *The maxim of quantity*: speakers should give as much information as is needed, and no more.
2. *The maxim of quality*: speakers should be sincere and say what they have evidence for or what they believe to be true.
3. *The maxim of relation*: speakers should try to be relevant to something which is already in the mind of the listener, or has recently been under discussion.
4. *The maxim of manner*: speakers should try to be succinct and orderly and to avoid ambiguity.

Fairly obvious problems exist with some of the maxims in real contexts. The maxim of relation ('be relevant') however is less easy to criticize and is currently at the centre of much theoretical work.

The maxims do provide some qualified suggestions for treatment and assessment: the maxim of relation (or relatedness) is clearly important as it helps the speaker to 'make sense'. What is said frequently relies on the thought processes of listeners for its effect. Speakers know, unconsciously, that they can rely on listeners and design their own contribution in the light of this knowledge. For example, pronouns and elliptical remarks take account of what listeners can be expected to supply in the way of grammatical components:

Polly: Where is it [the book we need]?
Jenny: [The book we need is] On my top shelf.

Many other communicative effects depend on similar *co-operative constructions* between conversational partners. Listeners have to know what to supply; speakers have to know what listeners are likely to know already.

Dore (1979) proposed a system for describing the different functions that communication can serve in the communication of pre-school children. His system, adapted by **Andersen** (1989), is presented in Table 1.

Conversational Management

Contextual influence

Communications take place within a context of some kind and it is that context which gives them their particular meaning on any given occasion. Pragmatics deals specifically with communication in context, whereas the rest of linguistics deals with the components and systems of language itself. An example may help to clarify how several different types of context operate to give words their meaning:

Ann and Mary are two school friends who meet at the school gate just before an examination. Ann says to Mary, "I'm really looking forward to this!" Mary replies, "Not half as much as me." Gritting their teeth, they both walk into school.

▶ The linguistic context for Mary's reply is created by Ann's statement.
▶ The environmental context for an informal interaction is provided by their being outside the school and well away from the exam room.
▶ The temporal context is provided by its being exam day, but not quite yet exam time.
▶ The personal context of an established relationship enables them to speak ironically for mutual comfort.

Who is speaking to whom, when, where and for what purpose (together with what has already been said) determines what it would be appropriate to say next and in what style it can be said. These factors also determine how what is said should be interpreted. The relevance of this as regards therapy is that clients need to be able to tailor their communications to any context in order to contribute appropriately. This is done by analysing the context as well as the utterances of communicative partners. In order to become able to do this, some clients require

Intent	Types	Example
Requests	Request information: yes/no questions	*Do you like apples?*
	Request information: 'Wh—' questions (Who, what, where, when, why?)	*What are you doing?*
	Request action or object	*Ball throw; me want it*
	Request permission	*Can I go out?*
	Make a suggestion	*Let's do it again*
	Other request types	
Statements	Label people, objects or events	*Ball; he's running*
	Describe objects/events	*It's a big ball; she's jumping high*
	Statement of emotions, sensations, intents (including expressing personal judgements or attitudes)	*I'm tired; I think that's silly; I'm going to go outside*
	Attributional statements	*I think you're sleepy*
	Predictions, reasons or rules	*It's going to rain; she hit him 'cos he took her toy*
Responses	Response to yes/no questions	*Yes; no; maybe; I don't know*
	Response 'Wh—' questions	*Nursery; Susan; today*
	Express compliance with requests	*OK; I'll do it*
	Acknowledge prior statements	*Mhm; yeah*
	Protest: expressing disapproval of partner's action or utterance	*No! Not there, daddy*
	Other response types	*Agreements; disagreements*
Conversation managers	Attention getters	*Hey; Jenny!; Look!*
	Clarification request	*What did you say?*
	Greetings and leave takings	*Hi!; Bye*
	Politeness markers	*Please; thank you*
	Exclamations	*Oh! Wow! Oh No!*
	Repetition: *own* prior utterance	
	Repetition: *others'* prior utterance	
	Other conversational managers: boundary markers and fillers	*You know; erm; Okay then; right*
Performatives	Teasing, joking, establishing rights, warning	*You're a banana; I'm Batman; watch out*

Table 1: Dore's communicative functions (as adapted by Andersen, 1989).

communication practice within encouraging and facilitative relationships. Such practice may be needed as well as or instead of work on speech and language. Moreover, such practice may be essential for the client to become able to interpret the speech of others correctly.

Where assessment is concerned, clients need to be observed in a variety of contexts if the clinician's view of their abilities is to be at all realistic. This is because people feel different and therefore perform very differently in different contexts. Various contexts in themselves also demand specific types of behaviour, (for example, job interview, classroom, auction room).

Coherence

'Be relevant' is one of the most robust conversational maxims. In order to be relevant, one has to form a clear idea of what a conversation is actually *about*. This presents difficulty to some speech and language therapy clients. On the other hand, confident communicators who know each other well are able to take risks with the need to be relevant. For example, one might say, "Oh, by the way, I didn't book the Paris flight" without introduction while discussing another topic. Close consideration will reveal that, while a new topic (such as going to Paris) may be quite unconnected to the subject under discussion, it can, in certain circumstances, be relevant to a current preoccupation shared by the conversational partners (in this case getting the Paris tickets booked). In this way a 'tangential' remark can be acceptable even though, as a rule, such remarks are not.

Deciding what is and what is not relevant at any given moment is part of making appropriate communicative contributions and interpreting the contributions of others. To avoid confusion, most normal communicators try to make the relevance of their contributions clear. They do this both in the case of short verbal contributions and in longer stretches of written or spoken discourse. The person who manages this successfully is thought of as a *coherent* communicator, as one who makes sense and is easy to follow.

As regards relevance to intervention, clinicians often regard 'topic handling', or coherent communication, as a skill-based set of abilities which can be instilled or corrected. Teaching clients to be as coherent as possible is clearly worthwhile. This can usefully be done by insisting on relevant utterances and teaching such skills as introducing, maintaining, switching and closing topics. However, this is not always possible or appropriate. Sometimes contributions that do have a relevance, but one which is not superficially obvious to the communicative partner or partners, will be dismissed as irrelevant — for instance, when reference is made to a previous conversation which the partner has forgotten. At other times the possible relevance of superficially 'strange' remarks will be sensitively identified by a listener who has noticed or remembered what is likely to have been intended. For example, a couple discuss the probability of getting 'caught' if they do not renew their TV licence. Later the wife spots a group of police officers and says, "I think they're after us!" The husband's response will depend on whether or not he recalls their conversation and sensitively connects it to her joking statement. These two types of response are likely to have different effects on relationships, for obvious reasons. Responding sensitively is important for building sound relationships with others (including clients). It promotes communicative confidence which improves performance. As is well known, success leads to success and the incoherent person can sometimes be led by encouragement towards more satisfactory conversational behaviour, whereas excessive criticism and correction can lead them further in the opposite direction.

Cohesion

Cohesion is the 'sticking together' of elements within a text or discourse. Certain cohesive devices in the linguistic surface enable this to happen. When these devices are missing, or are used inappropriately, it may be difficult to follow what a person has to say. Examples of cohesive devices include the following:

▶ **'Reference'**: this makes use of **deixis**, that is 'pointing' or referring to *someone, somewhere, or something* elsewhere in a text, discourse or context. Beyond its basic function in sharing attention, the purpose of deixis is often to do with brevity and the avoidance of repetition, as in 'After ***that**, **they*** left ***it there*** every day.' Reference of this type works well when all concerned are aware of what is, in fact, being referred to. It does not work at all when what is being referred to has not already been specified. There are other ways of referring: using the definite article to indicate that something has already been introduced, as with '**the frog**' (the one the princess was involved with, not just any old frog); or using comparative expressions such as '**a nicer one**' (than the one that was previously mentioned) or '**The same** day' (as the day previously mentioned).

▶ **Substitution:** this is often used to avoid repetition, especially in written texts. For example: "Simon likes ice hockey; ***violent games*** [that is, games like ice hockey] appeal to ***my son*** [Simon]."

▶ **Ellipsis:** this is used when there is thought to be no need to state in full what is already understood: "What do you think will happen to Peter?" "I really couldn't say …" (what I think will happen to Peter).

▶ **Conjunction:** this device can take many interesting forms. It serves to link 'chunks' of discourse together. Examples are '**on the other hand**' and '**finally**'.

▶ **Lexical cohesion:** this operates by reminding communicative partners of items and ideas by exploiting semantic connections between them. For example: "She dug up potatoes and carrots. When she got home, she put ***the vegetables*** on the table"; or "We walked through the snow for two hours. We didn't ***get warm*** until dinner time."

Maintaining cohesion is a complex task, and one which human beings take some time to master. There are many more devices than have been exemplified here and it will be noticed that, even in the limited examples above, connections can be made in both backward and forward directions across large and small distances within the discourse.

A case can be made for regarding cohesion not as part of pragmatics (making language work in context) but as part of syntax (arranging words so that they work together systematically). However one chooses to view it, cohesion clearly provides plentiful opportunities for failure and confusion on the part of speakers, writers, listeners and readers.

Perhaps the most crucial fact to bear in mind about cohesion is that information about this important area of ability is at present not widely available in the various professions dealing with communication disorders. Detailed information about the normal development pattern for using and understanding cohesive devices is scarce and yet individuals are sometimes identified as having educational problems, language disorders, thought disorders or interpersonal shortcomings partly on the basis of their weak or inappropriate use of cohesive devices. This is not done irresponsibly — such individuals may need help and sometimes even special placement — but more needs to be known about their specific difficulties so that the help they receive is appropriate.

One of the potential benefits of interdisciplinary co-operation in this area would be improved understanding of how to determine whether a person's difficulties with cohesion originate from a lack of knowledge and exposure, from cognitive disability, from language disability or from problems more akin to psychosis or social/emotional dysfunction.

Poor use of cohesive devices can create the false impression that a person is thinking and talking incoherently, saying, for example, "Looked, had gone it was raining" (**We** looked **and he** had gone **because** it was raining). This can lead to misdiagnosis. It is therefore important for clinicians to be alert to the possibility that language difficulties of this kind can exist and to promote interdisciplinary awareness of this problem.

The use and understanding of cohesive devices can usually be improved by tuition and practice, but some individuals do appear to find cohesion particularly difficult to handle. It is possible that problems of memory storage or access play a part in such difficulties. This is because items have to be remembered, at least sub-consciously, before they can be connected to one another. This is an area that would benefit from further research.

Clarification and repair

Competent communicators **monitor** the success of interactions as they proceed. They also monitor their own understanding of what is being said and its implications. When they notice that a problem has arisen, they normally attempt to repair the interaction themselves or ask their partner to do so, saying, for example, "I don't understand" or "Sorry, I should have explained better" or "Oh, I didn't mean to criticize you".

Furthermore, when competent communicators are alerted by their partners to the fact that a problem has arisen, they are often able to identify its cause and supply improvements. This can be a considerable achievement, requiring sophisticated linguistic knowledge and the ability to guess at the contents of one's partner's mind.

As regards intervention, the ability to repair and clarify can be improved considerably by tuition in the technicalities (for example, phrases to use, such as "I'm sorry", or behaviours to try, such as speaking more slowly). However, confidence, self-esteem and a realistic sense of obligation and entitlement may well play a part in promoting efficient clarification and repair. It has been found, for instance, that people with educational difficulties often fail to ask for clarification when they become confused (**Brinton & Fujiki**, 1989). It would not be wise to make assumptions about whether it is ignorance of the technicalities that handicaps them in this way. The reason might be that they have been discouraged; they blame themselves for the problem and fail to request help for this reason; or it may simply have escaped their notice that it is possible to ask for help.

Presuppositional Knowledge

Pragmatic theory will need to account for the ability of a speaker to consider listeners' needs when communicating a message. The better a person is able to imagine the **perspective** of his or her conversational partners, the more successful that person's communication is likely to be. Human cognitive abilities, memory and imagination make it possible, not only to take one another's perspective into account, but also to exchange meanings that are not apparent in the linguistic surface of what is written or said. Instead of being tied to the literal, or even the fixed idiomatic, meanings of words and phrases, people are able to notice humorous, ironic or suggested meanings. They can also build such meanings into their own messages.

Of relevance for intervention here is that clients need to be able to negotiate meanings in a creative and flexible way if they are to communicate naturally and effectively in the real world. They need to be able to produce and comprehend unpredictable messages and to take the perspective of their partners into account. It is therefore not sufficient to equip them with a knowledge of fixed meanings and syntactic constructions. They must learn to converse: to share negotiated meanings with others. They need to make the kind of suppositions their partners expect and to judge what others are likely to presuppose. That is to say, they need to empathize in various ways with their partners.

An important communication skill of this kind is that of deciding what can be regarded as **'given'**, that is, already known, and what will come to a listener as **'new'** information. When this matter has been perceived accurately the **informativeness** of what is said will satisfy the listener. When the perception has not been accurate, most listeners feel frustrated or confused, since they are not able to understand what is intended.

The imaginative inclusion of other peoples' thoughts in one's own communication plan is said to depend on one's being able to hypothesize that others have minds similar to one's own. This 'theory of mind' is thought to operate at several levels: I can guess what you think; I can guess what you think I think; I can guess what X thinks you think; I can guess what X thinks I think you think. Empathy with other people's feelings is thought to operate in a similar way (**Cox**, 1991, pages 113–91).

It has been suggested (**Baron-Cohen, Leslie & Frith**, 1985; **Happe**, 1994; **Sparrevohn & Howie**, 1995; **Boucher**, 1989) that people on the autistic continuum lack, or have in poorly developed form, a theory of mind and that this could account for so-called 'disorders of empathy'.

Clients whose difficulties seem to lie within the less severe sections of the autistic continuum (and this includes some with a diagnosis of Asperger's syndrome or semantic–pragmatic disorder) certainly appear to have difficulty taking the thoughts and feelings of others into consideration. As yet, it is not at all certain why this should be the case. These clients may fail to interpret facial expression correctly (prosopagnosia); they may lack sympathy with other people for emotional reasons; or a difficulty in hypothesizing, pretending or creating scenarios (imagining) may lie at the root of the problem. Addressing these problems in intervention is sometimes helpful, although it needs to be borne in mind that some clients may be unable to make progress in these areas for neurological reasons (**Cutting**, 1990; **Aicardi**, 1992; **Joanette & Brownell**, 1990).

Less disabled individuals can also have difficulties of various kinds with presupposition and therapy can be devised to tackle such problems directly (see Chapter 9). However only experience of real relationships and interactions can provide the *foundation* for acquiring these complex, person-related, features of communicative competence. Clients with various types of speech and language difficulty sometimes lack this experience. When this is the case, we have found that they benefit from intensive interactive therapy lasting six to ten weeks. This *pragmatics-centred therapy* can run concurrently with speech and language-centred therapy, or can precede it. In the latter case, the need for speech and language therapy is sometimes reduced, so it makes sense *not* to leave interactive therapy until all other problems have been dealt with and the client has still failed to become a successful communicator (**Fey,** 1986).

Summary

This chapter has described pragmatic approaches. We have attempted to examine some of the benefits and shortcomings of each approach and to make clear their contributions to the area of communication development and intervention with individuals with communication difficulties. It will be clear to readers that the writers favour a pragmatic approach to communication disorders.

Recommended Reading

Becker JA, 'Implications of Ethology for the Study of Pragmatic Development', Kuczaj SA, *Discourse Development: Progress in Cognitive Development Research*, Springer-Verlag, New York, 1984.

Brown G & Yule G, *Discourse Analysis,* Cambridge University Press, Cambridge, 1983.

Levinson SC, *Pragmatics,* Cambridge University Press, Cambridge, 1983.
Mey JL, *Pragmatics: An Introduction,* Blackwell, Oxford, 1994.
Stubbs M, *Discourse Analysis: The Sociolinguistic Analysis of Natural Language,* Blackwell, Oxford, 1983.

CHAPTER 3
PRAGMATIC DEVELOPMENT

Introduction/*16*
What Does Normal Pragmatic Development Mean?/*16*
Describing Pragmatic Development/*17*
Development of Pragmatics/*17*
    Functional (or Intentional) Communication/*17*
    Conversational Management/*18*
    Presuppositional Knowledge/*20*
Development of Pragmatics from Birth to Adulthood/*22*
    Up to One Year/*22*
    One to Two Years/*23*
    Two to Three Years/*23*
    Three to Four Years/*23*
    Four to Five Years/*24*
    Six to Seven Years/*24*
    Seven to Eight Years/*24*
    By Nine Years/*24*
    Adults/*24*
    Listening/*24*
    Developmental Information on Pragmatics in the Future /*26*
Summary/*26*
Recommended Reading/*26*

Chapter 3
Pragmatic Development

Introduction

There are three crucial questions concerning the development of normal pragmatics:

1. What is the normal course of development of pragmatic skills?
2. What are the processes involved in the acquisition of these skills?

In relating the normal development of pragmatics to the question of intervention with clients with pragmatic impairment, the third question presents itself:

3. What factors inhibit and enhance the processes of acquisition of normal pragmatic skills?

The second and third questions are addressed in Chapters 2 and 7, respectively. In this chapter we will address the first of the three questions above: What is the normal development of pragmatic skills? We will do this in several ways so that the discussion will be of value to readers with different backgrounds and purposes. First, we will examine some of the reasons why charting the course of pragmatic development is a difficult task that has not yet been completed. Second, we will look at the development of pragmatics by examining the different areas of pragmatics and developmental changes that occur within each. Finally, we will take a stage-by-stage approach and look at the child's pragmatic functioning at different stages of development from birth to adulthood. The reader will be aware that, as in all areas of development, variation exists within the age ranges of acquisition of pragmatic skill and knowledge.

What Does Normal Pragmatic Development Mean?

For those working with individuals who have pragmatic difficulties, it would be very helpful to know the range of normal pragmatic skills demonstrated at different ages. At present no means of reliably profiling pragmatic development exists. Despite numerous studies of particular aspects of pragmatic development, linguists, speech pathologists and psychologists are far from understanding the overall picture of normal pragmatic development. This is in sharp contrast to knowledge of syntactic and phonological development, where a clear view of the normal progress of children has made possible a principled approach to the remediation of disorders of language development. There are many reasons why comprehensive normative charts are not available currently and why it will be even more difficult to create charts with clinical usefulness. We explore three main reasons below:

1. *The relative newness of pragmatics as a field of study.* The field of pragmatics and clinical pragmatics is a fairly new one and therefore there is, relatively speaking, little developmental research data. There are pockets of research on specific pragmatic behaviours, such as requests, topic maintenance and eye gaze (including direction, intensity and duration of eye contact).

2. *The difficulty in defining concepts within the field.* Since the field is in its infancy, there is still much debate concerning the definition of pragmatics and what areas can legitimately be included within the field. Clinicians are similarly divided about the use of the term 'pragmatic disorder' and what constitutes such a disorder (**Smith & Leinonen**, 1992; **McTear & Conti-Ramsden**, 1992). Different disciplines have carried out research into pragmatics using many different approaches (which is a healthy thing) but this means that the data are not always easily comparable across studies.

3. *The variability of appropriate human communicative behaviour.* There is considerable variability of what is considered to be appropriate human communicative behaviour on differing occasions, between individuals, across cultures and over time (**Leinonen & Smith**, 1994). The range of normal pragmatic behaviour is not as easily defined as the range of usual grammatical and phonological performance as there is more individual variability in this aspect of

communication and there is less consensus as to what constitutes 'acceptable behaviour'. In addition, individuals have their own set of cultural, subcultural and family values. For example, groups of people create and follow similar pragmatic guidelines: such groups include guides and scouts, religious groups, toastmaster groups, Masonic lodges, working men's clubs and professional groups. Different age groups within adulthood may have their own sets of expectations, values and standards. For instance, the use of politeness forms in people in their 70s and 80s may be more common than for people in their 20s and 30s. Acceptance of behaviours and roles in society changes with time and situation.

Describing Pragmatic Development

The authors' knowledge of clinical decision making leads us to think that, without some developmental guidelines, clinicians are likely to be expecting too little or too much of clients and are also likely to be reluctant to accept that what appear to be infantile forms of behaviour may be developmentally appropriate. This is unfortunate since, for some individuals, acceptance has been found to foster communicative development more effectively than corrective approaches (**Smith & Leinonen**, 1992). For this reason we have taken a decision to include a sketchy and tentative outline of what urgently needed research may possibly confirm to be the normal pattern of events in the unfolding of pragmatic abilities. Short of postponing publication for several years, or omitting consideration of development, this appears to be our best option. Readers are urged to consult Chapter 4 in **McTear & Conti-Ramsden** (1992), together with the original source materials for that chapter, for a useful review of pragmatic development.

Development of Pragmatics

Roth & Spekman (1984a and 1984b) usefully described three different aspects of pragmatics: (1) functional or intentional communication/speech acts, (2) conversational management and (3) presuppositional knowledge.

Functional (or Intentional) Communication

Functional communication is concerned with what the speaker intends to communicate, how that intention is conveyed in an utterance or gesture and the effect of the utterance on the listener. Not surprisingly, the range and type of intentional communicative act changes with increasing maturity. Children's expanding world knowledge and increasing cognitive maturity mean that they have more ideas to communicate as well as increasingly sophisticated and indirect means of expressing them.

Several researchers have proposed frameworks for studying the development of intentional communication in childhood (**Dore**, 1978a and 1978b; **Tough**, 1977a; **Coggins & Carpenter**, 1981). **Dore** (1979) presents a classification scheme that describes 'conversational acts' or intentional communication in early childhood. He looked at the range of different intentions expressed by young children between the ages of two years seven months and three years seven months and reported that requests were the most commonly used form in this age group. Descriptions and responses were also found to be used commonly in this age range. A modified version of this scheme (**Andersen**, 1989) appears in Chapter 2.

Tough (1977a) proposes a system for classifying functional communication with particular reference to school-aged children. A simplified version of this system is illustrated in Table 2.

Using Tough's categories, **Retherford Stickler & Cannon** (1984) looked at the way a group of normally developing and a group of language-delayed children, functioning at **Brown's** (1973) stage V (approximately age 3–4 years), used language in a free play and in a cake icing activity. The percentage use of different functions seemed to be similar for both groups of children. A summary is presented in Table 3.

They found that the interpretative function (reporting on past and present experiences and reasoning) was the most frequently used (approximately 39 per cent of all functions) for all children in both situations. Both groups of children used the projective function (predicting, imagining or making projections about others) for approximately 20–25 per cent of functions in the free play situation, contrasting with a much lower percentage of use (approximately 9 per cent) while engaged in the cake icing activity.

Thus the existence of language delay appeared to make less difference to the range of

Function	Strategies	Description
Directive Directing actions and operations	Self-directing	Monitoring actions, focusing control, forward planning
	Other directing	Demonstrating, instructing, forward planning, anticipating collaborative action
Interpretative Communicating the meaning of events	Reporting on past and present experiences	Labelling, elaborating detail, comparison, recognizing incongruity, awareness of sequence
	Reasoning	Recognizing dependent and causal relationships, recognizing a principle or determining conditions
Projective Using imagination and experience to project and explore situations removed in time, space or reality	Predicting	Forecasting events, anticipating consequences, surveying possible alternatives, forecasting related possibilities, recognizing problems and predicting solutions
	Empathetic	Projecting into experiences of others, projecting into other people's feelings, anticipating the reactions of others
	Imagining	Renaming, commenting on imagined context, building a scene through language, language of role
Relational Establishing and maintaining social relationships	Self-maintaining	Expression of need, protection of self-interests, justification, criticisms, threats
	Interactional	Self-emphasizing strategies, other recognizing strategies

Table 2 Functional communication classification for school-aged children.

Function	Free play (%)	Cake icing (%)
Directive	15	11
Interpretative	37	40
Projective	23	9
Relational	11	23
Other	14	17

Table 3 Percentage use of communicative functions during two different activities (based on **Tough**, 1977a).

language functions used in interactions than the nature of the activity. We await further research using schemes such as Dore's and Tough's to see if it may be possible to suggest normative ranges of use of language in different situations in the future. This might enable clinicians to identify more objectively the value of different activities when attempting to increase the use of specific functions of language.

Conversational Management

Conversational management is concerned with the speaker's ability to take turns in a conversation; to introduce, maintain and switch topics; request and make clarifications (repairing conversations).

Turn taking

Turn taking skills develop from a very early age. During the first months of the child's life, parents engage in activities with their infant that may form the foundations of early turn taking skills (**Snow**, 1977 and 1995). Initially, turn taking is a non-verbal activity involving coordination of touching, smiling, looking and feeding. Later, it focuses additionally on timing of movements of objects. Still later, vocal and verbal turn taking develops. Three-month-old infants' communication was studied by **Bloom, Russell & Wassenberg** (1987). They found that, when adults responded to their child's vocalizations, the child's speech sounds increased relative to their non-speech sounds. **Collis & Schaffer** (1975) and **Ninio & Bruner** (1978) found that the young children in their study were skilled at taking turns. The children in these studies, aged between eight months and two years, rarely overlapped with their communicative partners.

Development of interruption skills, turns of increasing length and sophistication and other turn taking skills follow after about three years of age. **Gallagher & Craig** (1982) found that, by the age of three, children are able to recognize that a pause of longer than a second probably means that the listener is not responding for some reason. **Ervin-Tripp** (1979) reported that by the age of five years, children are able to use a sophisticated method, in instances when an initial attempt at taking a turn has failed, by stopping their utterance and waiting for a pause before taking their turn again. **Deffebach & Adamson** (1994) found that mothers used teaching strategies such as taking the child's role in a conversation, which may help to develop the child's understanding of turn taking skills.

Topic skills

The development of topic skills begins very early. During the child's infancy, parents often interpret what their child may be intending to say. For example, if the child is crying they say: "Are you sleepy, then?", even speaking words for the child: "I know what you're saying. You're saying: 'Mummy, pick me up!'" **Bruner** (1978) described this type of adult behaviour as 'scaffolding' as it constructs a scaffold for children to help them understand the world more easily. Later when children begin to be able to control their head movements more skilfully, adults and children are able to share a focus of attention on an object or event. Initially, the adult takes the major responsibility for drawing attention to objects, labelling them and manipulating them, but later children take more responsibility (**Foster**, 1981). Children begin to be able to make clear what they are interested in by gazing, making attention-getting noises and even later, by eight months or so, pointing to draw the adult's attention to things that interest them. At four to eight months they learn to look at an adult when an adult tries to draw their attention to something and then to look at where the adult is pointing or looking to see for themselves the focus of the adult's attention. By nine to ten months (and often much earlier) children are able to convey a message intentionally to another person.

By one year, most children are able to initiate topics by using gesture and single words to label objects: for example, "Sock", accompanied by holding a sock (meaning "Here is a sock"); to request objects: for example, "Bisibic", accompanied by pointing to the biscuit tin (meaning "I want a biscuit now"); to request actions: for example, "Up", accompanied by raised arms (meaning "Lift me up"); and to express emotions or states: for example, "Hot", accompanied by a rapidly withdrawn finger from the cup and a concerned facial expression (meaning "this is very hot").

Children as young as two are able to maintain the same topic as an adult (**Ervin-Tripp**, 1979). **Keenan and Klein** (1975) found that twins aged two years nine months and three years nine months were able to maintain topic in their interactions with each other both through repetition of the sounds the partner used and through meaningful utterance repetition. This ability to maintain topic within a conversation improves with increased age and probably with child-centredness of the topic (**James**, 1990, page 116). Thus 'tangential remarks' could indicate developmental delay. **Bloom, Rocissano & Hood** (1976) looked at the topic skills in children from **Brown's** (1973) stages I–V and found that children's ability to maintain topic increased from doing this 56 per cent of the time at Brown's stage I, 67 per cent at Brown's stage II and 76 per cent of the time at Brown's stage III. **Brinton & Fujiki** (1984) found that five-year-old children were able to maintain the topic 80 per cent of the time and produced an average of five utterances per topic, while adults maintained topic for 96 per cent of the time and had an average of about 11 utterances per topic. They also reported interesting developments in topic manipulation in their study comparing five-year-olds with nine-year-olds and adults. They found that five-year-old children tended to repeat information in the same or slightly different ways, whereas this was less common in nine-year-olds and even less so in adults. This type of information is crucial when assessing the topic skills of people labelled as disordered. See also **Hobbs** (1990) for a discussion of topic drift.

Requesting and making clarifications (repairing conversations)

Children as young as two seem to be good at revising their utterances when requested to do so by adults. **Gallagher** (1977) found that children who were functioning within Brown's stages I to III (20–30 months) were able to repair approximately 75–80 per cent of their utterances. Further, she found that the revision strategies that children used changed with increasing maturity. For example, children at stage I tended to make phonetic revisions; thus "Doggy eee i" would be repaired to "Doggy eat it". At stages II and III they tended to delete one of the elements in the utterance, presumably in the hope that it would become clearer to the listener. For example, "Doggy eat it" might become "Doggy eat". Stage III children additionally used a strategy of substitution to make their meanings clearer. For example, "Doggy eat it" might become: "Doggy eat bone". Interestingly, Gallagher found that these Stage

III children rarely made requests for clarifications from adults. This supports our own informal observations of children who rarely ask for clarification at four years but who seem to start to indicate when there has been a breakdown of communication between five and seven years by looking puzzled, repeating what the adult has said with a questioning intonation or directly asking the adult about a word that they have not understood.

Gallagher suggests that one of the reasons for children's reticence in asking for clarification may be their reluctance to imply to the adult that they have produced an inadequate message. It may also be that children are used to adults being relatively competent and just assume that the error is in their own comprehension skills. Alternatively, the child may not have learnt polite ways of making requests for clarifications or may have learnt that it often is not necessary to ask for a clarification because the message can become clear from the context or through other utterances conveyed by the speaker. **Wilcox and Webster** (1980) found that children aged between 17 and 24 months were more likely to simply repeat their 'failed' utterance when an adult said "What?" Those children who had larger vocabularies also tended to reword their utterances for the listener. This shows that very young children may have an awareness that the breakdown may be located in their own utterance. Further, it shows a willingness and ability to try to 'fix' the breakdown. In contrast, **Robinson & Robinson** (1976, 1977, 1978 and 1981) found that children up to the age of five or six tend to blame listeners if there is a breakdown in communication because of an inadequate message from the speaker. But seven to eight-year-old children blame the speaker for delivering an inadequate message. Interestingly, Robinson & Robinson found that these seven to eight-year-olds did not request a clarification from the speaker. Clinicians and teachers often encourage speakers to improve their repair and clarification behaviour as part of general social skills training.

Interrupting

Mastery of the skill of interrupting continues well into adulthood. Many adults experience difficulties with this skill. When one considers the complexity of manoeuvres required for skilful interrupting this comes as no surprise. **Sachs, Anselmi & McCollam** (1990) describe how children do improve their ability to interrupt in conversations with increasing age.

Presuppositional Knowledge

Presuppositional knowledge is concerned with the assumptions that one makes about the communicative context, particularly the listener's knowledge. **Sonnenschein & Whitehurst** (1982) and **McDevitt & Ford** (1987) suggest that children's ability to use presuppositional knowledge for communication may be influenced by many factors in addition to an ability to take the listener's perspective and knowledge into consideration. These factors include perception, memory, vocabulary, the child's level of arousal or involvement in a task, attention and utilization of feedback, and the goals of the speaker and listener.

Presuppositional knowledge involves taking account of the listener's knowledge, expectations and communicative needs. There are four different and interrelated elements in presuppositional knowledge:

1   general assumptions about how speakers feel and function in interactions;
2   use of appropriate reference and informativeness within interactions;
3   knowledge and use of appropriate politeness forms;
4   knowledge of social roles.

Developmental changes within these areas will be described briefly below. The reader is referred to Chapter 2 for more detailed descriptions of the importance of these areas for communication.

General assumptions about how speakers feel and function in interactions

Readers will remember from Chapter 2 that **Grice** (1975) proposed four maxims that speakers follow when taking part in a co-operative conversation:

▶ Quantity: be informative but not more so than necessary.
▶ Quality: be truthful.
▶ Relation: be relevant.
▶ Manner: be clear in your expression.

DeHart & Maratsos (1984) suggest that children have a natural basic ability to presuppose. In contrast, **Piaget** (1955) suggested that children of pre-school age are egocentric and are therefore *not* able to consider the listener's needs adequately. Researchers have since found data that suggest that children are able to consider the listener's needs within this age group.

For example, **Dunn & Kendrick** (1982) showed that two-year-old children talked in different ways when addressing adults or their younger brothers and sisters. **Guralnick & Paul-Brown** (1989) found that three- and four-year-old children modified their language when talking with peers who were mildly developmentally delayed. **Pynte, Girotto & Baccino** (1991) looked at children of about nine. When shown several pictures of, for example, boys sitting, including pictures where boys are sitting and performing another action at the same time, such as sleeping, reading a book or talking on the telephone, and then asked to choose the picture of the boy who is sitting, the children were able to pick out the one where the boy is *only* sitting and not also performing another action. **Pynte *et al*** argue that this illustrates that children of this age assume that speakers will make their message as informative as necessary but not more informative than necessary. **Brinton & Fujiki** (1989) propose that differences in the acquisition of presuppositional forms reflect the cognitive maturity of the child in areas such as information processing rather than presuppositional ability *per se*. Exactly which aspects of cognitive maturity are precursive to which specific aspects of presuppositional knowledge we do not yet know. Questions about the development of empathy also need to be further investigated (**Baron-Cohen**, 1991).

Use of appropriate reference and informativeness within interactions

Reference is the skill of referring appropriately to people, objects, places and ideas within discourse: for example, knowing that, once a person or place has been introduced as a topic of conversation, it is no longer necessary to use the specific name but pronouns (such as he, she or it) can be used instead, as in the following:

> Hasan visited Jody in Brighton last week. *He* told *her* about his plans to move *there* soon. *She* encouraged *him* to do *it* quickly, before prices start to rise.

The listener has to refer back to the information provided in earlier sentences in order to interpret the *italicized* words. There are many different kinds of referring, using personal pronouns, demonstrative pronouns, 'empty' terms such as 'whatshisname' to substitute for specific names, and so on.

The pattern of development of referring skills has received relatively little attention in research. It is clear that children's developing memory and linguistic systems will influence maturation of their referring skills. Using reference appropriately is not simply a matter of choosing pronouns to replace corresponding nouns. It involves appreciating the specific demands of a situation and being able to take the listener's perspective in interpreting a message. The following telephone conversation between a two-year-old boy and his grandma illustrates some of the difficulties in becoming aware of the needs presented by different situations:

> *Grandma:* Hello. Who is this?
> *Child:* It's me.
> *Grandma:* Oh! It's Sebastian, is it?
> *Child:* (silence)
> *Grandma:* And what are you doing?
> *Child:* This. (Pointing to the bowl of food he is eating.)

James (1990) suggests that children of three to four years possess the cognitive and linguistic abilities necessary to make certain presuppositions and adjust their communication accordingly. For example, she suggests that children adjust the *amount* of information that they offer to the listener according to whether the listener can see the object or event being talked about. Not all aspects of appreciating listeners' needs are acquired by this age. Using a referential communication task, **Krauss & Glucksberg** (1977) found that four-year-old children were unable to appreciate the listener's need for specifying referents that cannot be seen. See also **Leinonen & Letts** (1991 and 1992) and **Garton** (1986).

Knowledge and use of appropriate politeness forms

Bates (1976a) reported that two-year-old children were able to increase the level of politeness of their requests, when asked to, by adding the word 'please'. Our own observations of two-year-old children suggest that some children are also able to modify the volume, intonation and facial expression, so that a 'rude demand' becomes a 'sweet and polite request', imitating the model provided by a parent. **James** (1978) reported that children aged four and a half to five years, when playing with dolls, were able to change their level of politeness according to the listener's age and the situation. **Corsaro** (1979) found that children used more imperative forms with peers but forms with a higher level of politeness when addressing older children, parents or teachers.

It has been suggested that there are gender differences in the use of politeness forms

(**Tannen**, 1990 and 1993). For example, **Lakoff** (1973) suggested that women are more polite, saying "Thank you" or "Good-bye" and using indirect requests ("Would you mind passing the salt?" rather than "Can you pass the salt?") more frequently than men. **Ervin-Tripp, Guo & Lampert** (1990) found that five-year-old children were able to modify requests that were ignored to make them more polite ("Get that car" might be changed to "Could I have that car?") whereas three-year-old children simply repeated their initial request. Five-year-olds were also more sensitive to the inconvenience the request might cause the other person and showed more deference when they thought the other person was busy. Interestingly, **Ervin-Tripp *et al*** found that six to 11-year-olds did not make their requests even more polite than the five-year-olds when ignored or refused. Rather, they made their second request with added urgency or showed their aggravation with the listener. This may demonstrate the acquisition of a wider range of options in older children and possibly the strategy of appraising the outcomes of using different types of request. Readers who are interested in the developmental literature on children's requests are encouraged to look at **Becker** (1990) for a review.

Knowledge of social roles

Shatz & Gelman (1973) found that four-year-old children are able to modify their language according to whether they are talking to adults, peers or younger children. This suggests that they are aware of certain features of role-related language, though perhaps not consciously so. Similarly, **Corsaro** (1979) found that children aged two to five years used more imperative forms with peers ("Give me that car") and more permission requests ("Can I have that car?") with older partners.

Development of Pragmatics from Birth to Adulthood

Below we have grouped findings from the literature into age bands rather than topic bands so that clinicians can have an idea of the range of pragmatic skills and knowledge that they might expect to observe for a client at a particular age. It should be borne in mind that these are not well established norms of the kind one has come to expect for syntax or phonology. Also it will be seen that the important area of pragmatic comprehension requires further investigation at all age levels.

Up to One Year

In the earliest stages, before children show intentional communicative behaviour, adults tend to provide structure for the interaction (**Bruner,** 1982). Adults' more sophisticated skills mean that they usually take responsibility for ensuring that children have optimum opportunities to learn and develop relationships. In the first days and weeks the adult and child orient physically towards each other. Eye-contact and close attention are exchanged between parent and child. Later the adult–child pair transfer attention to external objects in their environment, such as other people, animals and toys. The adult generally follows the child's lead, but occasionally may draw attention to an object or event by making an interesting noise and or a facial expression, or by pointing to a toy, person or pet. The adult pays attention to the child whether or not the child demands it — but particularly if the child does demand it. In the early weeks the behaviour of adult and child is synchronous (**Trevarthen**, 1979). For example, the adult and child make noises simultaneously.

Later, adults begin to leave space for the child to take a communicative turn and reciprocity develops. Adults tend to attribute meaning to the child's turn and respond accordingly. For example, the infant 'smiles' as she makes a burp following feeding and the adult attributes meaning to the smile and the burp by saying, "Oh! You've had enough, have you? You liked that, didn't you?" The adult also brings attention to the fact that the child has taken a turn by imitating the child's turn. For example, if the child babbles or makes a vegetative noise the adult typically copies it. The process of imitation works in both directions. The child starts to show evidence of comprehension of a basic nature through anticipation of routines such as feeding, dressing and bathing, for example becoming excited on hearing the word 'dinner' and being placed in a high chair with a spoon and bowl in front of them. The child also starts to show understanding through the appropriate use of objects, rolling balls, brushing with brushes, drinking from a bottle or cup and so on.

Once the child engages in an action or vocalization purposefully (with an intended goal, however simple) we can say that the child has developed communicative intent. The fact that adults assume intention in the child's actions and vocalizations even before there is concrete evidence of intentionality may be essential for the development of true intention. The child starts to use proto-words towards the end of the first year. These are sounds or groups of sounds which are always, reliably, uttered in the presence of a specific stimulus. For example, a 12-month-old child says, "Upa upa" and raises his hands whenever his mother approaches him and he is not engaged in exploratory play. It is the adult's recognition of proto-words which, pragmatically, allows them to function in the same way that known words do in communication (**Snow**, 1977; **Bateson**, 1975).

One to Two Years

The range of communicative acts widens as children enter the second year of life. The child uses combinations of words, objects, proto-words and gestures, for example pointing to a car and saying, "Brum brum." Other features of the second year include an increasing ability to understand the communication of others in context and gradually out of context also. For example, a mobile child showed the following progression of comprehension:

At 12 months: "Get your coat." (Said in the context of a familiar routine as the older siblings are getting ready to go to school after breakfast. In addition, the child's coat is right in front of her and other family members are also putting on their coats.)

At 13 months: "Get your coat." (When the coat is not visible but the routine following breakfast is a familiar one and other family members are putting on their coats.)

At 14 months: "Get your coat." (When the coat is not in view and the context is not giving the child clues as to the appropriate behaviour for the situation.)

The child starts to understand the felicity conditions for the performance of communicative acts: that there are special circumstances under which a speech act will succeed. For instance, a request to go out will probably fail if it is raining and no-one is listening at the time. The child also starts to understand that utterances must be said clearly and begins to be able to integrate object knowledge, world knowledge, social knowledge and language. The child becomes skilful at gaining attention and begins to use simple politeness forms, such as 'please' and 'thank you'. The child shows that she is beginning to understand the use of register and can, for example, modify her voice when talking to a doll. The child has not yet learnt the finer points of turn taking and consequently overlaps (where the child and the communicative partner talk simultaneously) occur frequently.

Two to Three Years

From age two years the forms of language and non-verbal communication become both clearer and more elaborate. By age three, children are usually able to perform tasks that demonstrate the ability to understand that others possess minds with their own unique thoughts, feelings, beliefs and knowledge — the 'theory of mind' (**Shatz**, 1994). In addition, a greater awareness of felicity conditions is seen after two years. Children are able to modify their requests so that, for example, they can make a request more polite: "Give me the doll" becomes "Please give me the doll" or "Can I have the doll?" The three-year-old child is able to give simple explanations and to make some simple repairs to her own utterance. Fewer utterances are seen by the partner as irrelevant. There are the beginnings of the metalinguistic skill of using correct terms to talk about communication, such as word, sentence, your turn to talk and interrupt. For example, a child at age two years ten months had the following conversation with his mother:

> *Mum:* Do you want to draw on your board — I mean easel [pointing to the child's easel]?
> *Child:* No, it's not board. It's my easel. You said the wrong word, mummy.

Interrupting skills and skills at avoiding interruption by others when in a group are developing from the age of about two years six months. For example, Katy, at age two years nine months, used the phrase, "Excuse me", said repeatedly in a loud voice in order both to interrupt other children in a small group and to prevent other children from taking the floor from her. Using this strategy, coupled with taking very infrequent pauses, she was able to hold a turn for over 10 minutes. Later, most children learn that sharing turns is more appropriate behaviour in interactions.

Three to Four Years

Many children can make explicit statements about turn taking and about types of talk. Requests may involve strategies and several steps: "You know those biscuits? Well, if I'm good, after dinner and just one ..." Narrative comprehension and story telling should now be well developed (**Kemper**, 1984). Overlaps are fewer and children can now repair these (**Sacks, Schegloff & Jefferson**, 1974).

Four to Five Years

Repairs can be made, but 50 per cent of breakdowns are ignored. Clarifications of miscommunication are non-specific and tend to blame the listener. Referents begin to be clarified when not visible. Thus a child of two may say, "Want that toy" when the toy is not visible but a child of four is more likely to say, "I want my bear-hunt book from upstairs." More account is taken of the listener. Communicative routines are learnt, such as 'trick or treat', "What's the time, Mr Wolf?" Some understanding of threats and promises begins. Most of what is said by age four or five now seems relevant. At school or nursery, children learn more about politeness, persuasion, hints, rights (claiming and giving), justifying and explaining (**Tough**, 1977a). Gaps in interactions are now shorter (**Dewart & Summers**, 1995).

Six to Seven Years

Children can now make explicit reference to rules of communication and language (metapragmatics); they become less literal, though some literalness persists in certain situations. Repairs improve but clarification is still not sufficiently precise or insightful.

Seven to Eight Years

Clarification now often correctly locates the problem. Repairs can be made for the benefit of the listener. Children can now process conversations sufficiently swiftly to monitor their own comprehension and will therefore begin to request clarifications when necessary from both peers and adults. Higher level organization is evident in giving instructions and constructing narratives.

By Nine Years

Children become clear about threats and promises and cause and effect. They can use language to make predictions about likely outcomes. Account is now taken of listeners' thoughts and feelings, and also of their individual characteristics and history. This is not always altruistic. Role taking becomes more skilful and referents are usually made clear. What is said is now much more precise and specific. Fewer empty terms such as 'thingy', or 'whatsit' are used. The child is now able to be tactful and indirect. For example, a three-year-old child, on seeing another child with sweets, might say, "Mine! I want some", whereas a nine-year-old child with the same goal in mind might say, "I'm hungry" or "I wish I had some sweets as well", or might simply adopt a strategy of being nice and helpful in the hope of receiving a 'reward'. Several levels of politeness are understood and can be explicitly referred to (**McTear & Conti-Ramsden**, 1992).

Normally developing individuals may have difficulty well into adolescence with such matters as presupposition; implicature; inference; integration of different types of knowledge; skill in using what is known and understood; interpretation at various levels; humour and irony. There are no clear guidelines as to normality. School teachers report wide variation in the age at which children become confident and reliable in the achievements we have identified. It therefore seems appropriate to be cautious in labelling childrens' pragmatic mistakes as pathological. Despite this, those who have apparent pragmatic difficulties need to be identified as early as possible and appropriate intervention needs to be provided since their future social relationships and adjustment may be seriously compromised without such action.

Adults

Pragmatic skills continue to develop well into adulthood. Most of us are aware of certain things that we find difficult to do communicatively: for example, starting a conversation at a party with a stranger, making a complaint in a shop about faulty goods, remembering what someone has told us previously, giving a stranger directions and following a convoluted story. We all know certain individuals whom we regard as having extraordinary levels of social competence. We may not always agree about these individuals, but often we are able to do so. These people may be chosen as leaders in their field, or can be the jokers, or are just well liked by many people. It would be useful to gain a clearer picture of the skills and attributes these people have and to investigate the factors that have enabled them to develop such effective communication skills. In Tables 4 and 5 we have compiled lists of 15 positive and 15 negative characteristics of communication and possible effects on the communicative partner. (The lists are based on 20 students' responses to a simple questionnaire on effective communicators and should therefore not be viewed as a representative or comprehensive list.)

Listening

The developmental course of listening is a complex area of study and it is beyond the scope of this book to describe it in detail. The development of appropriate listening skills depends

	Characteristics of an effective communicator	Possible effect on communicative partner
1	Listening well	Speaker feels appreciated
2	Using appropriate eye-contact: looking a lot, but not too much	Partner feels listened to but not threatened
3	Clarity of articulation; not using unusual vocabulary	Partner does not have to concentrate hard to understand
4	Sequencing ideas clearly and logically	Partner can understand easily
5	Showing sensitivity and concern for conversational partner's feelings	Partner can relax, knowing the partner has no ulterior motives
6	Knowing when to end a conversation	Partner can leave when they want or need to
7	Having interesting things to talk about	Partner finds conversation interesting and rewarding
8	Leaving pauses and not interrupting	Partner feels listened to and does not have to fight to hold the conversational floor
9	Fixing breakdowns in the conversation skilfully	Partner feels at ease and not afraid of making errors
10	Displaying a sense of humour and laughing with the communicative partner	Rewarding for partner; feeling of shared emotions brings partners together
11	Using appropriate intonation (not monotone)	Helps understanding and pleasant to listen to
12	Remembering what the listener has said both within and across meetings	Confirms that listener is paying attention and may value what speaker has said
13	Standing close enough to the communicative partner	Partner does not have to struggle to hear speaker
14	Standing far enough away from the communicative partner	Partner does not feel threatened or uncomfortable
15	Showing that they understand the speaker by reflecting back	Confirms that listener is listening and understanding

Table 4 Effective communicators.

	Characteristics of a poor communicator	Possible effect on communicative partner
1	Looking bored or not listening	Speaker feels unappreciated
2	Touching or standing too close	Partner feels irritated or threatened
3	Staring or looking away	Partner thinks listener is not interested in the conversation
4	Mumbling	Difficult to understand speaker; may have to ask for repetition
5	Talking too much and not leaving a pause	Bores partner and does not allow partner to put own view easily
6	Talking too fast	Difficult to understand
7	Interrupting	Disrupts speaker's train of thought; indicates lack of interest in speaker
8	Talking in monotone or a voice that is too loud or too quiet	Irritates listener; listener has to try hard to hear speaker
9	Talking about self or own opinions all the time	Bores partner and makes partner feel undervalued
10	Looking at a watch or clock while listening	Partner feels listener is more concerned with other matters
11	Talking aggressively or unkindly during discussions	Listener feels threatened or upset
12	Not explaining jargon	Listener feels confused or may have to clarify terms
13	Rambling and waffling	Partner finds it difficult to understand and loses interest in speaker
14	Using patronizing tone or words such as 'pet' or 'love'	Partner feels annoyed, undervalued and patronized
15	Not understanding the speaker	Speaker feels frustration and a need to clarify or repeat

Table 5 Poor communicators.

upon many factors — cultural training and expectations (see **Blum-Kulka & Snow,** 1992 and **Clancy,** 1986), cognitive skills such as auditory perceptual skills, attention, memory, motivation and interest levels. As the child matures cognitively, listening skills increase and the ability to show the speaker that one is listening (through eye gaze, nodding, back channel responses, indicating understanding or lack of understanding) likewise improves with maturity.

Developmental Information on Pragmatics in the Future

We think that there is good reason to be hopeful of having a useful, fuller profile of normal pragmatic skills in the future. The reasons for this optimism are as follows. First, just as one knows intuitively when a grammatical error has been made, large numbers of people would be in agreement, we suspect, regarding what constitutes a pragmatic 'error'. There is more leeway in pragmatics than in syntax, but rules still exist. There is therefore the possibility of studying people's knowledge of rules and their rule-keeping or rule-breaking behaviour.

Second, the field of pragmatics is expanding rapidly and many researchers are currently investigating the development of specific areas of pragmatics. The CHILDES computerized data base set up by Brian MacWhinney and Catherine Snow (**MacWhinney**, 1991) provides a data bank of child transcripts from many large studies. If this data bank is fully utilized it may be possible to begin to build a profile of pragmatic behaviours within a variety of different situations.

Third, now that the diagnosis of pragmatic disorder is accepted more widely, more individuals who may have difficulties in this area are being recognized. This means that one can look more closely at disordered pragmatic behaviour. This close examination will help to refine the norms and gain a broader picture of the range of difficulties that individuals with pragmatic difficulties can suffer or create.

Finally, the work of ethologists (such as **Becker,** 1984 and 1990; **Crago & Cole,** 1991) is contributing useful methodological information for the study of pragmatics. This may mean that studies conducted will increasingly use enlightening methods.

Summary

The developmental information that we have presented here is necessarily patchy, but we think that it is sufficient to begin to provide clinicians with broad guidelines for normal pragmatic abilities. With further investigation into the area, and in particular with an increase in cross-disciplinary research, we feel hopeful that more comprehensive data will be available for clinicians in the near future.

Recommended Reading

Bates E, *Language in Context: The Acquisition of Pragmatics*, Academic Press, New York, 1976a.

Brinton B & Fujiki M, *Conversational Management with Language Impaired Children: Pragmatic Assessment and Intervention*, Aspen, Rockville, 1989.

Dewart H & Summers S, *The Pragmatics Profile of Communication Skills in Childhood*, NFER–Nelson, Windsor, 1995.

Dunn J, *Young Children's Close Relationships: Beyond Attachment,* Sage, London, 1993.

Foster SH, *The Communicative Competence of Young Children: A Modular Approach*, Longman, London, 1990.

Hulit LM & Howard MR, *Born to Talk: An Introduction to Speech and Language Development*, MacMillan, New York, 1993.

Kuczaj S, *Discourse Development: Progress in Cognitive Development Research*, Springer-Verlag, New York, 1984.

James SL, *Normal Language Acquistion,* Pro-Ed, Austin, Texas, 1990.

Myers Pease D, Berko-Gleason J & Pan BA, 'Learning the Meaning of Words: Semantic Development and Beyond', Berko-Gleason J (ed), *The Development of Language,* MacMillan, New York, 1993.

Ochs E & Schieffelin BB (eds), *Developmental Pragmatics*, Academic Press, New York, 1979.

Owens RE, *Language Development: An Introduction*, MacMillan, New York, 1992.

Snow CE, Perlmann RY, Gleason JB & Hooshyar N, 'Developmental Perspectives on Politeness: Sources of Children's Knowledge', *Journal of Pragmatics* 14, pp289–305, 1990.

Stephens MI, 'Pragmatics', Nippold MA (ed), *Later Language Development Ages Nine Through Nineteen*, Pro-Ed, Austin, Texas, 1988.

Warren AR & McCloskey LA, 'Pragmatics: Language in Social Contexts,' Berko-Gleason J (ed), *The Development of Language,* MacMillan, New York, 1993.

CHAPTER 4
PRAGMATIC DYSFUNCTION

Introduction/*28*
What is 'Normal' Pragmatic Functioning?/*28*
What are the Defining Characteristics of Pragmatic Dysfunction?/*28*
    Characteristics of Pragmatic Impairment/*29*
    Contributory Factors/*30*
How is Pragmatic Dysfunction Different from Other Disorders of Communication?/*31*
Pragmatic Knowledge and Skill/*31*
    Knowledge Required for Effective Pragmatic Functioning/*31*
    Skills Required for Effective Pragmatic Functioning/*31*
Motivation and Confidence/*32*
Causes of Pragmatic Difficulty/*32*
    Attributing Responsibility for Pragmatic Difficulty/*32*
    Identifying Causes of Pragmatic Difficulty/*32*
    What is Known about Causes of Pragmatic Dysfunction?/*32*
Diagnosis/*32*
    Labels Used in Diagnosis/*33*
Severity Rating/*34*
    What is a Severity Rating?/*34*
    What are the Advantages of Using Severity Ratings?/*34*
    Procedure for Severity Rating/*34*
    Positive Focus/*35*
Summary/*36*
Recommended Reading/*36*

Chapter 4
PRAGMATIC DYSFUNCTION

Introduction

This chapter will consider the defining characteristics of pragmatic dysfunction and examine it in relation to other disorders of communication. We examine the components of pragmatic knowledge and skill and we look at the impact of motivation and communicative confidence on the communication of an individual. Finally, we examine possible causes of pragmatic dysfunction and ways to describe the severity of a difficulty.

What is 'Normal' Pragmatic Functioning?

One of the limitations currently encountered by clinicians when confronted by pragmatic dysfunction is that, for both children and adults, there is a shortage of normative data. For example, most people regard tactfulness and a sense of humour as desirable, but there is little information available to guide the clinician as to whether or not the absence, or weakness, of these essentially pragmatic attributes is unusual. Similarly, use of 'unclear referents' is thought to be common in the utterances of people with pragmatic difficulties. For instance, a teacher asks an eight-year-old child to tell a story. The child begins, "They went up there to look for it." Unfortunately, the teacher has no idea who 'they' are, or what 'there' and 'it' refer to. Should this unclear referencing be regarded as abnormal? Are referents made clear by a minority of people or by the majority? What age groups would normally be expected to demonstrate this ability?

While there are developmental data emerging, these and many other similar questions await answers from research. This leaves clinicians in the position of being able to identify problems, *without yet being able to evaluate their significance.* This is rather like being able to identify grammatical errors without being able to state with confidence whether they represent disability, immaturity, illiteracy or dialect — a situation which present-day speech and language clinicians would find intolerable but which was not uncommon 30 years ago.

It may be useful to look at the developmental information presented in Chapter 3, but it should be kept in mind that, as yet, they can only be regarded as rough guidelines.

What are the Defining Characteristics of Pragmatic Dysfunction?

A list of specific types of superficial pragmatic difficulty, together with some possible underlying deficits, follows, derived from literature dealing with pragmatic disorder and the autistic continuum: **Lucas Arwood** (1991), **Sahlén & Nettelbladt** (1993), **Aarons & Gittens** (1990 and 1993), **Jordan & Powell** (1990), **Powell & Jordan** (1993), **Bishop & Adams** (1992), **McTear & Conti-Ramsden** (1992), **Smith & Leinonen** (1992), **Conti-Ramsden** (1991), **Gallagher** (1991), **HydeWright & Cray** (1991), **McTear** (1991), **Mogford-Bevan & Sadler** (1991), **Joanette & Brownell** (1990), **Adams & Bishop** (1989), **Bishop & Adams** (1989), **Bishop** (1989), **Byers-Brown & Edwards** (1989), **Morris** (1989), **Smedley** (1989), **Spence *et al*** (1989), **Tantum** (1988), **Abbeduto & Rosenberg** (1987), **Beveridge & Conti-Ramsden** (1987), **Browning** (1987), **Donahue** (1987), **Rapin & Allen** (1983 and 1987), **Conti-Ramsden & Gunn** (1986), **McTear** (1985a, 1985b and 1985c), **Friel-Patti & Conti-Ramsden** (1984), **Fey & Leonard** (1983), **Prutting & Kirchner** (1983), **Weintraub & Mesulam** (1983), **Lucas** (1980).

The following works from the field of psychiatry are also relevant: **Baltax** (1990), **Baltax & Simmons** (1988), **Gravell & France** (1991), **Hassibi & Breuer** (1980), **Rochester & Martin** (1979), **Wolff & McGuire** (1995). A review of the major part of the literature appears in **Smith & Leinonen** (1992).

From the length of the list, it will be apparent that *individuals are likely to manifest certain clusters of pragmatic difficulty rather than the entire possible range of symptoms.* We would like to stress that the list does only a little to clarify the conceptualization of these problems. It will be noted, for instance, that superficial behaviours and underlying factors have not yet been satisfactorily separated, although a start has been made.

Characteristics of Pragmatic Impairment

The following lists have been derived from the literature on pragmatic dysfunction. We have arranged the characteristics found in the literature into four main groupings: expressing communicative intents, conversational management, problems of presupposition, and pragmatic comprehension and knowledge base. Clearly, any one individual will exhibit only *some* of these features.

Expressing communicative intents

Does not attract attention to self.
Does not point (no deixis).
Seldom initiates interaction.
Does not make intent clear.
Echolalia (immediate or delayed).
Perseveration.
Poor non-verbal communication (eye signals, orientation to partner, body language, facial expression, gesture, signing).
Abnormal prosody (loudness, stress, rhythm, intonation, speed).
Unusual voice quality.
'Search behaviours' typical of word-finding difficulty (minor hesitations, false starts, neologisms, circumlocution).

Other features of speech and language such as articulation, phonology, syntax and major dysfluency may be implicated or may be normal. *Semantic problems* (uncertainty about the meanings of words – see page 42) *are noted and may be strongly associated with pragmatic difficulties*, but are not dealt with in this book.

Conversational management

Problems with basic interaction skills.
Poor attention and listening.
Poor turn taking (fails to take own turn, does not allow turns, pauses too long or overlaps). *Remember, turns may be verbal or non-verbal.*
Minimal turns (short utterances, few per turn).
Dominant turns (too many utterances).
Use of avoidance strategies.
Use of compensatory communication strategies (these may be mistaken for errors).
Speech act difficulties: use of only a narrow range of speech acts; overuse of one type of speech act (such as questions); speech acts performed inappropriately.
Problems of organization and relevance: difficulties with, or lack of interest in, narrative; thoughts not presented sequentially; disorganized behaviour; incoherence; poor use of cohesive devices; attention to details which others regard as non-salient or irrelevant; irrelevant replies to questions.
Topic management problems (possibly related to the above): clumsy introduction of topics; topic drift (does not maintain topic); 'tangentiality' (introduces irrelevant material without warning); 'obsessive' adherence to one topic; failure to follow (when partner seeks to switch topic); difficulty in closing topics politely; abrupt ending of interaction.
Weakness in conversational repair: failure to request clarification; failure to signal non-comprehension; failure or inadequacy in supplying clarification; poor spontaneous repairs (such as apologies).
Problems of interactive style: 'rudeness'; failure to adapt style to context; pedantic/formal/precocious style; overuse of clichés and stereotyped utterances; slowness in responding; over-hasty response.

Problems of presupposition (awareness of what may be assumed to exist in the minds of other people)

Ignoring the listener's perspective when speaking.
'Tactlessness'.
Apparent lack of empathic feelings.
Provision of more or less information than is needed.
Uncertain differentiation between 'given' (already familiar) and 'new' information.
Overuse of deictic terms or pronouns ('that', 'those', 'them', 'it', 'there', and so on) when the referent is not obvious to the listener.
Overuse of 'empty' terms, such as 'thing' or 'stuff'.
Use of full sentence forms rather than ellipsis.
Problems with constructing narratives.
Problems with the use of modal verbs.
Little use of metaphor, irony, humour, idiom.
A tendency to 'ramble'.
Use of jargon.
Paraphasia ('pork' for 'fork', 'hand' for 'foot').
Repetitiveness.

Pragmatic comprehension and knowledge base

Apparent difficulty in making sense of the world.
Difficulty in making inferences: appreciating the significance of words and events.
Tendency to interpret expressions literally.

Difficulty in keeping track of referents across stretches of discourse.
Failure to monitor own comprehension.
Difficulty in interpreting the communicative intentions of others (speech act comprehension).
Difficulty in interpreting indirect speech acts.
Difficulty in interpreting facial expression or other aspects of non-verbal communication.
Poor time sense and difficulty with temporal language and concepts.
Poor spatial awareness and difficulty with spatial language and concepts.
Poor comprehension of narratives.
Difficulty in understanding irony, humour, metaphor and idiom.

The following personal characteristics have also been noted and are thought by some writers to relate directly to pragmatic (and possibly semantic) impairment. We would prefer not to make this assumption since cognitive impairment, emotional discomfort or environmental factors might equally well be responsible.

- Obsessive interests
- Idiosyncratic style
- Gaucheness
- Shyness
- Inflexibility
- Non-cooperativeness
- Preference for 'off-task' activities
- Lack of empathy
- Lack of awareness of role and status
- Lack of respect for others
- Impulsiveness
- Distrustfulness

The present authors have noted several other commonly occurring features in people whose pragmatic abilities are impaired (however, the above reservations still apply):

- Aggressiveness
- Timidity
- A tendency to indulge in, or to attract, teasing or bullying
- Jealous and competitive attitudes
- Misunderstanding of competitive situations
- Excessive dependence
- An appearance of opting out or not making any effort

Further features mentioned in the literature could be viewed as *explanations* for some of the behaviours listed in the four groups. Much of the literature in which these features are mentioned lacks rigour. However, we have decided to include them in an effort to assist future researchers who are not familiar with the field. We also hope that there may be some benefit to interdisciplinary co-operation if the features are recognized.

Contributory Factors

The following factors possibly underlie, perpetuate or contribute to pragmatic difficulty.

Factors within the client

Neurological or psychiatric disorders
Slow cognitive or linguistic processing
Linguistic deficit
Immaturity
Personality factors

Social/emotional factors

Environmental factors
Low involvement with other people
Lack of confidence
Low self-esteem
Defensiveness

Factors in the self

Weak or absent sense of self
Weak or absent integrative ability
Weak or absent inner coherence

Imaginative factors

Poor imaginative ability
Weak or absent 'theory of mind'
Poor empathy with others

Cognitive style

Rigidity of thought/rigid concept boundaries
Disorganization
Short attention span; distractibility

Memory factors

Word finding difficulty
Short-term memory problems
Poor discourse tracking

Knowledge factors

Lack of world knowledge or social knowledge
Lack of specific pragmatic knowledge

How is Pragmatic Dysfunction Different from Other Disorders of Communication?

Pragmatic dysfunction differs from other disturbances of communication in that it primarily concerns communication *in context*. Linguistic, articulatory, vocal and other non-verbal abilities are involved, of course, but it is their *integrated use in real situations* which concerns us here.

Another important difference between pragmatic dysfunction and other communication dysfunctions is that, because the difficulty arises within an interaction, both partners in the interaction can contribute towards its failure or success. This makes diagnosis of pragmatic dysfunction more difficult than that of some other communication dysfunctions. As with language disorders, the dysfunction may affect both *expressive* pragmatic abilities (for example, acquaintances greeting each other appropriately) and *receptive* pragmatic abilities (such as friends understanding each other's jokes).

Pragmatic dysfunction may be found in individuals with or without speech and language disorders. What is noticeable to communicative partners is that, despite their having superficially normal speech and language, interactions with individuals with pragmatic dysfunction seem to be meagre, uncomfortable or simply 'odd'.

Pragmatic Knowledge and Skill

In order to function well pragmatically, people need to possess both knowledge and skill: (1) knowledge of possible speech acts (such as asking questions, responding, making a greeting or a joke) and how they can be performed; (2) skill in performing them; (3) knowledge about their appropriate use; and (4) knowledge of how they can be interpreted when performed by oneself or others.

Pragmatic functioning is disturbed in a number of circumstances or combinations of circumstances. First is when essential communicative knowledge is missing. This can be recognized by an individual performing poorly in formal and informal testing. Occasionally, an individual who has learnt specific social rituals may appear to possess the communicative knowledge underlying those rituals, but when observed in a wider range of situations the client's inability to generalize may highlight the superficiality of the learnt social rituals.

Second is when individuals lack skill in gaining access to, integrating and using knowledge which they do, in fact, possess. This can be recognized by observing that an individual performs less well in real situations than one might expect on the basis of test results.

Third is when people possess the necessary knowledge and the necessary skills, but behave as if this were not the case owing to lack of confidence or other emotional discomfort. This can be recognized on observing unexpectedly good performance in a person previously thought to lack both knowledge and skills because these were rarely used. Social shyness manifests itself through an individual performing well in comfortable circumstances but poorly in situations in which they feel uncomfortable.

Knowledge Required for Effective Pragmatic Functioning

Examples of the types of knowledge required for effective pragmatic functioning are:

▶ The knowledge that other people expect answers to their questions and that their questions can be interpreted in various ways.

▶ The knowledge of how to answer in a satisfactory way. This type of knowledge results from analysing the context and the question (both its literal meaning and its significance) then combining the result of this analysis with social and linguistic knowledge in order to design a suitable reply.

Skills Required for Effective Pragmatic Functioning

Examples of the type of skills required are:

▶ The skill to perform an appropriate combination of verbal and non-verbal behaviours in order to answer appropriately. This is achieved by analysing the question and the context, designing a reply, identifying the behaviours that are called for and then being able to perform them correctly and to *monitor* the performance.

▶ The skill to initiate a conversation. This is achieved by analysing the context, planning something relevant to say to the person, choosing the appropriate level of politeness and appropriate terms to use, then performing the initiation of the conversation correctly and being prepared for possible responses.

Motivation and Confidence

It is important to keep in mind the issue of whether or not a person is sufficiently *willing and confident* to communicate. This is important from the clinician's point of view, since it will influence not only diagnosis but also the design of intervention. Clearly, it would be unhelpful to label all instances of pragmatic dysfunction as evidence of true disability, since confidence is as crucial to conversation as it is to swimming.

When professionals are examining communicative competence and communicative confidence in an individual, consideration should be given to the following questions: (1) Does the individual sometimes perform better than they habitually do? (2) What are the possible reasons for the individual's underperformance? (3) Does the individual possess the requisite knowledge and skills? (4) Is the individual able to gain access to, integrate and skilfully employ the requisite types of knowledge in any given context?

Causes of Pragmatic Difficulty

Attributing Responsibility for Pragmatic Difficulty

Clinically, it is usual to attribute any failure in interactions to disability in one partner, the client, and to state that the client has a 'disorder'. We suggest that it is more helpful to acknowledge that superficial difficulties in communication can arise for a variety of reasons, *not all of them* to do with deficits in the client's abilities. However, there is a need to examine the fact that some clients, for whatever reason, do appear to experience unsatisfactory interactions quite frequently. This is thought to be due to their having pragmatic difficulties which their communicative partners find it hard to accommodate.

Identifying Causes of Pragmatic Difficulty

Thorough academic investigation of the mechanisms and causation of pragmatic dysfunction is urgently needed for the following four reasons:

1 Treatment and counselling can become more appropriate.
2 Preventive measures can be considered.
3 Research can become more clearly focused.
4 Insights with possible wider applications can be shared with other disciplines.

What is Known about Causes of Pragmatic Dysfunction?

The causes of pragmatic dysfunction are not fully understood. This is partly because these dysfunctions have only recently been identified as essentially pragmatic and have thus not been systematically investigated as potentially linked phenomena. Potential causes of pragmatic dysfunction are discussed in detail by **McTear & Conti-Ramsden** (1992) and by **Smith & Leinonen** (1992). Possible causes of pragmatic dysfunction that have been suggested in the literature include the following:

1 semantic deficits;
2 impairments of cognition;
3 impairment of imagination;
4 institutionalization;
5 negative environmental influences (**Rutter**, 1981);
6 lack of social experience possibly playing a part in the development of inappropriate styles of interaction;
7 certain neurological conditions, particularly those affecting the right cerebral hemisphere (**Bryan**, 1988; **Rapin & Allen**, 1983; **Starratt Myrers**, 1984; **Shields**, 1991).

As stated above, it is not yet clear which difficulties are fundamental to other, more superficial, manifestations. For example, a person might fail to use polite forms of speech because of hostility, lack of social knowledge, lack of empathy or ignorance of the polite forms themselves. A person might produce unsuitable responses, either because of uncertainty about social rules and pragmatic obligations or because the intention of their partner's initiation had been misunderstood.

Diagnosis

The identification of pragmatic dysfunction itself is not as difficult as the discovery of its cause. One of the most important identifying features is subjective experience of discomfort on the part of communicative partners and this is usually easy to detect. Objectively identifying the source of that discomfort, however, is a demanding professional task which requires the clinician to make detailed observations. Clinicians involved in diagnosis should be aware of a number of possible complications when identifying the causes of pragmatic dysfunction.

First, the origin of communicative difficulties may lie in the behaviour of either partner, or in the relationship between them. For instance, a disturbed parent may influence the pragmatic performance of his or her children, or a tired clinician may not stimulate clients to do their best.

Second, the situation or the activity within which the communication is taking place may be influencing the behaviour of one or other participant. For instance, working on jigsaw puzzles tends to reduce people's verbal output, whereas presenting an interesting problem to be solved tends to increase it.

Third, group interactions present multiple relationships which make it more difficult to identify the origins of breakdowns. Making judgements about the appropriacy of contributions is also more difficult in a group since expectations differ between individuals (cf **Leinonen & Smith**, 1994).

Fourth, it is possible that one's expectations may be coloured by cultural or subcultural prejudice (**Leinonen & Smith**, 1994).

Finally, any combination of the multiple pragmatic problems listed below may be present to varying degrees in different communication situations.

Labels Used in Diagnosis

In view of the wide range of possible pragmatic difficulties and their multiple possible causes, we regard the use of simplifying labels such as 'semantic–pragmatic disorder' as potentially misleading. This label also serves to remove attention from an important group of clients — young children whose comprehension is adequate but whose conversational skills are poorly developed.

A term which is sometimes used to designate what are essentially pragmatic difficulties is 'high level language disorder'. The term has some appeal, in that there are certain difficulties at the discourse level which do not become apparent until the basics of speech, language and communication are in place. Also certain skills, for example the use and comprehension of irony or certain kinds of implicit meaning, develop late in childhood and appear to call for cognitive maturity and the integration of several areas of sophisticated knowledge. An objection arises as follows: the term 'high level' has connotations of developmentally advanced skills. This may be misleading because children who are in the early stages of communication development perform many complex feats of pragmatic integration. For instance, three-year-olds can from time to time remember their parents' request for polite behaviour in grandparents' houses and adapt their verbal and non-verbal communications accordingly. They can combine linguistic and social knowledge with their knowledge of the world in order to ask us, very persuasively, for their favourite dinner. They can perform some of the functions which adult speakers perform and should be expected to do so. What is needed is developmentally appropriate treatment based on an understanding of which high, and low, level functions are normally present at certain developmental stages. When young children whose pragmatic skills are weak attend speech and language clinics, they should be helped with communication (pragmatics) as well as with speech and language.

The term 'high level language disorder' is probably best reserved for those difficulties which suggest that an individual is not yet fully able to make use of inductive reasoning, for instance difficulties with implicit meaning, humour and irony. We prefer to use the more open expressions 'pragmatic difficulty' or 'pragmatic difficulty associated with ...' and then to name the associated condition, such as language delay, dysfluency, semantic disorder (comprehension deficit), aphasia, autism, developmental delay, and so on. However, we also accept that a simpler, catch-all term such as 'semantic–pragmatic disorder' may be viewed as desirable for purposes such as clinical audit or for the allocation of resources and as clinical shorthand.

As to whether pragmatic difficulty, or indeed pragmatic disability, exists in a pure form, we remain uncertain. Careful description of presenting problems and associated factors will, we suggest, prove more valuable than 'diagnosing' an unclear condition. Whatever terminology is favoured, important distinctions need to be made, in both children and adults, between the following:

1 Pragmatic difficulties which are associated with early speech impairments (articulation, dysfluency, voice) or expressive language problems (phonology or syntax) which have eroded communicative confidence and/or prevented normal social interaction.

2 Pragmatic difficulties associated mainly with environmental or emotional problems, for example those experienced by people who have been mistreated or denied opportunities for social interaction (**Law**, 1992; **Law & Conway**, 1991 and 1992; **Smith & Leinonen**, 1992).

3 Pragmatic difficulties associated with Asperger's syndrome and autism (**Aarons & Gittens**, 1992; **Frith**, 1989 and 1991; **Baron-Cohen & Bolton**, 1993).
4 Pragmatic difficulties associated with psychosis (**Baltax**, 1990; **Hassibi & Breuer**, 1980; **Baltax & Simmons**, 1988).
5 Pragmatic difficulties associated with semantic impairments (developmental or acquired: **Bishop**, 1989; **Rapin & Allen**, 1983 and 1987).
6 Pragmatic difficulties of a specific nature thought to be associated with right hemisphere dysfunction (**Bryan**, 1988 and 1994; **Shields**, 1991; **Starratt Myers**, 1984).

The consequences of misdiagnosis can be very serious for the individuals concerned, therefore there is a pressing need for improved interdisciplinary co-operation in this matter.

Severity Rating

What is a Severity Rating?

Pragmatic difficulties can result in varying degrees of disruption to communication and varying degrees of distress to the speaker and their family. A severity rating is a clinical judgement that classifies an individual's difficulties into a descriptive category according to how severe the pragmatic difficulty is considered to be. Any severity rating will have an element of subjectivity, but we feel that broad ratings of severity (mild, moderate and severe) can be made when consideration of a wide range of factors and perspectives is taken by the rater.

What are the Advantages of Using Severity Ratings?

A simple description of severity rating for pragmatic difficulties can be advantageous for the following reasons.

Planning and prioritizing treatment

A severity rating can assist clinicians who want to create compatible and complementary groups of clients for small group work, for example. Clinicians may need to plan the clinical caseload in such a way that those clients who have the most severe difficulties are given a higher priority than those with less severe difficulties. Clinicians who are less experienced with clients with pragmatic difficulties may want to use a severity rating system to ensure that those clients with moderate to severe difficulties are seen for a second opinion by a colleague who is more experienced within the area of pragmatics.

Predicting outcomes

Knowledge of the severity rating of a particular client can give guidance as to the most likely outcome for the client. *In general*, the more severe the pragmatic difficulty the poorer the predicted outcome may be. (It will be obvious to clinicians that this is an oversimplification and that each client's predicted outcome will need to be considered individually.)

Sharing information with clients and their relatives

Since clients and relatives will not have the context of broad experience of the range of pragmatic difficulties, it can be useful to put a pragmatic difficulty into context by using the descriptive labels 'mild', 'moderate' or 'severe'.

Sharing information with professionals

In addition to describing the specific difficulties that a client or group of clients is experiencing, it can be useful to have a system for describing the overall severity of the problem in a mutually comprehensible manner.

Procedure for Severity Rating

One way of arriving at such a rating is to gather objective facts about the impairment and consider these together with what is known of the client's personality, temperament and environment. Consideration of the following factors will assist the clinician in forming a judgement of severity:

1 The extent to which the client's thinking and emotional life are being disrupted. For instance, difficulty with forming hypotheses or short-term memory problems can cause a severe disruption to communication. Similarly, difficulty in integrating information and then thinking about past events is likely to affect a person's ability to see matters clearly and to act rationally.
2 The extent to which the client's social relations are being disrupted.
3 The extent of the disruption caused for the client's family and others in the immediate environment.

The type of information concerning the actual impairment that needs to be gathered in order to decide on a severity rating includes the following:

- The *specific type of difficulties* encountered by the client, some being more disruptive than others. For instance, using a pedantic style of speech is not likely to be so disruptive of social relationships as poor turn taking or extreme rudeness.
- The *frequency* with which the difficulty becomes apparent. The difficulty may be one that is observed only once in a day (for example, inappropriate use of humour) or it may be one that occurs several times within every interaction (for example, using unclear referents in conversations, so that the listener becomes confused).
- The *range of difficulties* encountered by the client: for example, the difficulties could be concentrated around a relatively narrow range of communicative difficulties such as greetings, leave-takings and initial starting up of conversations, or the range may be very broad, including difficulties in turn taking, taking the listener's perspective and using politeness markers appropriately.
- The client's degree of *insight* and their skill in *repairing and clarifying*. The client may be very aware of their difficulties and be able to assist listeners by providing corrections to their messages or by offering explanations to smooth breakdowns in communication. For example when a client is using the pronouns 'he' and 'she' without prior explanation they might explain this apologetically to the confused listener: "Sorry, I'm so excited about telling you what happened at Joe's party that I forgot that you haven't met the people I went with — Sue and Andy." Conversely, the client may be unaware that they have a difficulty with pragmatics. A common difficulty that occurs throughout the population but is frequently unrecognized by the individual concerned involves a failure to introduce topics that will be of interest to the listener as well as the speaker (as when talking about oneself or about one's own hobbies exclusively).
- The extent to which successful *communication strategies* are used.

The issue of severity rating is discussed in more detail in **Smith & Leinonen** (1992, pages 162, 181–3, 203–4). Examples of how people and their pragmatic problems might be grouped within three levels of severity follow. However, it needs to be recognized that the severity of problems can change from one situation to another (see 'context', page 40) and also over time, as in the case of those neurological disorders which vary from day to day.

Severe pragmatic difficulties

People with autism and some types of psychosis.

Moderate pragmatic difficulties

People on the autistic continuum, for instance those with Asperger's syndrome.
People diagnosed as having 'semantic–pragmatic disorder' or 'high level language disorder'.
Some institutionalized people.
Undiagnosed people regarded as communicating poorly or 'oddly'.
Some people with learning difficulties whose particular cognitive limitations affect pragmatics.
Some right hemisphere stroke patients.
Children with speech/language delays or disorders who lack basic communicative competence.

Mild pragmatic difficulties

It is important to note that these mild pragmatic difficulties can be encountered in the absence of any pathology. Most of us will experience some difficulty in communicating successfully at some time in our lives.

Any of us experiencing a breakdown in communication with another person and not being able to repair it smoothly.
People who want to improve their management skills.
People who lack conversational 'know-how'. (This can include people with or without a history of language disorder or dysfluency.)
Students who produce incoherent essays.
People who shout inappropriately.
People who feel the need for social skills: classes, communication courses or assertiveness training.
Mildly unempathic people.
People who become boring (for example, lecturers or writers).

Positive Focus

While it can be helpful to focus on what clients can *not* comfortably achieve and to consider how their difficulties may be rated as mild, moderate or severe, a more therapeutic approach is usually to work from strengths. This focus, after all, contributes to the client's communicative confidence. Many clients who do experience some difficulties with the pragmatics of communication nonetheless avoid many of those listed above (**Byers-Brown & Edwards**, 1989).

Few of us would claim never to encounter any pragmatic difficulties of any kind and most of us are aware of how discouraging it can be to have our strengths overlooked. This needs to be kept in mind when the severity rating of clients' problems is considered, and also of course when planning treatment. Some of the strategies which people use to compensate for difficulties are unacceptable, for instance kicking the listener to get attention. Often, however, clients are able, given the necessary confidence and self-esteem, to compensate in some more positive way. Examples of more positive compensatory strategies include the following:

▶ repeating back to the speaker what the client has understood them to say.

▶ making minimal contributions when a 'turn' is called for.

▶ combining verbal and non-verbal methods of communication.

▶ echolalia or telegraphic utterances can be used by a client in an attempt to join in conversation and these contributions can be encouraged to begin with and then gradually improved.

Good compensatory strategies and a supportive environment, or even a supportive conversational partner on specific occasions, can reduce the impact of a person's disabilities and difficulties. These strategies need to be recognized and welcomed. Sometimes, however, they are simply regarded as evidence of inadequacy and are then discouraged or corrected, which has a poor effect on the client's confidence and interactive skills. Explaining the validity of such 'communication strategies' to clients' associates can reduce the impact of pragmatic difficulties on relationships and social functioning (**Smith & Leinonen**, 1992; **Lesser & Milroy**, 1993). Helping relatives to 'correct' clients' speech and language only when it is appropriate to do so has traditionally been part of the clinician's role and becomes even more necessary where there are pragmatic difficulties.

Sadly, the impact which these difficulties have on a person's social functioning can be increased by the critical and sometimes hostile response of others. Unfavourable reactions range from simple misunderstanding, through teasing, discourtesy and disrespect to outright ostracism or aggression. Needless to say, further difficulties can develop in reaction and these can be mistaken for intrinsic disability.

At a time when there is growing awareness of the wide range of pragmatic 'faults' which could be 'corrected', it is essential for clinicians to retain their understanding of the importance to clients of positive communicative experiences.

Summary

This chapter has described the difficulties in defining normal pragmatic functioning that were highlighted in Chapter 3. We have presented a very detailed and lengthy list of features that have been described in the literature as being characteristic of pragmatic dysfunction. The scale of the problem of identifying and classifying pragmatic difficulties and their underlying causes has been discussed, as have the further problems associated with forming a diagnosis of a pragmatic difficulty. Finally, we have discussed the issues involved in describing the severity of a pragmatic difficulty — an area that will be taken up once more in Chapter 8, where we present a severity rating scale.

Recommended Reading

Of the references mentioned at the beginning of this chapter, we suggest that the following will provide a basic reading list for pragmatic difficulties. (See also Appendix I.)

Bishop DVM, 'Autism, Asperger's Syndrome and Semantic–Pragmatic Disorder: Where are the Boundaries?', *British Journal of Disorders of Communication* 24(2), pp107–21, 1989. Also reprinted by the National Autistic Society (UK).

Friel-Patti S & Conti-Ramsden G, 'Discourse Development in Atypical Language Learners', Kuczaj S (ed), *Discourse Development*, Spinger-Verlag, New York, 1984.

Harris PL, *Children and Emotion: The Development of Psychological Understanding*, Blackwell, Oxford, 1989.

Lucas Arwood EV, *Semantic and Pragmatic– Disorders*, 2nd edn, Aspen Systems, Rockville, 1991.

Mogford-Bevan K & Sadler J (eds), *Child Language Disability Vol 2: Semantic and Pragmatic Difficulties*, Multilingual Matters, Clevedon, 1991.

Rapin I & Allen D, 'Developmental Language Disorders: Nosological Considerations', Kirk U (ed), *Neuropsychology of Language, Reading and Spelling*, Academic Press, New York, 1983.

Rutter M, *Maternal Deprivation Reassessed*, Penguin, London, 1991.

Chapter 5
Introduction to the Assessment of Pragmatics

Introduction/*38*
What is Pragmatic Assessment?/*38*
Why Assess Pragmatics?/*38*
Problems in Assessment/*38*
    Lack of Normative Data/*39*
    Subjectivity of Observations/*39*
    Inconsistencies in what is Acceptable Behaviour/*39*
    The Influence of the Assessor, Situation and Activity/*39*
    The Difficulty of Separating Clients from their Environments/*39*
    Evaluating Skills as Positive or Negative/*39*
    A Client's Lack of Ability versus Failure to Demonstrate Ability/*39*
    Overassessment/*40*
    A Narrow Viewpoint/*40*
    Context/*40*
    Depth of Assessment/*41*
Methods of Assessment/*42*
Formal Assessments/*42*
    Semantic Comprehension Assessment/*42*
    Pragmatic Comprehension Assessment/*42*
    Production/*43*
Summary/*45*
Recommended Reading/*46*

Chapter 5
INTRODUCTION TO THE ASSESSMENT OF PRAGMATICS

Introduction

In this chapter we will examine the importance of the process of assessment and will describe *formal* pragmatic assessments that are currently available. In Chapter 6 we will present *informal* assessment methods and provide guidelines to assist the transition from the assessment process to intervention planning. Although we have dealt with formal and informal assessments separately, we wish the reader to be aware that our belief is that a **combination** of formal and informal assessments is appropriate for most clients.

Assessment is one of the most important stages in the process of assisting clients with communication difficulties. It is essential when contemplating an assessment to include consideration of the pragmatic skills and knowledge of the individual. A person's communicative use of speech and language skills is crucial to the success of their interactions and relationships. The ability to integrate various types of knowledge, as described in Chapter 2, allows individuals to experience success in the areas of education, employment and personal life. It also plays an important role in their inner life of thoughts and emotions.

What is Pragmatic Assessment?

In our view, pragmatic assessment is a continuing process which provides an objective and representative picture of a client's communication in everyday life. A pragmatic assessment should be done for the benefit of clients and their families. Because of this client focus, the aims of a pragmatic assessment should be to discover: (1) the client's pragmatic strengths; (2) the client's pragmatic difficulties; (3) what the client needs to be able to do communicatively to function adequately in their particular environment; and (4) what the client hopes and wishes to be able to do communicatively to function more effectively.

A complete picture of *all* of the client's communicative behaviours and knowledge is not essential (thankfully) at an initial assessment. However, a good assessment will be sufficiently thorough to allow the therapist to plan intervention *logically* and with a *sound scientific basis*. An initial assessment can capture the *main* characteristics of communication and later continuing assessments can provide more detailed information as and when necessary. The latter provide the therapist with an opportunity to monitor continually the success of intervention.

Why Assess Pragmatics?

There are several different reasons for carrying out assessments:

1. Screening relatively large populations for pragmatic difficulties in order to offer a preventive service.

2. Providing a diagnostic description of clients by comparing them with their peer group and describing their strengths and needs.

3. Planning intervention. Without the foundation of an accurate assessment, the client's intervention plan will perhaps be inadequate for their needs. Important areas of strength, weakness or preferred learning methods may be overlooked.

4. Establishing a baseline from which progress in intervention can be measured. Motivation can be maintained through referring the client back to previous levels of skill or knowledge.

5. Providing information for caregivers and clients about strategies that they can employ to assist communication in the short term while intervention is being planned or the client is on a waiting list.

6. Accountability: to ensure that managers are aware of the quality and value of the service that is being provided, thus indirectly influencing budgeting and management decisions. (See Chapter 6 for more information on accountability.)

Problems in Assessment

Although we believe that assessment is of paramount importance, it would be naïve to suggest that it is a straightforward process. On the contrary, it is full of potential problems that need to be borne in mind both when preparing for the assessment and when involved in the process itself.

Lack of Normative Data

There is, as yet, a shortage of normative data upon which judgements of suitability to ages and stages of development can be based (see Chapter 3). **McTear & Conti-Ramsden** (1992) and **Leinonen & Smith** (1992) have pointed out that unacceptable behaviours such as overinitiation or excessive questioning may well be developmentally determined. If children normally pass through stages of dominating conversations or of asking an uncomfortable number of questions, for whatever reason, it may be unwise to inhibit such behaviour before clients are developmentally ready to move on.

Subjectivity of Observations

It should be remembered that, no matter how hard one tries to remain objective, observation is a subjective activity. It is difficult for even skilled clinicians accurately to identify clients' true intentions. However, subjective information about how the clinician feels when interacting with a client has its place in collecting observational data since communicative success depends on producing the desired subjective effect in a partner. Linked to this problem is the practical difficulty in obtaining observations of the client with a variety of communicative partners, each able to describe the success (or lack of success) of their interaction with the client.

Inconsistencies in what is Acceptable Behaviour

Cultures, subcultures and individuals differ in their estimation of what is appropriate in communicative behaviour. However, it is easy to assume, incorrectly, that all right-thinking people share one's own view (**Leinonen & Smith,** 1992).

The Influence of the Assessor, Situation and Activity

The behaviour of the communicative partner involved in assessment will have an effect on the person designated as the 'client' for speech pathology purposes. This fact must not only be acknowledged but be kept in the forefront of one's mind when assessing the client's performance and estimating the client's knowledge. Only if this is done and if the client is observed in several different settings and engaging in a variety of activities can a realistic assessment be made.

The Difficulty of Separating Clients from their Environments

Abnormal pragmatics may indicate an abnormality within a client or a particular environment. As with any other behavioural abnormality, abnormal pragmatic behaviour cannot be assumed to indicate an abnormality within the client. There is also a possibility that the client's environment may be contributing to the creation and/or perpetuation of the abnormal behaviour. For instance, children who are ill-treated or neglected may communicate poorly even though no pathology is present (**Law & Conway,** 1991 and 1992; **Smith & Leinonen,** 1992; **Leinonen & Smith,** 1994). Also clients who have spent much time living in institutions may display inappropriate behaviours that are not frequently seen outside the institutional setting, such as inappropriate friendliness, demanding rewards after certain ritualized communications or unnecessarily repeating requests.

Evaluating Skills as Positive or Negative

Certain unusual communication characteristics may be useful compensatory strategies for a client. For example, echolalia can allow a person to take a turn despite failing to communicate a meaningful message.

A Client's Lack of Ability versus Failure to Demonstrate Ability

When observing communicative behaviour with a view to determining underlying pragmatic ability, it is important not to assume that disability exists when communicative behaviour appears to be inadequate. There are four main reasons for this. First, circumstances may have prevented the demonstration of a person's full repertoire: an adult may fail to demonstrate turn-taking ability because of excessive eagerness to recount an exciting event, or a child may fail to demonstrate the ability to stay on topic because of anxiety or excitement.

Second, individuals do not always choose to employ their full range of abilities. For example, a client may fail to respond adequately to questions because of discomfort with the setting, the activity, the communicative partner or the assessor.

Third, the need to develop or employ certain skills may not have become apparent to the person concerned. Once the need is apparent, the skill may be demonstrated. Thus a client who is able to take another's perspective into account may have been living in circumstances where this was never expected. Examples may include people who have been institutionalized, or, conversely, overindulged.

Finally, prerequisite skills and items of knowledge are sometimes missing but, once these have been taught, the client is able to perform certain pragmatic functions which were thought to be impossible. Thus a client may appear to lack the ability to use politeness skills but these may start to be regularly employed after the expected forms have been taught and the appropriate situations for their use have been pointed out.

Overassessment

Clients may be assessed by several different professionals or teams over a period of months or years prior to their difficulty being recognized as one primarily with the social use of language. It is important that the therapist maintains sensitivity to the stress that assessment causes to clients and their families. Assessment should only be carried out where it is clear that the client stands to gain significant benefits. Wherever possible, previous assessments should be used and duplication should be avoided. It is worth spending some time discussing previous assessments with the caregiver and (with the written permission of the caregiver) obtaining copies of previous assessments and progress reports from teachers or therapists. This includes obtaining assessments and records from health and education authorities in situations where the client may have relocated.

A Narrow Viewpoint

It is necessary to take account of those who know a client best, such as caregivers and relatives. It can also be valuable to obtain the views of several other people who know the client, for example teachers and friends, as well as eliciting information directly from clients themselves. It can be useful to decide which people would be able to give helpful information in joint consultation with the client (where appropriate) rather than deciding in advance whom you would approach. It may be appropriate to give the pre-assessment questionnaire described below (page 48) to those people chosen. Alternatively, clinicians can easily design on a word processor their own questionnaire which could be customized for each client or each client group. This avoids the problem of people being asked questions that are not appropriate to their circumstances. This can be particularly bothersome and may result in unreturned questionnaires if, for example, a spouse of a client is asked to fill in one that has many items that apply primarily to children, or a teacher is asked questions about activities that occur only at home.

Context

Attention is drawn here to the variability of pragmatic performance. When considering how people understand and participate in communication in context, the vital role played by context itself has to be kept in mind. This is especially important when clients are being assessed. **To determine whether or not individuals are experiencing pragmatic difficulties, and also to estimate their potential,** it is essential to observe them in a variety of activities, situations and relationships.

The following illustrations of various aspects of 'context' may help to clarify its complex nature.

Culture and subculture

Different cultures, and even subgroups within one culture, have differing expectations about politeness and what constitutes 'rudeness'. Specific social norms and conventions may or may not be appreciated by every client, but they can exert an influence through the expectations of the communicative partner. For instance, clients who are seen as rude because of a cultural mismatch may experience unfriendly attitudes from others as a result. This can lead to a worsening of social behaviour which is not entirely attributable to the client's disorder.

Situation

Some individuals are frightened of medical settings and behave differently in them. Others perform well only in their own homes or in familiar territory.

Activity

Some activities place greater demands on people's pragmatic skill than others. Two people tidying a cupboard might interact satisfactorily since everything that is being spoken about is visible and at hand. There is no need, here, to specify what is being referred to or to refer back and forth within a stretch of discourse. Even turn taking in this situation can be mediated by the physical activities involved. However, if the same two people were to attempt a discussion of their previous evening's television viewing, it could well emerge that one of them was struggling to recall, describe or interpret what had been seen. Similarly, some activities give little opportunity for people to demonstrate abilities which they have. Pragmatic abilities are frequently over- or underestimated in assessment for these reasons.

Role

Different role relationships call for different styles of interaction. For instance, authority figures are not addressed in the same way as peers. People with pragmatic difficulties cannot always appreciate this, but it will nevertheless affect the partner's response, which will, in turn, affect the client.

Relationship

If a relationship already exists between people who are interacting, that past relationship forms a special part of the context for the current interaction.

Current state of relationship

Relationships are not static but are updated on the basis of the most recent encounter. Most people do not behave identically with two friends if one of them has recently been behaving in a disconcerting way.

Knowledge of partner

One behaves differently if one knows that a communicative partner is currently upset or has special knowledge of the topic under discussion.

Topic

One speaks more freely on some topics than others. Some topics call forth greater creativity than others. For instance, compare 'What I did at the weekend' or 'What I had for Christmas' with 'How I escaped from the snow-drift', 'What fascinates me about X—' or 'How to get started on the word processor'.

Linguistic context

Contributions must fit the grammar of the current discourse. That is to say, they must not only be grammatical in themselves, but must fit the form dictated by what has been said in the rest of the interaction. Long stretches of language have syntactic rules, just as sentences do (**Longacre**, 1979). For instance, "He looked under the hat" fits the linguistic context of "I don't know what Peter did next" *if* both interactive partners already know who Peter is and which hat is being referred to. Similarly, "Under the hat" fits with "I can't remember where he looked next" and "All this looking for things made him tired" fits into a continuous narrative.

Contributions are made to fit, partly by understanding what has gone before and partly by grasping the structural rules which operate beyond the level of sentences.

Inferential context

Contributions to any interaction need to indicate that one has understood the partner's apparent intention. In order to understand for oneself what is going on, one considers the significance, as well as the literal meaning, of what has already been said, on both sides. This inferential understanding provides part of the context for designing and interpreting further utterances. For instance, supposing a person says, "My mother was truly a saint", it would not be appropriate to take the statement literally and reply "That's amazing! You must have been very proud." Keeping track of the inferential context presents direct pragmatic challenges which many clients find it difficult to meet.

We hope it will now be clear that the successful use and reception of communicative behaviour in real life calls for the ***analysis of various types of contextual information***. Furthermore, ***the outcome of that analysis has to be integrated with several other types of knowledge and skill***. It is perhaps not surprising that difficulties can arise in this complex task.

Depth of Assessment

It is difficult to judge how much information is necessary to construct a useful profile of clients' skills. If the purpose of the assessment is simply to screen for pragmatic difficulties then a much broader and quicker assessment will be required than with a diagnostic assessment which contributes to placement decisions and within which intervention goals will be rooted. The depth of the assessment will be constrained by the following factors:

1. The relative importance of the pragmatic aspects of communication in the particular client's communication difficulty;
2. The amount of testing already completed;

3 The severity and breadth of the problem;
4 Constraints on the therapist's time. (However, we would suggest that the quality of the assessment should *not* be compromised because of time constraints. Rather, a solution that maintains a high quality of client service should be negotiated.)

Methods of Assessment

Choosing the most appropriate methods of assessment for a client is a task that requires considerable thought and preparation. If pragmatic assessment is a relatively new or little explored activity within a department or for an individual professional, an investment of several hours or days may be required to construct assessment questionnaires and informal procedures. In addition, a vital component of the successful integration of pragmatic assessment within any setting is the joint negotiation and agreement with colleagues and managers of both a philosophical rationale for introducing pragmatic assessment and the practical requirements needed to carry it out reliably. These practical requirements include ensuring that there is an appropriate location, personnel involvement, suitable recording and playback equipment and assessment materials, including any formal assessments that are to be purchased, budgeting for additional travel time, analysis time and secretarial support.

Formal Assessments

Semantic Comprehension Assessment

This is not a book about semantics. However, semantic issues underlie everything that is discussed in the book. Therefore it is crucial to remember that the assessment and description of clients' semantic knowledge is an essential part of understanding their pragmatic functioning. This may be one reason why it is difficult to disentangle semantic and pragmatic disorders. Another reason is that, if clients fail to understand what has been said to them for semantic reasons, they cannot respond appropriately and may therefore appear to be pragmatically disordered (**Leinonen**, 1995).

For semantic comprehension, four main areas require investigation:

1 Lexical knowledge and skills. This includes word recognition as well as receptive vocabulary.
2 Semantic relations. This includes knowledge and skill in understanding and using word combinations (syntax) to produce meaning.
3 Knowledge of idiomatic expressions. Fixed idioms, such as 'in a mess' and 'What are you up to?' have become an inseparable part of the semantic system, whereas newer inventions such as 'I could murder a curry' required pragmatic processing, at least on the first occasion of hearing.
4 Interpretation. This includes knowledge of the implications and personal significance of word choices and combinations. Interpretation requires knowledge of connotative as well as denotative meaning and thus also involves **pragmatic skills** such as analysis of context and recognition of speech acts: for instance, the recognition that a speaker intends to joke rather than to threaten, or vice versa.

There are several assessments of the various areas of comprehension available. The *PPVT (Peabody Picture Vocabulary Test)* (**Dunn**, 1965) and the British version, the *BPVS (British Picture Vocabulary Scale)* (**Dunn & Dunn**, 1982), assess receptive vocabulary primarily for nouns, verbs and adjectives and can be used for children or adults. *The Boehm Test of Basic Concepts* (**Boehm**, 1971) looks at a variety of spatial, temporal and numerical concepts through pictures. Other examples are *PRISM (Profile in Semantics L & G)* (**Crystal**, 1982), *TROG (Test for the Reception of Grammar)* (**Bishop**, 1983) and *The Word Finding Vocabulary Test* (**Renfrew**, 1995). For a thorough text on semantic issues the reader is referred to **Nelson** (1985).

Pragmatic Comprehension Assessment

Specifically pragmatic issues in comprehension concern the negotiation of meaning between communicative partners and the ability to make reference back and forth within stretches of discourse. This negotiation and referring to the future and to the past enables people to make *inferences* and to interpret the communicative intentions of others within specific situations. In order to do this really successfully, people have to integrate pragmatic skills with their knowledge of the world and their knowledge of language. There are several factors that can adversely affect pragmatic comprehension:

1 deficits in short- and long-term memory;
2 speed of processing;
3 perception of self and others;
4 affective considerations (emotional issues);
5 true pragmatic disabilities.

It will be apparent to clinicians that identifying clients' strengths and needs in the above areas will have considerable value, even if done informally.

For helpful discussion of comprehension issues, the reader is referred to **Chapman** (1981), **Miller *et al*** (1980), **Bishop** (1982 and 1987), **Crystal** (1982), **Dewart** (1995) and **Landells** (1995).

Production

It should be remembered that successful production usually depends on having comprehended both the social and the linguistic context within which the utterance is made. There are a variety of procedures available for describing pragmatics which generally focus on the productive aspects of communication. Below are listed guidelines for analysing transcripts, observations, assessment procedures and recordings. They have been subdivided into the following areas for ease of reference: pre-linguistic clients and children up to school age; school-aged children within the classroom; adults and older children; people with learning disabilities; adults with acquired dysphasia. Some clinicians may find the method of subdivision used in **Smith & Leinonen** (1992) preferable.

Assessments for pre-linguistic clients up to school age

Halliday (1975) and **Dore** (1975) present methods of viewing early communicative functions. These methods have the advantage of being *descriptive* approaches rather than *deficit-centred* approaches.

The *Pre-verbal Communication Schedule* (**Kiernan & Reid,** 1987), which is suitable for any age group, examines six key aspects of communicative functioning.

Coggins & Carpenter (1981) provide a method of analysing conversational data which may be applicable to any age group, including the elderly.

Wetherby and Prizant (1989) present guidelines for the assessment of communicative intent in children.

The Pragmatics Profile of Early Communication Skills (**Dewart & Summers,** 1995) is a lengthy questionnaire that is administered to caregivers in the form of an interview. It is designed for use with individuals from the earliest stages in communication to the later school years. It very helpfully provides the clinician with examples of possible responses for each question. It can be used as a questionnaire that is sent out prior to a more thorough assessment or as a context for instruction.

The communication assessment profile by **McLean & Snyder-McLean** (1978) is a transactional approach to early language training.

Ecoscale is a profile of adult and child interaction by **MacDonald & Gillette** (1986 and 1988).

The *Pragmatics Observation List* devised by **Johnston, Weinrich & Johnson** (1984) explores the level of adequacy demonstrated by children's pragmatic functioning.

The *Pragmatics Protocol* (**Prutting & Kirchner,** 1983) is one of the more familiar devices for identifying appropriately used and inappropriately used areas of communicative skill in all age groups. The problem of differing opinions as to what is 'appropriate' complicates the use of this assessment.

The *Bristol Language Development Scales* (**Gutfreund,** 1989) include an element of pragmatic analysis. A 'syntax-free' scale caters for groups who cannot hear or comprehend.

A method of systematizing observation of pragmatic behaviours which clinicians find helpful is presented in **McTear** (1985a).

The *Social Interactive Coding System* (*SICS*, **Rice, Sell & Hadley,** 1990) is a procedure for structuring observations of the communicative interactions of children in a naturalistic setting. The observer watches the child in segments of five minutes followed by a five-minute break for a total of 40 minutes (that is, 20 minutes of observation time). The observer fills in an observational coding sheet which provides space for noting time, activity area and type, addressee and the interactive 'status' of the child. The interaction codes include *initiations* (questions, statements, exclamations, requests and so on), *responses* (one-word, multi-word or non-verbal), *repetitions* — the child's repetition if her first attempt fails, and *ignoring* — the child ignores or is ignored. Once a description of the child's activities and interaction status is obtained, the clinician may see patterns emerging that can suggest possible intervention targets and strategies.

Menyuk, Liebergott & Schultz (1995) present a set of procedures for transcribing vocal turn taking and systems for coding child-directed speech: 'Measurement and coding rules of mother's speech' and 'Mother's requests for non-verbal action coding sheet.' They developed both schemes for research purposes in their longitudinal study into early language. However the procedures could usefully be adapted for clinical use with prelinguistic clients and those in the early linguistic stages.

Assessments for school-aged children within the classroom

Tough (1977a and 1977b) offers a framework for identifying the functions fulfilled by school-aged children's use of language in the school setting.

Weiss (1981) describes the comprehensive *INREAL* (*Inter-reactive Learning*) analytical framework for examining dyadic interaction.

Heublein & Bate (1988) describe an excellent method of exploring interactions: *INREAL*.

The information scale of the *Bus Story Test* of continuous speech **Renfrew** (1997) has been recognized as a valuable tool in research which may predict whether or not a child's early language difficulties will resolve by age five years six months (**Bishop & Edmundson,** 1987). This may be because it examines integrative abilities which underpin language development or because it reveals short-term memory deficits which impede pragmatic and linguistic functioning. Alternatively, it may be that failure to understand the story is a major reason for poor performance in the test and that it is this which predicts persisting language difficulty (**Paul,** 1992). See also **Andersen *et al*** (1996) for a description of a communication rating scale used in conjunction with Renfrew's *Bus Story*.

A procedure devised by **Blank & Marquis** (1987) which lies somewhere between a probe and a checklist provides easily presentable information which is useful in the preparation of individual educational plans.

The *Test of Pragmatic Skills* (**Shulman,** 1985) is suitable for three to eight-year-olds. This standardized test looks at the range of intentional communicative acts demonstrated by children in a range of different short play activities. **King's** (1989) paper on this test will be found helpful.

The *Pragmatics Screening Test* and *Teacher Ratings Scale* of **Prinz & Weiner** (1987) are designed for ages three years six months to eight years six months. There is a disadvantage to these procedures in that they have to be scored and analysed by the publishers in the USA.

Simon's (1986) *Evaluating Communicative Competence: A Functional Pragmatic Procedure* is suitable for school-aged children. The results of a prompted interview can be conveniently displayed on a reproducible table.

The Behavioural Inventory of Speech Act Performances (*BISAP*) (**Lucas,** 1980) looks at the ability of school children and people with learning disabilities to perform elicited speech acts. Lucas stresses the importance of 'felicity conditions', that is, suitable conditions (see page 23) for the successful performance of communicative acts; thus the assessment attempts to establish the client's knowledge of such conditions. These issues are further discussed in **Lucas Arwood** (1983).

Dewart & Summers (1995) present *The Pragmatics Profile of Communication Skills in Childhood*.

Assessments designed for use with adults and older children

If one is attempting to construct one's own system, familiarity with two important papers will be useful. **Roth & Spekman** (1984a and 1984b) explain, with special reference to children's assessment, how to categorize behaviours and focus upon crucial aspects of receptive and productive pragmatic functioning.

Damico (1985) discusses a system which can be used for adults and older children (eight years plus). A total of 17 problem behaviours are identified and discussed within the basic supposition that co-operation is fundamental to successful interaction and that these behaviours violate co-operative principles.

Wiig and Semel (1984) have suggestions to offer which are valuable in assessing adults and older children. See also **Semel, Wiig & Secord** (1993) and **Wiig & Secord** (1988).

Brinton & Fujiki (1989) also discuss assessment and present particularly interesting ideas in the areas of topic skills and clarification request skills.

See also **Coggins & Carpenter** (1981) and **Dewart & Summers** (1995 and forthcoming).

Assessments specifically designed for people with learning disabilities.

Wirz (1981) provides a checklist which, though dated, presents some useful ideas.

Coupe *et al* (1985) describe a method, which could be adapted for videotape analysis, of identifying communicative intent in the observed behaviours of pre-verbal people with severe learning difficulties. See also **Coupe & Golbart** (in press).

The *Communication Assessment Profile (CASP)* **Van der Gaag** (1988) is a carefully validated measure intended to be used jointly by speech and language clinicians and care staff to produce a realistic view of clients' strengths and needs.

For further discussion of the assessment of this client group, **Calculator & Bedrosian** (1988) and **Lucas** (1980) are recommended.

Tests and assessments concerned with adult dysphasia

The *Functional Communication Profile* (*FCP*, **Sarno,** 1969) explores functional performances in everyday situations.

The *Edinburgh Functional Communication Profile* (**Skinner *et al*,** 1984) includes attention to the intention of speakers and to non-verbal behaviours in a variety of contexts.

The test of *Communicative Abilities in Daily Living* (*CADL*) (**Holland,** 1980) is designed to provide realistic assessment of aphasic adults who are able to role-play. Although it is soundly based (on research/theory), clinicians have raised questions as to whether its design allows its use in a variety of cultures.

The profile of *communicative appropriateness* (**Penn,** 1988) suffers from the previously mentioned problems with regard to a lack of consensus in appropriacy judgements. However, it does examine features which other assessments neglect, such as coherence, cohesion, politeness and sarcasm.

The *Communicative Effectiveness Index* (*CETI*, **Lomas *et al*,** 1989) specifically addresses the measurement of change during treatment. For this reason it is of particular use in monitoring the success of an intervention programme.

The *Right Hemisphere Language Battery* (**Bryan,** 1988 and 1994) brings into focus much that has been previously suspected about the effects of right hemisphere damage, or possibly whole brain dysfunction. Its use should be investigated by any clinician doubting the pragmatic abilities of an adult client. Concepts from the battery are also helpful in thinking about younger clients.

For further reading in the assessment of adult aphasia, see **Green** (1984), **Smith** (1985), **Blomert *et al*** (1987), **Lesser & Milroy** (1987 and 1993), **Crockford & Lesser** (1994), **Rosenbeck, LaPointe & Wertz** (1989). See also *PACE* (**Davis & Wilcox,** 1981 and 1985) for investigation of specific deficits.

Many of the above tests and systems are capable of adaptation to the needs of various age groups and client groups. Some of them could also be of use to clinicians working with non-verbal or non-oral communication.

Summary

This chapter has introduced the process of assessment of pragmatics. We have discussed why we believe it is essential to investigate the individual's pragmatic skills in any assessment of communicative functioning. There are many problems involved in carrying out assessments appropriately which have been discussed above. Finally, we have listed formal pragmatic assessments that are currently available, focusing on general assessments, clients who have learning difficulties and adults with dysphasia. The following chapter will continue the theme of assessment but will investigate informal approaches.

Recommended Reading

Golinkoff R, Hirsh-Pasek K, Cauley K & Gordon L, 'The Eyes Have It: Lexical and Syntactic Comprehension in a New Paradigm', *Journal of Child Language* 14, pp23–45, 1987.

Howard S, Hartley J & Muller D, The Changing Face of Child Language Assessment 1985–1995, *Child Language Teaching and Therapy* 11(1), pp7–22, 1995.

Lesser R & Milroy L, *Linguistics and Aphasia: Psycholinguistic and Pragmatic Aspects of Interaction,* Longman, London, 1993.

McTear M & Conti-Ramsden G, 'Assessment of Pragmatics', Grundy K (ed), *Linguistics in Clinical Practice,* Taylor & Francis, London, 1992.

Chapter 6
Informal Assessment

Introduction/*48*
Questionnaire Data/*48*
Interview Data/*48*
Observational Data Collection/*49*
    Recording Observational Data/*49*
    Interactive Situations Used for
        Observations/*50*
    Assessment of the Communicative
        Partner/*50*
    The Interaction Record/*51*
    Pragmatic Rating Scale/*58*
Summary/*60*
Recommended Reading/*60*

CHAPTER 6
INFORMAL ASSESSMENT

Introduction

Formal assessments provide valuable information to allow professionals to make judgements about the existence and extent of a difficulty. However, on their own, formal assessments cannot provide clinicians with sufficient information to allow in-depth understanding of an individual's pragmatic difficulties. Informal assessments present opportunities for clinicians to explore a client's communication in a variety of situations and thus can provide more useful information to assist with planning intervention. In this chapter we will describe three methods of assessing clients informally, using questionnaires, interviews and observational data collection. These methods can be used on their own or perhaps more productively in combination with each other and with formal assessments.

Questionnaire Data

A pre-assessment questionnaire, such as the one designed by **Gallagher** (1983), may be completed with caregivers prior to observational assessment. These questionnaires are intended to reveal optimum situations and circumstances for more detailed assessments and to assist the caregivers and professionals in identifying relevant areas of inquiry. Some thought needs to be given to the practicalities of completing the form, including who should be present when the questionnaire is completed. It may be valuable to have the client present in some circumstances or it may be better for a caregiver or spouse to be interviewed in private in other circumstances.

We recommend a client-focused approach where the assessment is designed to address each client's situation and particular needs individually. Below, we discuss the importance of assessing the communicative partner as well as the client. We highlight the importance of the communication style of the partner (therapist, teacher, parent, caregiver, nurse, relative, friend and so on) and the active role that professionals and family can play in facilitating successful communication, or sometimes in concealing a client's difficulties.

More detailed questionnaires, for example **Dewart & Summers** (1995), can be an excellent aid in gaining a picture of a client's communication from the perspective of a parent or caregiver. The questionnaire can be completed in the privacy of the family home and done at a time to suit the family. If it is returned to the clinician by post this can help save time for both clients and clinicians. (It is suggested that enclosing a stamped addressed envelope will increase the likelihood of busy families returning the form promptly.) In many cases, it is preferable for the questionnaire to be completed jointly with a clinician since one of its purposes is to provide a context for the caregiver to learn about pragmatic development. Clinicians will, as usual, need to judge each client's circumstances individually when making a decision about the preferred method of collecting data through using a questionnaire.

Interview Data

Although some clinicians will find a pre-assessment questionnaire valuable for certain clients, not all clinicians and not all clients will feel comfortable using this tool. Even if a pre-assessment questionnaire has been completed it is still important to have a face-to-face initial meeting, even if it is fairly short. It is important to interview the client directly or, if the client is too young, to interview the family in order to clarify information gained from a questionnaire and in order to start to build a relationship. Some questions are more easily asked and answered in a direct interview than on a questionnaire. For most children under four or five it will probably be most valuable to gain interview data from the parent rather than asking the child for information. For older children there are pros and cons for having an open discussion initially about communication. The disadvantage is that it can make the client feel self-conscious at a time when the clinician hopes to increase confidence and self-esteem in the child as a communicator. One of the advantages of an open discussion, however, is that children will feel that they can reveal things about their relationships and communication that have perhaps been a source of anxiety and the therapist can gain insights quickly into clients' perceptions of themselves. Working with adult clients almost always requires an interview directly between the client and the clinician to discuss communication. Only in circumstances where the client's cognitive functioning is not sophisticated enough to follow an interview would it be appropriate to omit this stage.

Observational Data Collection

Observational data collection methods are especially helpful in assessing clients' true strengths and needs. Being confronted by a variety of conversational contexts allows the clinician to observe how successful the client is at meeting the demands of the situation. Observational data collection also allows us to assess the style of communicative partners and the role they may be playing in maintaining a communicative difficulty or in facilitating communicative success. We will describe the range of recording tools available for observational data collection, from simple pen and paper to video relay systems. The advantages of using a variety of different observational settings in assessment will be addressed and the benefits of assessing communicative partners' interaction style will be discussed in some detail. Finally, a procedure for assessing both communicative partners within an interaction (the Interaction Record) will be presented.

Recording Observational Data

Pen and paper recording

Pen and paper recording can be used where it is not possible or desirable to use mechanical recording devices (for example, if a client has a particular fear of the video camera or simply does not want to be video-taped). A useful alternative to having clinicians write down observations themselves is to have a colleague who is experienced in observation sit unobtrusively within the room and write down observations in freehand form or on a checklist.

Audio recording

Audio tape samples are easier to obtain, but omit the visual information (such as nodding, eye signalling, body posture and proximity and facial expression) which can be so important for judgements of communicative appropriacy (**Smith & Leinonen,** 1992; **Leinonen & Smith,** 1994). More natural recordings are obtained if the audio tape recorder is constantly present than if it is introduced for the purpose of the assessment.

Video recording

Video tapes of the client's behaviour in a variety of different settings can be obtained, for example in the home, at school, at the nursery or play group, at a stroke club or stammerers' club, in the clinic or in the training workshop. The only limit on the setting is the client's and family's feelings of comfort within the different settings. Video-taping where clients are made to feel singled out or odd in some way in front of their peers is obviously counterproductive and must be avoided.

Video tapes can be a valuable record of a client's (or caregiver's) performance which can later serve many purposes, including reminding clients and their families of the amount of progress that has been made. They can also help clinicians to note changes in clients and develop themselves professionally, and allow shared observation with other clinicians and professionals. (Remember to obtain permission from the client and/or caregiver.) It is particularly important to capture eye gaze, posture, proximity and facial expression (**Leinonen & Smith,** 1992 and 1994).

The video operator needs to have some understanding of how data are going to be used. If an untrained operator is used then focusing in too closely on the interaction or too far away to see facial expression can be a problem. A wide-angled lens can be helpful in capturing the interactional aspects of a situation, particularly in a small room, but clinicians should be aware that the quality of the picture may deteriorate a little with certain of these lenses.

Analysis of the video tape should ideally take place within a matter of hours or days. If a week or longer is allowed to pass, it is more difficult to recall the interaction details. Various systems of analysis may be applied to a video-taped sample (and samples recorded by other means). These procedures are especially valuable when transcripts are available, since the analysis can then be more detailed and reliable. The time-consuming nature of the procedures is outweighed by their value. A quick but superficial assessment may appear to be an efficient use of time in the short term, but can often prove to have been a false economy in the medium to longer term if it results in important areas of communicative difficulty being overlooked. For example, areas that are not so important are made targets for intervention, or areas that are developmentally inappropriate are dealt with, leading possibly to frustration, lack of progress and wasted time for all (**Crystal,** 1995).

Video-relaying facilities

Another useful means of collecting data that is rarely available in most centres is video-relaying equipment. A video camera can be placed unobtrusively within the observation room and relayed back to any number of observers sitting in another room. This arrangement could save a client from feeling 'overassessed' within a clinic setting. The interdisciplinary team as a group could observe a client, with just one member of the team co-ordinating the assessment. Individual assessments could be considerably shortened, saving time for both client and professionals. In addition, this system allows team discussion to include at least one shared observation. This means that differences in professional evaluations can be resolved through scrutinizing the video tape in conference.

One-way windows

Those clinicians who have access to a one-way window can take advantage of this useful facility. In addition to removing the problems of clients feeling inhibited by the presence of the video or audio-tape machine, there is the advantage of being able to have the parent or spouse observe the clinician interacting with the client without causing the client to feel inhibited. As always, informed consent from the client and family will be obtained by the clinician.

Interactive Situations Used for Observations

Communicative behaviour changes according to the demands of the specific context. Different behaviours are observed with changes in location, interactive partner and type of activity. Observing the client in different locations such as home, the park, school, hospital, work, community centre or nursery allows the clinician to build a clearer picture of functional strengths and needs. It is useful to have several observations of the client with different partners. Suitable interactants will depend on the individual circumstances of the client and the preferences of the client. Some obvious choices for partners are, for a child client, a parent, a clinician, a nursery teacher and a peer or small group of peers; for an adolescent client, a peer (or sibling) or group of peers, a parent and a teacher or the clinician; and for an adult client a spouse or close friend, a son or daughter. Within each observation setting it is important to observe the client engaging in several different types of activity: for instance, formal testing, informal conversation, engaging in a favourite activity and being asked to follow instructions to complete a construction task.

Assessment of the Communicative Partner

In any interaction the partners share responsibility for communicating effectively. The balance of responsibility may not be shared equally. For example, a person who has a learning difficulty with an accompanying problem with intelligibility and awareness of listener needs may require a listener to be patient and to ask questions to verify an unclear message.

Both partners can do things that help or hinder the process of communication (**Smith & Leinonen,** 1992). Because of the important part that communicative partners play in facilitating or hindering communication development and recovery in clients, we feel that it can be important to assess the styles used by significant communicative partners. **Wood *et al*** (1986) demonstrated the benefits of examining questioning style in their work with teachers of the deaf working with young deaf children. (See Chapter 8 for further discussion of this.) Since clinicians spend much time in the role of communicative partner with a wide range of clients, it may be especially important for clinicians to monitor their own skills and to be aware of their more facilitative interaction modes, as well as strategies that they use which may be less helpful to clients. Thus the communicative partner may be the client's parent, spouse, friend or teacher, or it may be the clinician herself.

Why assess communicative partners?

Communicative partners may develop an increased awareness of their importance in the process of development or rehabilitation. Particularly useful facilitating strategies already being used by the communicative partner can be identified and highlighted to give the partner confidence that the client is being helped to learn or relearn communication. Doubt about their helpfulness in interacting with their child or spouse can be a source of anxiety for caregivers which may be transmitted unintentionally during communication.

If the communicative partner is using strategies that are unhelpful for the client but finds it very difficult to use alternative strategies, then an objective demonstration of ways in which the strategy is not helpful (accompanied by support and encouragement for positive aspects) can be valuable in assisting partners to modify their style. For example, if the caregiver is giving many commands to the child and the child is refusing to co-operate, the caregiver could decrease the commands and increase comments.

Analysis of communicative partner style

The caregiver's responses can be analysed in many different ways. The method of analysis chosen by a clinician will depend upon her level of skill, the time available and the purpose of the assessment. There are no procedures, as far as we are aware, that have been accepted as standard. However, we have mentioned many procedures that could be used in an interactive analysis. In particular, conversational analysis (**Sacks, Schegloff & Jefferson,** 1974; **Coggins & Carpenter,** 1981) and the *INREAL* (**Weiss,** 1981) system lend themselves to this purpose. Clinicians can of course construct their own rating scales.

Methods of communicative partner assessment

Our preferred method of assessing the communicative partner is using a video camera. This is because as well as providing an accurate copy of the interaction that can be analysed in detail for assessment purposes, tapes can be used easily as a training tool to develop facilitative styles for communicative partners. Tapes can also be used to provide a 'baseline' measure which may be useful in demonstrating change/progress. No other method can do these things so successfully since every detail is available for scrutiny.

The Interaction Record

We have developed an Interaction Record that readers may find useful in guiding their transcription and analysis of the video-taped interactions. The chart provides a method of rapidly constructing a visual record of brief extracts of dyadic interaction in a way that identifies the communicative behaviour of both participants. It enables the possible contribution of each partner to the success or failure of the interaction to be identified and thus helps clinicians to share the outcome of their observations with others.

The benefits of using the Interaction Record (IREC)

The shared nature of communicative responsibility is apparent in the record. This can help all involved to take their share of responsibility for communicative success as well as failure. A written record helps to highlight the potential of any participant whose contributions are not being noticed or rewarded.

This simple visual means of presenting information will make it easier for clinicians to show clients and their associates how interactions could be improved. It also becomes possible to demonstrate what clients are capable of, given a facilitative partner. When clients are shown to be more capable than has previously been believed, a 'snowball' effect in communicative skills frequently appears to take place. This may be because raised expectation on the part of others, together with recognition of positive communication strategies that are being employed, produce instances of success. These, in turn, raise clients' expectations and confidence. Self-esteem may also be improved, which further benefits communicative behaviour.

Sample length

The length of interaction that should be transcribed is not predefined. It goes without saying that, the more data analysed, the more sure we can feel that our impressions and conclusions are accurate. Transcription is a time-consuming activity (roughly 10 minutes for each minute of conversation is needed — more if intelligibility is reduced). However, the time spent can be justified since proper analysis can improve treatment effectiveness. Long transcriptions are, of course, the most revealing, but by using the IREC it is possible to take a short cut. A brief (say three-minute) sample of interactive behaviour can be presented in such a way as to highlight the sources of failure and success.

Who can use the IREC?

Analysis of the transcript can be used by the clinician alone or with students for training and development purposes. It can also be used with caregivers of children and adults and some clients as part of intervention. The caregiver and/or client and the clinician watch the video tape and use the IREC to analyse the interaction together. Obviously, this approach requires a reasonable level of skill on the part of the caregiver or client and therefore would not be suitable for young children or for adults who have low levels of comprehension.

IREC can be used with clients with dysfluency problems, adults with right hemisphere damage, adults with mild levels of dysphasia, adults or adolescents with mild or moderate learning difficulties, clients with mental illness or social skills problems and with young children.

Different methods of using the IREC

The interaction record can be used in any way that is helpful for the clinician. It can be used to make a transcription record of an interaction for the clinician to analyse and plan intervention. It can also be used to demonstrate to clients, caregivers and colleagues certain pertinent aspects of interaction to help focus intervention. For the latter purpose, the clinician would proceed as follows:

1. select the shortest possible section of a video-taped or audio-taped interaction which illustrates specific difficulties or successes in interaction;
2. transfer this to the Interaction Record chart with as much or as little detail as is required;
3. add comments to the chart as appropriate and supplement with further information if necessary.

For example, if the caregiver is using a very high number of questions during the interaction you may wish to focus on question types and frequency and add a column that allows you to illustrate this aspect in more detail. Conversely, you may want to focus on a behaviour which could be used more often, such as commenting.

How to complete the IREC

The Interaction Record is arranged as follows:

Date Here the date of the interaction is recorded so that it is possible to see progress by comparing records made on later occasions.

Location It is important to assess communicative performance in a variety of settings, such as hospital, home or playground; therefore this is crucial information to include on the chart.

File or tape number Here the client's file reference or video tape reference code can be written to help keep track of records easily.

Page number The page number is useful as the record may extend over several pages and it is naturally vital to keep track of the sequence of utterances within the discourse.

Turn number The turn number will enable one to locate utterances rapidly and to identify turn-taking activity.

Utterance number The utterance number reveals whether participants confine themselves to single utterances per turn, which is often the case in clinical interactions, or whether either of the interactants is producing multiple utterances per turn.

I, R or R/I The clinician records whether each utterance functioned as an initiation, a response or a response/initiation. Initiations and responses need to be identified so that uneven distribution between the partners can be noted. Such unevenness can occur for a variety of reasons, some of which call for remediation. Response/initiations are important because their use indicates skill in responding in a way that keeps the interaction going and carries it forward (**McTear,** 1984). Examples of R/I would be: "No I didn't. Did you?", "What?" or "Well, what would you have done?"

Speech act type Here one records the specific speech act (questioning, agreeing, refusing, negating and so on) for each utterance produced by the participants. The speech act refers to the purpose or intention behind what is being said. 'Speech' acts (that is, communicative functions) can also be accomplished by non-verbal means. For instance, the speech act 'refusing' or 'denying' can be performed by shaking the head. This can be recorded further across the row, as described below. In some circumstances, the clinician may be interested purely in the speech act type of one of the participants and not the other.

Participants The Interaction Record is designed for use in dyadic interaction but it would be a simple matter of adding a further series of columns to the form should users wish to record triadic or group interactions. The participants could be two children, a teacher and a child, a doctor and a patient, a trainer and a client with learning difficulties, a speech and language therapist and a dysfluent client, a nursery nurse and two children, and so on. It will not always be appropriate to include similar types of detail, such as date of birth, for every participant. This is why the 'details' are left open.

Observer The observer is the person completing the Interaction Record. The comments of this person may or may not need to be recorded in the column provided after the spaces for the verbal and non-verbal contributions of the participants. This space could be used for a variety of purposes, such as to record whether a particular communicative interaction was a successful one or not, or to note helpful and unhelpful strategies that are used by communicative partners. It could be helpful to keep 'side notes' of additional comments.

Verbal Refers to the actual words that the participant says. Any level of transcription can be used here. Where useful, a phonetic transcription could be used and stress marks included. Where that information may not be particularly revealing it can be omitted and an orthographic transcription used.

Non-verbal Refers to any pertinent behaviours that the observer wishes to record, such as eye-signalling, proximity and body posture, head shaking and nodding, pointing and other gestures. It can also be useful to record here a description of any objects or pictures that form the focus of the discussion, sharing of laughter, joint referencing and so on.

An IREC blank record form (which can be photocopied) and two examples of completed IRECs are included below.

Example 1

In this dialogue participant A is a speech and language therapy student who has been told that participant B never speaks. She is alert to B's tentative attempt to communicate and willingly abandons her therapy plan in order to respond to him. She builds on an initial success by introducing a personally relevant topic. It might be argued that the student overuses directives and questions. However, an encouraging exchange takes place and one is left with the impression that the child will continue to communicate.

Example 2

In this interaction, participant A is a speech and language therapy student who regards B as an almost non-communicating child with seriously disordered syntactic development. This is on the basis of formal testing. From the point of view of the observer, it is A who appears to be the poor communicator. He talks about matters which do not interest B and fails to listen or respond to what B has to say. When he speaks to the observer about the child, he appears to be unaware that the child has uttered an appropriate and complex sentence.

Analysing communicative partners

Following on from creating an IREC, clinicians may want to analyse the interaction in more detail. This can be done in several ways. For example, the clinician can simply look at the Interaction Record and discover patterns for each of the partners. Thus the observer may see from an IREC where the two participants were a teacher and a teenager with learning difficulties that the teacher appears to initiate more frequently than the teenager. It may further be seen that the teenager's most usual response is a non-verbal one of shaking or nodding her head to indicate no or yes. The IREC can also be used to help the teacher to identify his most facilitative options. This would be done by examining with the teacher what activity was taking place at times when the client produced verbal contributions or took longer turns than usual, as well as looking at the teacher's own interactive behaviour.

Another observer may be interested in identifying the range of different speech acts produced by one of the participants in the interaction. In order to do this, the observer may construct a separate table (see *Table 6* for an example). Tables can be used to look at any area of communicative performance of interest to the observer.

Pragmatic Rating Scale

Occasionally, observers may want to have a system for rating the participants' performance on a scale to give an idea of how their performance compares with others. Since we have very few data on norms this is a subjective process, but one which can be of particular value when observations are validated by several observers and when comparisons are made over time. We have constructed a *Pragmatic Rating Scale (PRS)* for clients (see page 58) that can be photocopied or adapted by clinicians for use with specific client groups.

Speech act type	Verbal	Non-verbal	Total
Requests for information			
Requests for action			
Other requests			
Statements			
Exclamations			
Refusals			
Negation			
Unintelligible			
Other			

Table 6 *Assessing or observing speech acts.*

Interaction Record

Date				Location			File Tape No			Page No						
				Participant A			Participant B			Observer						
Turn No	Utt No	I,R or R/I	Speech Act Type	Name	Details		Name	Details		Comment						
				Verbal	Non-verbal		Verbal	Non-verbal								

© Andersen-Wood & Smith, 1997. You may photocopy this form for instructional use only.

Interaction Record

Date 30.1.97			Location Special school			File Tape No 1			Page No 1
			Participant A Student clinician			Participant B 'Non-speaking child'			Observer Tutor
Turn No	Utt No	I, R or R/I	Speech Act Type	Name A F	Details		Name D K	Details	Comment
				Verbal	Non-verbal		Verbal	Non-verbal	
1	1	I	Directing	Brush Dolly's hair	Smiles				Positive controlling
2	1	R	NV Agreeing				Unintelligible utterance	Brushes doll's hair	Willing compliance
3	1	I	NV Joking				Unintelligible utterance	Puts coat on head	Looks doubtful (child)
4	1	R	Exclaiming	Oh! A hat!	Laughs				Student did well
5	1	I	Switching topic	Just a minute	Touches child				Child still happy
6	2	I	Directing	Sit down	Maintains touch				What's she doing?
7	3	I	Request info	Is your nose better?	Points to own nose				Nice personal touch
8	1	R	Give info				Unintelligible utterance	Nods	Comprehension (?)
9	1	I	Request info	Who hurt it?	Looks concerned		Staring at student		"
10	1	R	Give info				Tammy (loud)	Smiles	Has not spoken before
11	1	R/I	Request confirmation	Tammy?	Looks shocked			Smiles	Seems happy
12	2	R/I	"	Did she; the dog?	Looks doubtful			Smiles	"
13	1	R	Gives info					Nods	"

Example 1 Interaction Record

Interaction Record

Date				Location			File Tape No *1*		Page No *2*
				Participant A			Participant B		Observer
Turn No	Utt No	I, R or R/I	Speech Act Type	Name *A F*		Details	Name *D K*	Details	
				Verbal		Non-verbal	Verbal	Non-verbal	Comment
14	*1*	*I*	*Request info*	*What did she do?*		*Looks concerned*			*Can he answer?*
15	*1*	*R*	*Gives info*					*Mimes info*	*Yes, very well*
16	*1*	*R*	*Checks info*	*Pushed you over?*		*Looks surprised*			*Student did well*
17	*1*	*R*	*Confirms info*			*Smiles*		*Nods and smiles*	*Cheerful again*
18	*1*	*R*	*Exclaims*	*Well, I don't know!*		*Smiles*		*Smiles*	*They are sharing*
19	*2*	*I*	*Sympathizes*	*You better now?*		*Smiles*			
20	*1*	*R*	*Gives new info*					*Smiles and mimes*	
21	*1*	*R/I*	*Checks info*	*Hurt your foot too?*					*They're really in tune*
22	*1*	*R*	*Confirms info*					*Nods*	*OK to switch now*
23	*1*	*I*	*Offering*	*Who wants this?*		*Offers ball*			
24	*1*	*R*	*Claiming*				*M M M*	*Reaches for ball*	*Wow!*
25	*1*	*I*	*Prompting*	*Can I have the …*		*Gives ball*			
26	*1*	*R*	*Labelling*				*BALL*	*Smiles*	

Example 1 Interaction Record (continued)

Interaction Record

Date 15.02.97			Location Clinic		File Tape No 3		Page No 1
			Participant A *Student clinician*		Participant B *Child with delayed speech and language*		Observer *Clinician*
Turn No	Utt No	I, R or R/I	Speech Act Type	Name		Name	
				Verbal	Details Non-verbal	Verbal	Details Non-verbal	Comment

Turn No	Utt No	I, R or R/I	Speech Act Type	Verbal	Non-verbal	Verbal	Non-verbal	Comment
1	1	I	Command	Put the man on the plate	Points			They have done a lot of this today
2	2	I	Command	Put him on it	Points hard			Very firm
3	1	R	Comply (-)			Unintelligible utterance	Puts plate on man	He's bored
4	1	I	Correction	No, put him <u>on</u> the plate	Frowns			Doesn't understand
5	1	R	Comply (+)			Unintelligible utterance	Puts man on plate	That's enough
6	1	R	Praise	Good, very good	Smiles			Good encouragement
7	1	I	Command	Now put the ...	Smiles			Oh dear, not another
8	1	I	Statement/threat			⟨I do one more, I go home⟩	Frowns. Gets up	The child is speaking well
9	1	I	Command	Sit down and listen	Points to chair			Student ignores child
10	2	I	Command	Put the girl under the cup	Points to cup			What will happen?
11	1	R	Comply			Unintelligible utterance	Puts girl in cup	Well done!
12	1	R/I	Complain	Listen, did I say <u>in</u>?	Frowns		Frowns	
13	2	I	Complain	He still can't really communicate				Not with you, evidently

Example 2 Interaction Record

Pragmatic Rating Scale

Name			Participants				
DOB			Activity				
DOA			Location				
Client details							
Pragmatic skill		Skill absent			Demonstrates skill well		Comments
1 Pre-verbal Communication	NA	1	2	3	4	5	
Smiling							
Getting attention vocally							
Imitates sounds adults make, eg. dada, baba, ooo							
Looks at desired objects							
Pointing to objects or events							
Expressing like/dislike							
Waves hello/bye-bye							
Plays pat-a-cake or peek-a-boo games							
2 Intentional Communication	NA	1	2	3	4	5	
Naming objects/people, eg. ball, mummy							
Commenting on objects, people or events, eg. big ball, mummy there, car bang							
Asking questions (Where? What? When? Why? Who?)							
Making requests, eg. dummy please? Up up? Me go outside?							
Responding to questions							
Saying hello							
Saying bye-bye							
Expressing feelings, eg. tired, hungry, cross							
Offering help to others							
Using humour appropriately							
Introducing self appropriately							
Understanding others							
3 Managing Conversations	NA	1	2	3	4	5	
Responding to questions at an appropriate speed							
Taking turns in a conversation							
Starting up a conversation with a friend							
Keeping the conversation going							
Knowing when to end a conversation							
Showing others that you are listening to them							
Asking for clarification when you don't understand							
Giving clarification to listener when she doesn't understand							
Interrupting politely							

© Andersen-Wood & Smith, 1997. You may photocopy this form for instructional use only.

Pragmatic skill		Skill absent				Demonstrates skill well	Comments
4 Awareness of Listener's Needs	NA	1	2	3	4	5	
Being specific when necessary, eg. "Here's Marie, my friend"; *not* "Here she is."							
Acting politely when necessary							
Using appropriate vocabulary							
Providing background information when necessary							
Sequencing ideas logically so listeners can follow							
Saying things that are relevant to the listener							
5 Non-verbal Communication	NA	1	2	3	4	5	
Eye contact/gaze							
Appropriacy of body position and distance from conversational partner							
Appropriacy of facial expression							
Melody (intonation) of voice							
Appropriacy of volume of voice							
6 Complex Skills	NA	1	2	3	4	5	
Using telephone							
Making purchases							
Using public services eg. transport							
Contributing to a group discussion							
Comments							

© *Andersen-Wood & Smith, 1997. You may photocopy this form for instructional use only.*

Communicative Partner Profile

We have created a photocopiable profile of the communicative partner's interactions with a client called the *Communicative Partner Profile (CPP)* for those individuals (parents, clinicians, nurses, caregivers and teachers) who want to facilitate the communication of a client.

The profile has a section for personal details at the top. Below this there are four areas of interaction that can be profiled. The clinician will consider each area and simply put a tick in the yes or no column according to whether or not the partner is currently demonstrating each particular skill. Comments can be placed in the next column along, where it may be noted that this area is especially facilitative for the client, for example, or that for this particular client the skill is not appropriate. In the last column, clinicians can indicate whether this area is one that may benefit from further training. Finally, under section 5, specific goals can be set for assisting communicative partners to change certain behaviours or attitudes within interactions. For example:

Area 1	Decrease number of questions asked
Method	Practise role-play with clinician
Area 2	Give client longer time to respond in conversation
Method	Use video-tape to observe effect of not giving client sufficient time to respond
Area 3	Talk about the 'here and now' rather than abstract concepts
Method	Observe clinician demonstrating how to talk about concrete concepts (here and now)
Area 4	Share enjoyment and humour with communicative partner
Method	Observe client with others engaging in enjoyable activities, which client and other person can share

Summary

In this chapter we have examined a range of informal assessment methods that can be used to examine pragmatic difficulties. We have looked in particular detail at questionnaire, interview and observational data collection methods and have suggested a format (the IREC) for structuring observations of informal interactions.

Recommended Reading

Brinton B & Fujiki M, *Conversational Management with Language-Impaired Children: Pragmatic Assessment and Intervention,* Aspen, Rockville, Maryland, 1989.

Calculator SN & Bedrosian JL, (eds), *Communication Assessment and Intervention for Adults with Mental Retardation,* College-Hill, Boston, 1988.

Fey ME, *Language Intervention with Young Children,* College-Hill, Boston, 1986.

Pellegrini AD, *Applied Child Study: A Developmental Approach,* Lawrence Erlbaum Associates, Hillsdale, New Jersey, 1987.

Prutting CA & Kirchner DM, 'Applied Pragmatics', Gallagher TM & Prutting CA (eds), *Pragmatic Assessment and Intervention Issues in Language,* College-Hill, San Diego, 1983.

Roth F & Spekman N, 'Assessing the Pragmatic Abilities of Children: Part 1: Organizational Framework and Assessment Parameters', *Journal of Speech and Hearing Disorders* 49(1), pp2–11, 1984a.

Roth F & Spekman N, 'Assessing the Pragmatic Abilities of Children: Part 2: Guidelines, Considerations and Specific Evaluation Procedures', *Journal of Speech and Hearing Disorders* 49(1), pp12–17, 1984b.

Communicative Partner Profile

Name of client (C)	
Name of partner (P)	
Relationship to client	
Date of profile	
Activity	
Location	
Details	

	NA	Yes	No	Comments	Train
1 Facilitating Relationships					
Demonstrating positive affect towards C					
Demonstrating interest in C					
Praising C					
Listening to C					
Using appropriate touching (hugging etc) with C					
Giving feedback in positive manner					
Disciplining appropriately					
Sharing humour					
2 Facilitating Conversational Interaction					
Following C's lead					
Allowing plenty of time for responding					
Leaving silence when appropriate					
Asking for clarification when necessary					
Noticing when C doesn't understand					
Interpreting behaviour/affect accurately					
Assisting/encouraging communication					
3 Facilitating Communication Development					
Using language at appropriate level					
Using clear speech					
Giving commands					
Asking questions					
Making statements and comments					
Making suggestions					
Making requests					
Repeating self for clarity					
Repeating back what client has said					
Sequencing ideas logically					
Staying on child's topic					
4 Non-facilitative Strategies					
Controlling C's interests and activities					
Missing attempts to communicate					
Difficulty setting boundaries consistently					
Overinitiation					
Overusing questioning					
Overusing commands					
Creating punitive or overly permissive atmosphere					
Blaming C					

© Andersen-Wood & Smith, 1997. You may photocopy this form for instructional use only.

5 Training for Communicative Partners	
Behaviours/attitudes to maintain, increase or decrease	**Date**
Area 1	
Method	
Area 2	
Method	
Area 3	
Method	
Area 4	
Method	

Training progress/problems

Notes

© Andersen-Wood & Smith, 1997. You may photocopy this form for instructional use only.

CHAPTER 7
PRINCIPLES OF INTERVENTION

Introduction/*64*
Past Approaches to Intervention/*64*
Philosophies of Intervention/*64*
    Linguistic Approaches/*64*
    Behaviourist Approaches/*65*
    Interactionist Approaches/*66*
    Approaches Based on Social Learning
        Theory/*66*
    Communication-Centred (Pragmatic)
        Approaches/*66*
Pragmatic Intervention/*66*
    Prevention/*67*
    Training Caregivers, Ourselves and
        Others/*67*
    Naturalistic Approaches/*72*
    Facilitating Pragmatic Development
        through Special Activities/*72*
    Metapragmatic Awareness Training/*72*
    Accepting the Communication
        Difficulty/*73*
Summary/*73*
Recommended Reading/*74*

CHAPTER 7
PRINCIPLES OF INTERVENTION

Introduction

We are going to present the intervention section of this book in four separate chapters. Chapter 7 will cover the principles of intervention, past approaches and discussion of philosophies underlying various intervention methods. Chapter 8 will present current intervention approaches and more detailed therapy suggestions that clinicians can use with a range of clients. Chapter 9 will describe ways of facilitating pragmatic development through the use of special activities, metapragmatic awareness teaching and accepting the pragmatic difficulty. Finally, Chapter 10 will give a range of ideas for working with specific client groups and ways of intervening with specific pragmatic difficulties.

Past Approaches to Intervention

Therapy approaches in the past often tended to be goal-centred rather than communication-centred. Behaviourism and structural linguistics have had a strong influence on clinical methods, encouraging clinicians to focus on pronunciation and grammatical structures within a clinical rather than a more natural setting. Clients have usually been seen individually because the ideal learning situation was believed to be one free from distractions (**Warner, Byers-Brown & McCartney**, 1984). Cognitive processes such as auditory discrimination, attention control, sequencing and categorization have been given prime consideration in intervention rather than social and emotional factors.

Nevertheless, past approaches have not completely neglected pragmatic skills. For example, goals in intervention with dysfluent clients frequently included focusing on appropriacy of eye-contact, facial expression and body language. Functional communication has been a focus for work with adult dysphasic clients for many years and clinicians were trained to recognize signs of boredom, particularly in younger clients. However, although short periods of conversation and play were often included within the therapy session, these were regarded as lead-ins, rest periods and rewards rather than as essential parts of the therapeutic process. Naturalistic interaction, though sometimes used in order to obtain a language sample for assessment purposes, was seldom seen as a valuable educational experience for the client.

Philosophies of Intervention

It is important that clinician's who are engaging in the complex process of intervention understand what they are doing and why. This understanding and the flexibility that it allows is what differentiates a clinician from a technician. Beliefs concerning the development or recovery of communication and beliefs concerning the role of the environment in that process will have a profound effect on the way in which clinicians work. The location of intervention, the goals of intervention, the priority given to training others, the preference for group therapy, individual therapy or consultative models of therapy and the styles of interaction adopted when with a client will all be affected by these beliefs. The spectrum of philosophical approaches to intervention is wide. We will describe five of the most important (linguistic, behaviourist, interactionist, social learning and communication-centred [pragmatic] approaches) and their implications for the working practices of clinicians. For a more detailed discussion, the reader is referred to **Fey** (1986), **Smith & Leinonen** (1992) and **Gallagher** (1991).

Linguistic Approaches

Linguistic approaches suggest that language is acquired by the child in much the same way as other genetically pre-programmed abilities such as motor co-ordination. Linguistic approaches have little of value to offer the clinician working with the pre-linguistic client as they stress the teaching of specific grammatical structures in production and comprehension and have little to say about the precursors to language. Since subscribers to this approach believe that the child is pre-programmed to acquire grammar with minimal input from the environment, it follows that the importance of the clinician is restricted in this model. In cases where grammatical acquisition has been disrupted, clinicians do, however, provide children with structured input specifically directed towards semantic or syntactic acquisition.

Behaviourist Approaches

Traditional behaviourist approaches hold that language is merely one of many behaviours that can be shaped and reinforced by caregivers. The implications of this approach for clinicians are that

- Behavioural change is the aim of therapy;
- Clinicians simply need to create the correct reinforcement schedule for clients to acquire or relearn those language structures taught;
- imitation is an appropriate method of learning for the client; and
- generalization of skills is achieved by presenting stimuli in a wide range of settings.

Much that happens currently in speech and language intervention appears to be founded on these beliefs.

Behaviourist approaches to pragmatics are many and varied. Some can use a very structured programme of learning with specific steps to follow and strict schedules of reinforcement. In a less rigid approach to behavioural training one chooses specific target behaviours within play or other 'naturally occurring' activities, models the behaviour, reinforces the desirable behaviour through praise and possibly tangible rewards and extinguishes undesirable behaviour by ignoring it or removing desired activities or objects. Teachers working in classroom settings have often adopted behavioural principles with normally developing children and those within special classes. Behavioural training can take place individually or within a group setting. In Chapter 9 we will describe four different approaches to increasing awareness of pragmatic skills that use behaviourist principles to a greater or lesser extent. Teaching metapragmatic awareness involves some principles of behaviourist approaches as it encourages imitation and correction of behaviours as well as bringing an awareness of pragmatics. Pragmatic skills training is more obviously based on behavioural principles with its skill components, practice and praise. We will introduce assertiveness training which similarly, through role-play, incorporates many behavioural principles to useful effect. Finally we describe direct instruction.

Advantages of behaviourist approaches

Some of the advantages of behaviourist approaches to training are the following:

1. Behaviours can be taught with reasonable ease and so 'progress' within the therapy setting can be seen quite quickly.
2. Many different behaviours can be treated in this way.
3. The focus of the therapy is on success and praise; therefore it can be a confidence-building activity for clients.
4. Clients with particularly limited abilities can be seen to make progress as behaviours can be split up into small units rather than being seen as a complex set of behaviours.
5. There is a wide variety of behavioural training programmes available that can be very time-saving as original schemes do not have to be created. For a description of a range of behaviourally focused schemes, the reader is referred to **Blank & Marquis** (1987); **Rustin** (1987); **Jackson, Jackson & Monroe** (1983).
6. Accountability issues can be important. Progress on behavioural measures can be easily presented to managers who judge effectiveness of therapy. It can be more difficult explaining the less tangible benefits of indirect or naturalistic therapy, though the most crucial step of all is to write pragmatic aims into the treatment plan.

There is healthy controversy over whether a behaviourist approach to working with clients with pragmatic or social skills difficulties is effective or not (**Matson & Ollendick**, 1990). Given that no single approach to therapy has received unanimous recognition as being the most effective method, and that very little work has been done comparing the effectiveness of different approaches, it is too early to advocate just one.

Disadvantages of behaviourist approaches

It is important also to stress some of the main disadvantages of a behaviourist approach:

1. Skills may be learnt in only one situation and generalization to other situations may be slow to occur or may not occur at all (**Leonard**, 1981).
2. There may be a tendency for the clinician to adopt a highly directive role, which may mean that the client is often placed in a subordinate role. This may have the effect

of limiting the range of possible interactions (see Chapter 8, pages 86–7).

3 There is more to functioning communicatively than simply acquiring all the requisite skills and items of knowledge piecemeal. Integrating everything that has been learnt is the key feature of successful pragmatic performance (**Craig**, 1983). Communication may be such a complex process that it cannot be taught behaviourally.

4 Behaviourist approaches to pragmatics tend to work most effectively in group situations because clients are able to practise and observe skills in real and role-play situations with peers. It may be difficult, however, to match clients with complementary skills.

5 Groups can be enjoyable to facilitate but can also be quite daunting if one is not experienced in this. Training in group facilitation skills is necessary in order to run a group successfully.

We see the behaviourist approach to pragmatics as one of a number of possible approaches that can be useful, provided that the advantages and disadvantages are clearly understood. Combinations of approaches may offer the best way. In Chapter 9 we will describe four behaviourist approaches that are currently used to teach pragmatics: metapragmatic awareness teaching, pragmatic skills training, assertiveness training and direct instruction.

Interactionist Approaches

Interactionist approaches (**Fey**, 1986; **Craig**, 1991; **Bloom & Lahey**, 1978) stress the interaction of three aspects of communication: language form, language content and language use. Communication develops by children interacting with their environment and inducing the relationships between non-verbal events and states and their corresponding verbal labels. Implications for clinicians are that the clinician is viewed as a facilitator of language rather than a teacher; that the child needs to acquire the underpinning cognitive precursors prior to being able to learn appropriate linguistic concepts; that clinicians should model language within a natural context; clinicians should be aware of the developmental level of the child so that input can be pitched at an appropriate level; and that activities should be naturally occurring ones or those chosen by the child rather than the clinician, since this will make the activity more motivating and relevant for the child.

Approaches Based on Social Learning Theory

Approaches based on social learning theory stress the complexity of communication and the importance of considering the social aspects of communication as well as the linguistic and cognitive aspects. Language is acquired through the observation of modelled events and outcomes. The processes of attention, retention, motor reproduction and motivation are viewed as crucial in the acquisition process. The developmental level that the child has achieved determines the level at which she is able to learn from the observation of models. The implications of this approach for intervention is that it is important for the child to learn from someone with whom she has a motivating social relationship. The clinician's role is to model communication and to motivate the client to experiment with language forms. Linguistic goals should be chosen that are within the client's capabilities from the point of view of attention, retention and motor reproduction. It will be seen that the social learning and the interactionist theories are similar, though not identical.

Communication-Centred (Pragmatic) Approaches

We recognize that goal-centred approaches (such as linguistic and behavioural approaches) have a place within speech and language therapy. However, for the client whose difficulties are principally pragmatic, there are two major disadvantages to goal-centred therapy: first, the clinician, not the client, controls the interaction, thus preventing the client from learning how to initiate; second, the client has little opportunity to experiment with the performance of speech acts or to learn about co-operative interactions through experimenting with them with the clinician. Intervention that encompasses a range of approaches is required if clients are to improve their communicative competence. A pragmatics-based communication-centred approach aims to provide these opportunities for clients.

Pragmatic Intervention

We present below six strategies that can be usefully employed in pragmatic intervention: prevention; training caregivers, ourselves and others; naturalistic approaches; facilitating pragmatic development through special activities; metapragmatic awareness training; and accepting the communication difficulty.

Prevention

There is a growing interest in the prevention of communication disorders. Professionals can do much to foster prevention of pragmatic disorders within their community and to help caregivers and teachers to forestall the development of serious pragmatic problems. Suitable action in the case of early or minor difficulties can obviate the need for later therapy. Further details of ways in which clinicians can undertake a preventive role are detailed in Chapter 8, but examples of preventive activities that clinicians can initiate are the following:

1. giving informative talks on the causes and characteristics of pragmatic dysfunction;
2. offering advice to all new and potential parents of infants through talks at antenatal classes, parentcraft classes, schools and clinics;
3. ensuring that fellow professionals are aware of your expertise in this area and are clear about the procedure for asking for advice and making referrals to you;
4. taking part in multidisciplinary assessment teams to ensure that pragmatic assessment is an integral part of a rehabilitation or developmental assessment;
5. offering training or information to professionals, such as health visitors, paediatricians, psychologists, psychiatrists, playgroup workers, nursery nurses and teachers, or nurses, doctors, physiotherapists and occupational therapists within hospital settings, who are most likely to come into contact with individuals who may be showing pragmatic difficulties;
6. offering to give talks to charitable organizations and parent-run groups such as Mencap, AFASIC, stroke clubs and so on; and
7. providing a screening service within schools.

Training Caregivers, Ourselves and Others

One widely used approach to intervention is the training of those in closest contact with the clients themselves, such as parents, spouses, nursery nurses, hospital nurses, training centre staff, physiotherapists, teachers and peers. We strongly advocate this approach, especially with motivated parents and staff. Since the caregivers usually spend most time with the client, it is sensible, where possible, for them to take a major role in the facilitation of communication. The problems of generalization are overcome more easily in this way and caregivers and others can feel empowered. In addition to training others, it is valuable to update our own clinical interaction skills so that our practice is in line with current research findings. Four styles of interaction with clients are presented below. It may be valuable for clinicians to examine their *own* style with a view to identifying aspects of their own interactions that will help clients and those aspects that may be less helpful. In Chapter 8 we will present further ideas for training ourselves and some specific methods of training others who live or work with clients with communication difficulties.

Modifying clinicians' intervention styles

Many courses that train professionals to work with children teach the importance of being in control of the teaching situation. This leads to an assumption that professionals need to be in control of what the clients do at all times when 'working' with them. Many of us have been taught the importance of preparing lesson plans with materials and activities that we decide in advance will interest the client. Although training of this type offers much of value, it also has the disadvantage of making it difficult for clinicians to use a variety of interaction styles and to respond to clients' current interests and moods. In particular, clinicians may find it difficult to use the more co-operative ways of interacting that seem to be most helpful with individuals with pragmatic difficulties.

As clinicians, the majority of us have been trained to direct clients fairly firmly for their own good. Clinical behaviour (intervention style) of this kind could be described as directive, controlling or even coercive. Training does of course include the information that negative or hostile directiveness is not regarded as therapeutic and that hostile coerciveness is unprofessional and unacceptable.

With little training in co-operative approaches, clinicians have sometimes felt at a loss as to how an interactive or co-operative approach can be reconciled with their professional responsibility for clients' communicative improvement. In these confusing circumstances, clinicians have experimented with different approaches, sometimes successfully, sometimes less so. It may be useful here to consider some examples of interaction styles so that they become easier to recognize.

Figure 1 illustrates a range of different styles that therapists can at times adopt in their interactions with clients. It is not likely that individuals always fall at the same point on the

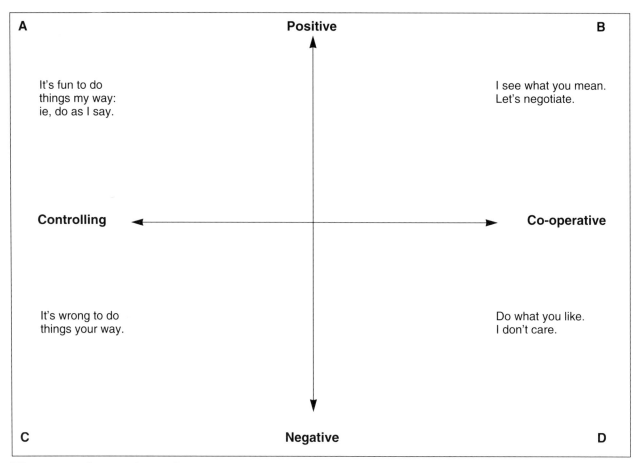

Figure 1 *Interaction styles.*

chart in all interactions. Rather, one is likely to vary one's style within each interaction and with different clients. Clearly, the two positive styles are recommended, while the negative styles are regarded as mistakes by most clinicians.

Type A: 'Positive controlling'

This is the most commonly encountered clinical approach. Over the years it has proved successful in helping adults and children with a wide variety of speech and language difficulties. The clinician is firmly in charge. Clients know that they are expected to co-operate.

Advantages

▶ A curriculum can be devised for the client which allows all involved to have access to the planned intervention.

▶ The client can be guided through the curriculum and thus is helped to acquire and practise the necessary skills.

Disadvantages

▶ Clients can be passive learners who may not fulfil their true potential because of the limits imposed by the curriculum.

▶ Skills acquired in this way may not generalize to situations in which the client is expected to operate independently, creatively and spontaneously.

Figure 2a *"It's fun to do things my way."*

The 'positive controlling' intervention style is illustrated in *Figures 2a* and *2b*.

Clinician: Here's a teddy. Say 'Teddy'.
Thomas: Teddy.
Clinician: OK. Good boy. Now teddy is sitting. Say, 'Teddy sitting'.
Thomas: Teddy sit.
Clinician: Good. Listen, teddy sitting. Now dolly's sitting. Say, 'Dolly sitting'.
Thomas: Dolly sitting.
Clinician: Good boy. Well done. Now I'm going to make teddy fall down and you tell me what he is doing. Look! Teddy's falling. Say, 'Teddy falling'.

Figure 2b *"It's fun to do things my way."*

Clinician: What's this?
Rebecca: Bus.
Clinician: Yes, and what colour is it?
Rebecca: Red.
Clinician: Yes, good girl. It's a red bus. Can you say 'red bus'?
Rebecca: Red bus.

Type B: 'Positive co-operative'

The positive co-operative approach is commonly used by clinicians on an occasional basis, for instance when gathering a language sample or giving the client a break between tasks or at the end of a 'working session'. The clinician is more silent than usual, observes the client carefully and responds to the client's reasonable wishes and initiations. The client is, to some extent, in charge (though the clinician retains ultimate responsibility) and has somewhat restricted choices where the activities and topics are concerned. The reason for extending clients' freedom is, as we discussed earlier (page 31) that a good deal of knowledge has to be acquired and integrated in order to communicate successfully. Clients need experiences of freely interacting with a supportive partner in order to acquire such knowledge and we now know that even the most affectionate families do not always provide such experiences in sufficient quantity (**Law & Conway**, 1991 and 1992). Unfortunately, we also know that unhelpful experiences within families have to be considered as a real possibility for some clients (**Rutter**, 1989; **Wells**, 1985). The seriousness of this possibility is born out by figures provided by the NSPCC (UK): in March 1996 the total number of children in England on child protection registers was 32,351 (29 per 10,000 under 18-year-olds). These are children deemed to be at risk of significant harm as defined by the Children Act, 1989 (**Department of Health**, 1997).

Advantages

▶ The clinician is able to model good communicative and ***listening*** behaviour for the client as well as good language.

▶ Both child and adult clients experience the power of successful communication.

▶ Clients are placed in the position of having to take some responsibility for the interaction.

▶ Clients are free to experiment with their use of language and actively to discover more of the complex rules of interaction than it would be possible to teach them in controlled situations.

▶ Skills acquired in this way have been observed to generalize to other situations, possibly because clients achieve what educationalists call 'ownership' of the skills.

Disadvantages

▶ If clients receive *only* this type of intervention (that is, no curriculum-based work) they can be deprived of access to important areas of teaching and some of their needs may not be met.

The 'positive co-operative' intervention style is illustrated in *Figures 3a* and *3b*.

Figure 3a *"Let's negotiate."*

Mina: Ooo! water!
Clinician: Oh what fun! Splash, splash.
Mina: Splash water. Splash splash.
Clinician: Oops! I think we have splashed it on the floor a bit too much. Let's take it outside to play, then we can do lots more splashing and

	we won't make a mess. Can you help me to carry it outside?
Mina:	Outside. Splash splash.
Clinician:	Yes. Come on.

Figure 3b *"Let's negotiate."*

Charlie:	Want car.
Clinician:	OK, let's find it. It might be in the big box.
Charlie:	Box.
Clinician:	Here's the big box. Oh, there's the car, look. [Remains silent while the child starts to play.] Oops! The car bumped the big box.
Charlie:	Bump.
Clinician:	My car's bumping the little box.
Charlie:	Naughty.
Clinician:	Yes, naughty car.

Type C: 'Negative controlling'

Negative controlling approaches are not intentionally used by most clinicians. What can inadvertently happen is that the need to be, or perhaps to be seen to be, in control of the client's learning temporarily dominates the clinician's thinking.

Advantages

▶ Clients might be *compelled* to learn when they have shown little natural inclination to do so.

Disadvantages

▶ Most clinicians would agree that clients who are treated in this disrespectful manner may learn only a limited amount.

▶ Clients may cease to be active and fully engaged in the interaction.

▶ Clients may not become confident in using what they have learned in their everyday lives.

▶ Clients may cease to attend for treatment.

The 'negative controlling' style of intervention is illustrated in Figure 4.

Figure 4 *"It's wrong to do things your way."*

Anna:	Splash.
Clinician:	**No.** Say, "Water". George is pouring the water.
Anna:	Splash water.
Clinician:	**No, not quite.** Try again. George is pouring the water. Pouring water.
Anna:	George.
Clinician:	Yes. And what is George doing?
Anna:	George splash.
Clinician:	Yes, that's right, but I want you to say, "George is pouring the water." You be a good boy now and say it for me nicely.

Covert Type A and C (controlling) styles

Covert Type A and C approaches can occasionally be observed. Here the clinician tries to give the impression that the client is sharing control of the interaction while not in fact allowing this to happen:

Clinician	What would you like to do today?
Petra:	I'd like to play rockets.
Clinician:	Well, I think I've got a picture of a rocket in here. Should we look at these cards?
Petra:	No.
Clinician:	Well, let's just do my pictures and then you can have a break and play rockets.

Type D: 'Negative co-operative'

This is an excessively permissive approach which allows the client almost total freedom and does not provide what most people would see as realistic communicative input and appropriate limit setting. For example: "Why are you climbing on the table, Megan? Is it fun?"

Advantages

▶ The client may learn something through taking responsibility for what occurs and through behaving in a more exploratory way than usual.

▶ The clinician may learn, by allowing herself to experiment with degrees of freedom, how to share control of the interaction in a more sensible way.

▶ There is also a highly skilled permissive approach used by specialist play therapists within which children are protected but allowed to explore their feelings freely. This is *not* what we have in mind when we describe the 'negative co-operative' approach.

Disadvantages

▶ The client may get into danger.

▶ The client may be deprived of opportunities to benefit from specifically targeted teaching.

▶ The client will not have opportunities to learn from realistic interactive contributions from the clinician.

▶ To engage in this approach at all frequently would not really be consistent with professional responsibility.

▶ Clients may assume that, because you are not imposing any rules, they can behave as they like in other situations where rules need to be followed.

The 'negative co-operative' style of intervention (permissive) is illustrated in *Figures 5a* and *5b*.

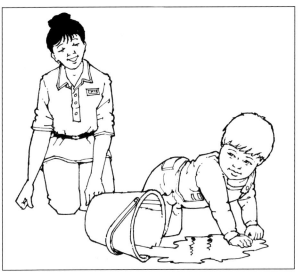

Figure 5a *"Do what you like. I don't care."*

Sam: Oooh! Water!
Clinician: Yes. Lots of water. Oops! It's gone all over the floor.
Sam: Splash.
Clinician: Oh dear! I think it's soaking the carpet. Oh well, you are enjoying yourself aren't you?
Sam: Splash.
Clinician: Oh no! You've tipped the whole bucket over. I bet you're going to do lots more splashing now, aren't you?

Figure 5b *"Do what you like. I don't care."*

Karl: Want scissors.
Clinician: OK. I'll just get on with my writing, you play with the scissors.

We hope that clinicians will spend some time thinking about their own range of intervention styles with the above models in mind and that they may feel inspired to experiment with different styles in intervention.

Naturalistic Approaches

Naturalistic therapy involves planning relevant meaningful situations or activities for the client. This can be done by clinicians themselves or by caregivers who have been trained by clinicians (**MacDonald & Gillette,** 1988; Hanen Program — available through Winslow; see also **Elder**, 1995). The clinician will work out specific and more general aims to incorporate within these activities. Feedback is provided regarding the success of the interaction only as a natural consequence of the success or failure of the communication. The clinician aims to encourage the development of a relationship based on principles of equality and trust with the client. The clinician ensures that the client's everyday environment provides frequent opportunities for communications that are naturally reinforcing. Naturalistic therapy aims to give the client genuine experiences of interaction. It has the following advantages:

1. The client absorbs knowledge concerning language and the rules for its social use unconsciously.
2. The clinician recognizes and rewards minimal communicative attempts. This encourages the client to communicate further.
3. The clinician provides practical (non-explicit) feedback as to degrees of communicative success and failure for the client.
4. Clinicians can enable caregivers to provide early interactive experiences which may have been missing or unsatisfactory for that particular client.
5. The demands which the situation makes upon the immature abilities of the client are gradually increased so that discouragement is avoided and yet challenge is provided.
6. The client becomes motivated to experiment with communicative behaviours and to seek new knowledge about language and its use.
7. The client gains confidence as a communicator through experiencing satisfying interactions.

In naturalistic therapy, clinicians provide opportunities for genuine interaction. Activities, equipment and the behaviour of the clinician are, however, carefully tailored to the needs of the individual clients.

Facilitating Pragmatic Development through Special Activities

Symbolic activities

It is well established that learning to play symbolically, for instance with small cups and saucers or with dolls and miniature cars, is related to the development of linguistic communication (**Reynell**, 1977; **Piaget**, 1955; **Lowe**, 1975; **Sachs**, 1984; **Garvey**, 1977; **Gould**, 1986). Learning to see two-dimensional pictures as representations of the real world is also an important developmental step. A further stage in the growth of symbolizing ability is the use of objects to represent others which they do not resemble: for example, a piece of wood can become a car. Drawn and written symbols, too, may bear no resemblance to the objects and ideas that they represent. These latter types of symbolization require human beings to 'pretend', for instance, that the wood is a car. Other forms of pretending, such as dressing up, enable people to place themselves in the role of others or to manipulate imaginary people and events. These uses of the imagination may also be involved in pragmatic functioning. Pretending and symbolic activity are potentially useful for remediating pragmatic difficulties. In addition to play, clinicians have used painting and drawing, puppets, narrative, drama and role-play to encourage the development of pretending.

Non-symbolic activities

Non-symbolic activities such as construction and motor play can form useful media for stimulating basic communicative interactions such as pointing. Motivation and excitement can run high in motor play, leading to spontaneous expression in clients who are usually reticent and perhaps to an awakening of the client's dormant sense of self and others.

Metapragmatic Awareness Training

Metapragmatic awareness teaching

Metapragmatic awareness teaching involves helping the client to become consciously aware of communicative rules and knowledge. The therapist achieves this through discussion, explanation and giving examples of those rules and items of knowledge. Developing metalinguistic awareness is thought to be an important step in children's transition from oral language to literacy (**Garton & Pratt,** 1989; **Chaney,** 1994; **Paul,** 1992). However, this conscious awareness cannot be expected until a child is sufficiently mature.

The basic steps involved in metalinguistic awareness teaching are as follows:

1 The clinician identifies a specific deficit in the communicative performance of the client.
2 The clinician explains to the client why this is causing problems.
3 The clinician provides opportunities to practise.
4 The clinician gives constructive feedback on the client's performance.

Focusing metapragmatic awareness on clients' communicative strengths is particularly useful. If the client has no true disability, but is failing to perform satisfactorily for reasons such as lack of awareness, habit, lack of helpful experience or lack of confidence, improvement can be rapid. If, on the other hand, the client is *unable* to function in the desired manner, more developmentally suitable approaches may be needed.

Some clients are not able to benefit from direct explicit instruction and can have their communicative confidence and self-esteem undermined by attempts to focus consciously on communication difficulties. It is important for clinicians to be able to recognize this and to have the confidence to try more subtle approaches when necessary, rather than making inappropriate and potentially damaging demands on these clients.

Pragmatic skills training

One common variation of metapragmatic teaching is social skills training. This form of training involves the client acquiring conscious knowledge of social skills, such as making eye-contact, but it also incorporates an element of practice, often through role-plays and in groups. One form of social skills training that we are calling 'pragmatic skills training' will be expanded on in Chapter 9.

Assertiveness training

Another form of metapragmatic awareness teaching is assertiveness training which has many similarities with social skills training or pragmatic skills training but generally involves more focus on communication situations that can be especially difficult or may involve a conflict of goals, such as making a complaint or refusing a request. In addition, assertiveness training holds as central the acceptance of certain beliefs about the rights of individuals: for instance, the right to have an opinion and to express it, though not necessarily to change other's opinions or to win every argument.

Direct instruction

Direct instruction involves activities such as drills or working on referential communication tasks. Drills involve engaging the client in practical exercises where specific behaviours are demonstrated by the clinician and practised repeatedly with the client. Drills help the client to learn how to choose appropriate communicative behaviours within a limited range of specified contexts. Explicit feedback is offered to the client in the form of praise and constructive criticism for improved performance. Self-evaluation may also be encouraged. Drills are usually carried out in a speech and language clinic on a one-to-one basis, often for short periods of time (20–40 minutes per week). While not suitable for all clients, direct instruction of this kind can be usefully combined with a pragmatics-based approach in some circumstances.

Referential communication games can be a useful way of helping the client to appreciate listener needs. Typically, the client and clinician sit opposite each other with an identical picture or set of objects and a screen or barrier to prevent partners seeing each other's picture or array. The first communicative partner gives directions to the second to create an image or form that is identical to their own. The task can involve, for instance, drawing a picture, building constructions with blocks of various colours and shapes or creating a village.

Accepting the Communication Difficulty

For some clients intervention may not lead to improved communicative performance, or progress may be frustratingly slow. In such cases, one option for clinicians and clients is to validate and maximize those positive communicative strategies used by the client and to work on improving communicative confidence. This will be discussed further in Chapter 9.

Summary

This chapter has described approaches to intervention – both current and past. We have examined the ways in which the philosophy behind different intervention approaches affects the teaching role of the clinician and the focus of intervention. We have introduced a range of approaches describing their advantages and disadvantages for communication improvement.

These approaches will be examined further in Chapter 9 and specific intervention strategies, activities and ideas will be presented.

Recommended Reading

Fey ME, *Language Intervention with Young Children*, College-Hill, Boston, Mass, 1986.

Gallagher TM (ed), *Pragmatics of Language: Clinical Practice Issues*, Singular Publishing Co, San Diego, 1991.

Lucas Arwood EV, *Semantic and Pragmatic Language Disorders*, 2nd edn, Aspen, Gaithersburg, 1991.

Smith BR, 'Communication Therapy: the Application of Pragmatics and Discourse Analysis to the Work of Speech Pathologists', Grunwell P and James A (eds), *The Functional Evaluation of Language Disorders*, Croom Helm, London, 1989.

Chapter 8
BASIC INTERVENTION & TRAINING

Introduction/*76*
Prevention/*76*
Training Others and Ourselves/*77*
    Training Caregivers/*77*
    Principles to Guide Parents/*78*
    Older Children and Interacting in
        Groups/*84*
    Modifying Clinicians' Interactive
        Style/*84*
Naturalistic Intervention/*85*
    Aims of Naturalistic Therapy/*85*
    Benefits of the Naturalistic Approach/*86*
    Directive Behaviour v Contingent
        Responding/*86*
    Facilitating the Development of Speech
        Acts through Naturalistic Therapy/*87*
    Further Development of Speech Acts/*89*
Summary/*89*
Recommended Reading/*89*

Chapter 8
BASIC INTERVENTION & TRAINING

Introduction

This chapter will expand on the approaches to intervention introduced in the previous chapter. Practical guidance for intervention with a range of client groups and age groups will be given, focusing especially on the fundamental issues of prevention, training ourselves and others and assisting the development of basic pragmatic skills and knowledge. The intervention approaches we are suggesting that clinicians can choose from in this chapter are prevention, training others and ourselves, and naturalistic therapy.

Prevention

The benefit of investing professionals' time and expertise in the area of prevention of communication disorders can be difficult to quantify accurately. For this reason, prevention work does not always receive the attention or, more significantly, the resources necessary for programmes to be instigated and valued. In the fields of coronary disease, cancer and childbirth there has been considerable work carried out on prevention. It seems logical that a preventive approach to communicative disorders will not only reduce the distress and suffering of those who experience communication difficulties but also save resources when taking a medium-to-long-term perspective.

Essential first steps in promoting preventive work are to incorporate prevention as an integral component of the curriculum for students' training courses; for professionals concerned with disorders of communication to spend a proportion of their working week in directly addressing prevention issues; or for one member of a team of professionals to have special responsibility for co-ordination of preventive work. It can also be useful to document the apparent effects of *not* preventing problems, for instance failure at school and emotional dysfunction. We have found the following approaches to preventive work to be of value:

1. Educate parents about the importance of communicating with their children so as to optimize their development.
2. Educate spouses and family members through individual discussion or workshops about enhancing communication within the family.
3. Educate parents and carers about communication disorders, so that early identification and referral are facilitated.
4. Educate other professionals who may come across individuals with communication impairments to minimize misdiagnoses and increase early referrals. Such professionals will include health visitors, nursery nurses, adult training centre staff, care of the elderly staff, paediatricians, physiotherapists and psychiatrists.
5. Support team evaluations for children with communication impairments so that again a thorough and wide-ranging evaluation is carried out, with increased opportunities for cross-disciplinary discussions and referrals.
6. Support and offer professional input to organizations that provide opportunities for social interactive situations, such as play groups, stroke clubs, laryngectomy clubs, stammering clubs and so on.
7. Prepare written materials for dissemination of information regarding pragmatic impairments and their prevention. Use opportunities to discuss prevention in community forums as frequently as possible: for example, at schools, hospital open days, support groups, careers conventions or shopping centre displays, talking to groups such as pregnant mothers, school children and other community groups.
8. Use radio, television, newspapers, magazines and journals or health and education professional newsletters to disseminate information on prevention and early referral of clients with potential pragmatic difficulties.
9. Encourage a more responsive and accepting attitude towards individuals with poor communication skills by dissemination of information.

10 Encourage fellow professionals and students to investigate interactive and responsive intervention methods and to try to use directive approaches only where they are truly beneficial.

Research looking at the effectiveness of the various approaches to prevention is required so that professionals and managers are able to choose those methods that are proved to be most effective for different groups of individuals.

Training Others and Ourselves

How clinicians and caregivers interact with clients will inevitably affect their pragmatic development. In Chapter 7 we described four styles of interaction and their advantages and disadvantages and in Chapter 6 we described a simple method of evaluating and monitoring caregiver interactions through use of the interaction record (IREC). We are going to suggest further ways in which clinicians and caregivers can become aware of and modify their interaction styles in order to help the communicative confidence of clients.

In presenting training of caregivers and ourselves as an approach to intervention we do not want to imply that clients' pragmatic difficulties are necessarily *caused* by caregivers. Certainly, caregivers should not receive blame if their interaction style is unhelpful to clients. Realistically, however, it is wise to acknowledge that, through no fault of their own, some caregivers do fail to provide what is needed. We find that interactors can often be trained to become more sensitive and helpful communicators. Research (**MacDonald**, 1978) has shown that training caregivers, especially parents, can have beneficial effects for clients and their caregivers. Similarly, training peers to interact with communicatively impaired children has shown some benefits (**Strain, Shores & Timm**, 1977).

Training Caregivers

Research and common sense tell us that those who are closest to clients and who spend most time with them will have the best chance of facilitating the client's communication. The approach we are presenting here focuses on training the family and caregivers.

Relationship building

Parents and infants normally enjoy sharing activities and emotions with one another. From the earliest days of infancy parent and child engage in simple, non-verbal turn-taking behaviour which lays the foundation for the infant's later conversational development. Communication continues to develop within relationships, (**Fogel**, 1993; **Stern**, 1977). This is the starting-point for caregivers of very young children who want to help the child's pragmatic development. If, from the time that the infant first experiments with a simple pointing gesture, she experiences a warm, responsive and reliable caregiver who makes communication an enjoyable experience, it seems likely that she will have positive expectations of communication with others.

Relationships are built up over time from infancy and through routine activities such as feeding, bathing, dressing, holding and playing (**Bruner**, 1975; **Kaye**, 1982). Sharing humour as well as sharing interests, ideas and feelings makes a relationship special. Engaging in games that provoke shared smiles and laughter can be helpful for clients and their caregivers, especially when the caregiver is not confident about engaging in interactive games naturally. They may not be engaging in these games for a variety of reasons — lack of experience of being with infants and young children, feeling embarrassed to play and use 'baby language', lack of energy, depression, difficulty in forming a relationship with the child, poor experience of parents themselves or simply a lack of awareness of the benefits of these games. A supportive and encouraging clinician can often improve parent–child relationships.

Some activities that, in our experience, can be very rewarding for both partners are presented in *Table 7*. Relationships with adult clients are developed through different age- and interest-appropriate activities. The qualities of responsiveness, sharing humour, interests, ideas and feelings, are equally essential, however, for rapport building with clients of all ages. For a useful resource of ideas for enjoyable activities for infants and children readers are referred to **Fisher** (1988); **Matterson** (1989); **Mackay & Dunn** (1989); and **Gee** (1986).

Attention giving and routines of joint attention

The quality of attention given to a poor communicator is variable in everyday life. One of the special contributions which a clinician is able to offer is undivided and supportive attention. *Receiving attention* prior to being expected to *pay attention* to tasks themselves provides encouragement fand an example for children; it appears to be at the same time motivating and rewarding. When a child feels secure with the clinician, predictable routines in which both people share an external focus of attention such as dances, rhymes, activities or simple games (peek-a-boo, round and round the garden, hide and seek, blowing raspberries, bathing and feeding activities, and so on) encourage communication (**Ratner & Bruner**, 1978). Joint attention to less predictable stimuli such as toys, animals, books or television will also be helpful. Useful though it is to teach children how to control their attention and divide it between adults and activities (**Cooper, Moodley & Reynell**, 1978), there is a possibility that undue eagerness to compel the child to pay attention may lead to passivity and deceptively compliant behaviour with problematic pragmatic development. Attention levels, like motivation levels, vary according to the interest level of the material and the tiredness level of the child.

Interactive games

Table 7 includes simple games that can help foster relationships and provide activities for sharing attention with a child aged 3–36 months. Some of the activities are more suitable for younger infants and some more suitable for the older age range. Many of these games can be modified for use with an adult whose cognitive and social functioning is within this developmental age range. All of these games require that the adult be in very close proximity to, and preferably facing, the child. This is something which can give rise to some problems and anxieties. Since physical closeness is essential in the early stages of communicative development, clinical policies with regard to touching clients need to be thoroughly thought through. An 'open door policy', video monitoring or treating in the presence of parents or colleagues can prevent any possible accusations of abuse on the part of the clinician.

Even though these interactive games are well known to most parents, it can still be valuable to give them a written list of games like this. Parents are busy people who may spend much of their time feeling exhausted and who may not have the time or the creative energy to think of new games to play with their child. There are many baby books available that describe these and other simple games and routines (**Buhai Haas**, 1987; **Gee**, 1986; **Cooke & Williams**, 1985; **Lynch & Cooper**, 1991). Clinicians and parents will know many other games that can be used to similar effect.

Responsiveness

In all of these activities a responsive partner is essential for the child to enjoy the activity and gain maximum benefit. The role of responsiveness in the development of children's communication has been studied by **Ainsworth** (1974) who concluded that four aspects of a parent's responsiveness correlate positively with the later development of children's conversational skills. These are described in *Table 8*, along with our suggested implications for clinicians' and parents' interactions with infants and young children. **Snow** (1984, pages 87–91) discusses the issue of parental responding and states that, in the very early stages of communicative development, responses need to be contingent upon what the child has said or done rather than the introduction of new topics or reflecting the parents' own ideas. She also provides a helpful summary of other work on semantically contingent speech.

It seems clear that having a responsive communication partner who responds contingently plays an important role in at least the early stages of communication development (**Snow**, 1994; **Pine**, 1994).

Principles to Guide Parents

Helping parents and caregivers to learn ways of communicating with their child can have beneficial effects for both partners. There are some specific and more general principles for working with clients that are particularly useful for parents to bear in mind when trying to communicate with their child. **MacDonald** (1985) proposes three principles of communicative interaction:

1. Every behaviour can communicate: a glance at a carton of juice can communicate that a person would like to drink the juice; moving towards a toy can be interpreted as expressing interest in that toy. Children can be encouraged to express their interest through increasingly more conventional means.

2. Communication functions as a feedback loop: responding positively to a child's communicative attempt will further encourage the child to initiate communications and respond.

3. Expectancies play a role in determining the way others communicate: expecting a child to communicate may increase the likelihood of communication, whereas having low expectancy may diminish communicative attempts.

Activity	Procedure
Peek-a-boo	Hide your face behind your hands for a few seconds, then remove your hands and say, "Boo" with a wide-eyed expression. *Variations*: use cloth/furniture to hide behind or hide the child under a small blanket, then lift it up.
Dancing	Dance a waltz or a faster dance with the child. Spinning around and galloping while being held very securely by the adult can be great fun.
Spider/mouse walking	Move your fingers in a spider/mouse-like walk towards the child, saying: "Here's a little spider/mouse." Eventually, make the spider/mouse tickle the child on her tummy or toes.
Fish game	Open and close your mouth like a fish, so that you create a nice, gentle, popping noise.
Bouncing	Hold your baby's hands and allow her to bounce up and down on her knees. If she is too young or too old for this game, put her on your knee and bounce or make her ride on your knee or ankle as if it were a horse. Varying the speed and height can build excitement and lots of laughter.
Raspberry game	Blow raspberries on your hands. Encourage the child to do the same. *Variation:* blow raspberries on the child's tummy.
Cheek popping	Put your finger inside your mouth towards your cheek. Then quickly pop it out, making a loud popping noise. Alternatively, puff out your cheeks and then 'pop' them by pressing your fingers on them.
Making funny voices	Talk in a low or a high voice. Imitating cartoon character voices can be successful but amateur attempts will probably be just as good.
Making funny faces	Press your nose and stick out your tongue. Encourage the child to touch your tongue and, as soon as she gets close, retract it. Then press your nose again and continue the routine. *Variation:* eyes can blink if the chin is pressed.
Chasing	Say to the child, "I'm going to get you", then chase her by crawling. Tickle or hug her when you catch the child.
Tug of war	Give the child a cloth or string to hold and then gently tug at it. *Variation:* 'tease' your child with a string or object by putting it within her reach then just as she touches it, moving it away suddenly. After a few 'teases', let her get it. Do not do this to the point of frustration. Only continue if the child enjoys it.
Funny walk	Do a funny walk: do bunny hops, shuffle your feet, walk like a soldier, waddle like a duck, crawl like a baby, and so on.
Nursery rhymes	Sing any nursery rhyme to the child while they are sitting on your knee. Rhymes with repetition, finger and body movements are especially nice for children in the pre-linguistic stages as they will enjoy watching you and being manipulated (gently). Later they can begin to join in the actions and words. (Heads, shoulders, knees and toes; Tommy thumb; This little piggy; Round and round the garden; The wheels on the bus; and Old MacDonald had a farm are very good.)

Table 7 Interactive games.

Responsive parent behaviour	Implications for interactions
Awareness of the child's communicative signals.	Focus on the child to pick up *even very subtle* signals.
Interpretation of the child's communicative signals.	Be aware of the child's possible needs, wants and ideas to increase the likelihood of interpreting the child's communicative signals accurately.
Appropriateness of response to the child's communicative signals.	Assess the child's developmental level and be aware of the current interests of the child so that responses are rewarding and developmentally appropriate.
Promptness of response to the child's communicative signals.	Respond immediately and realistically to the child's communicative attempts.

Table 8 Responsive parent behaviour and implications for interactions.
Source: Adapted from **Ainsworth** (1974).

We have found that the general principles of interaction outlined in table 9, below, are helpful for parents and professionals to keep in mind when attempting to enhance communicative interaction with a child.

Some additional techniques, especially those at the linguistic and complex language stages, are slightly more structured and more appropriate for developmentally older children than the activities described above. However, if used naturally in a relaxed environment, they are suitable for children of all ages and even for adult clients with learning difficulties if modified appropriately to take into account the adult's needs.

Communication facilitation techniques

Communication facilitation techniques (CFTs) are simple ways in which therapists can modify their style of interacting with a client in order to facilitate the natural communication acquisition process. Many researchers have suggested that the use of certain adult communication strategies, such as using expansions of the child's communication, help to facilitate the child's language production (**Furrow, Nelson & Benedict**, 1979; **Hoff-Ginsberg**, 1985 and 1986; **Farrar**, 1990; **Richards**, 1990; **Richards & Gallaway**, 1993; **Richards & Robinson**, 1993). The precise value of using each 'facilitative' technique for specific developmental levels has yet to be researched and we are not in a position to claim that all techniques will be successful with clients. However, the techniques that we are suggesting as facilitative are consistent with what research is available currently and with our own clinical experience. Several authors in the clinical literature (**Weybright & Rosenthal Tanzer**, 1986; **Fey**, 1986; **MacDonald**, 1978) describe CFTs (sometimes termed 'language stimulation techniques'). The labels we have given to the CFTs are those we feel are most descriptive of the technique, but the reader will come across a wide variety of labels in the literature and in clinical practice to describe essentially the same techniques.

How might CFTs help communication?

The usefulness of CFTs lies partly in their focus on clinicians changing their behaviour rather than any pressure on the client to perform. The well known story about the contest between the wind and the sun to get the man to take off his cloak illustrates that force can be less powerful than gentle encouragement. All parents know that children often refuse to perform when they are asked to do so. The CFTs aim to encourage the adult to shift attention away from the speech performance of the client and direct it towards the client's interests and choice of activities.

Because the adult starts to pay more attention to what the child looks at, touches and communicates about, the relationship can become closer as the adult begins to tune in more closely to the child's world. In common techniques (such as imitation training: "What's that?" No response. "It's a fork. Say 'fork'." "Fork." "Good, fork.") where the focus is on the child's talking, relationship building can be hindered, particularly when children become conscious that their acceptance (shown by praise) is dependent upon talking or behaving in certain ways.

Always focus on your *relationship* with the individual, rather than on using a technique.
Focus on the *child*, not on yourself.
Leave *space* (silence) for the child to talk.
Accept all the child's communicative attempts.
Eliminate non-essential questioning.
Use vocabulary at the appropriate level for the client.
Never demand or necessarily expect a *verbal* response.
Try not to be too quick to point something out to the child; rather, *wait* to see what she finds interesting about an object or action.
Show that you have a *genuine interest* in the child by listening, watching what she does and involving yourself in her interests.
Do not correct pronunciation or grammar: you can say it correctly (later, in a natural situation) without pointing out that the child has made an error.
Letting children run wild is not necessary, but they do need to become active explorers, so set reasonable limits and expect the child to conform, but do not expect her to become the passive recipient of 'stimulation'.
Adults naturally have to retain enough power to protect the child, but need not dominate *all* the time.

Table 9 *General principles of interaction.*

The techniques

We have identified 16 CFTs from clinical experience and literature. We have subdivided the techniques into three different groupings according to the *stage* of development of language of the client. In the *pre-linguistic stage* there are techniques that we think are especially useful for individuals at this stage in their communication development. Pre-linguistic techniques are also helpful for clients who begin to show self-consciousness and even resistance through feeling pressurized to talk. The second group contains techniques suitable for clients who are at a *linguistic stage* of communication development: for example, clients who attempt single words and who put two or more words together. The third group of techniques in the *complex language stage* is qualitatively different from the first two groups in that, although no performance is required from the client, the techniques do naturally provide scaffolding for a response if the child is ready and willing to offer one. These techniques are suitable for clients who are able to understand and produce language.

The CFTs from each group will be described by providing examples of interactions incorporating the techniques. Although we have split the techniques up into groups, any technique can be used with any client. In particular, it is expected that as clients move into the linguistic stage, techniques from the pre-linguistic stage will not be dropped but rather will be built upon by adding techniques from the linguistic stage group.

Pre-linguistic stage

1 Sharing attention This technique involves adults noticing the client's focus of attention and then making the client aware that they too are attending to it. If the client is able to switch gaze from the object to the adult or is able to point, the adult needs to be alert to signals from the client that she wants them to share her attention to the object.

Example:
   Child: [Looking intently at a large, brightly coloured ball.]
   Adult: That's a ball [pointing to it and looking alternately at the client and the ball]. Here it comes! [rolling the ball towards the client and continuing to look alternately at the client and the ball].

2 Sharing emotion This technique is similar to sharing attention, but in addition to sharing interest in the same object or action the adult and client share surprise, laughter and excitement. It is valuable to share eye-contact during the expression of emotion.

Example 1:
   Child: [Sees a cat come into the garden unexpectedly and vocalizes/points.]
   Adult: Oh! There's a cat [looks at the cat and at the client alternately].

Example 2:
   Child: [Puts a hat on her head, with mirror next to her].
   Adult: Ha, ha, ha. Look at your hat! [pointing to the hat and looking at it].

3 Making associative noises or gestures This technique, used by parents universally, involves making a noise or gesture to accompany the action made by the client. The clinician is careful to leave enough space for the client to imitate sounds or gestures spontaneously.

Example 1:
   Child: [Pushes a toy car along the floor.]
   Adult: Brum, brum. [Perhaps also gets own toy car and continues to make the noise.]

Example 2:
   Child: [Eats food herself or pretends to feed a doll.]
   Adult: Num, num, num [makes eating noise and licks lips].

Example 3:
   Child: [Picks up a toy dog.]
   Adult: Woof! Woof! [and pants like a dog].

4 Describing actions or states of mind This technique involves focusing on what the client is doing. If the client is not doing anything, then focus on what you think she can see or hear or what she might be thinking about. A variation on this technique is where adults play alongside children and describe what they are doing to the child.

Example 1:
   Child: [Drinks her juice from a cup.]
   Adult: You like that don't you?

Example 2:
   Child: [Client is doing nothing, but you both hear the telephone ring.]
   Adult: You can hear the telephone.

Example 3:
   Child: [Client looks tired.]
   Adult: You're sleepy.

Example 4:
   Child: [Playing with a basket of clean clothes from the washing line.]
   Adult: I'm folding Jill's T-shirt. I'm folding my shorts. I'm folding your trousers.

5 *Describing objects* This involves the adult noticing what object the child is looking at and then describing the characteristics of the object to the child. The salient characteristics will vary with the stage of conceptual development that the child has attained, but examples would include name, size, location, shape, colour, texture, temperature and ownership. This technique also helps clients to practise the early stages of topic introduction.

Example 1:
   Child: [Looks at a budgie.]
   Adult: That's a budgie. It's granny's little blue budgie.

Example 2:
   Child: [Having a swim at a swimming bath.]
   Adult: The water's cold.

Linguistic stage

Many of the CFTs in this stage allow clinicians to facilitate the development of a variety of speech acts (communicative functions or intentions) that may be absent or poorly established in a client's repertoire. As with all of the CFTs, it is worth remembering that the clinician will be following the child's interests primarily, rather than following an agenda of certain techniques. The CFTs should be used carefully to preserve the natural flow of conversation and the clinician's concentration on communicating ideas rather than grammatical constructions.

1 *Confirmation/agreement* This technique involves letting the client know that you heard and understood what was said by repeating it and that you agree with what was said.

Example:
   Child: Hot [points to a hot cup of tea].
   Adult: Yes. It is hot.

2 *Repeating* As the title of this technique suggests, it involves simply repeating what the client says. This allows the client to hear a clear version of the utterance, provides a model of a simple form of clarification and shows that the utterance has been recognized. Further, it communicates to the client that the topic of conversation that they initiated is being maintained by the clinician conveying interest in them.

Example:
   Child: Big boat.
   Adult: Big boat.

3 *Reformulation* Reformulation involves repeating what the client says, as in 'Repeating' above, but reordering the words slightly or substituting more accurate words so as to more closely approximate adult norms. This technique serves the same pragmatic purposes as the previous one but in addition provides an unsolicited repair that reflects back to the child the adult's understanding of the communication.

Example 1:
   Child: Boat out [while putting the boat in the bath].
   Adult: Boat in.

Example 2:
   Child: Car mummy [pointing to mummy's car].
   Adult: Mummy's car.

Example 3:
   Child: Juice more [frowns and pushes juice away].
   Adult: No more juice.

4 *Expansion* Expansion involves repeating what your client says and expanding it a little so that it more closely approximates adult norms.

Example 1:
   Child: Train chu chu.
   Adult: Yes. The train says 'chu chu'.

Example 2:
   Child: Rain.
   Adult: It's raining.

Example 3:
   Child: Bottle down.
   Adult: Put the bottle down.

5 *Addition* Addition involves, first, expanding what the client says and then adding one or more related utterances. This CFT can help clients to learn about topic expansion.

Example 1:
   Child: Rain.
   Adult: It's raining. It's very wet.

Example 2:
   Child: Daddy sleeping.
   Adult: Daddy's sleeping. He's tired.

Example 3:
   Child: Tiger goes like this: grrrr.
   Adult: The tiger goes like this: grrrr. He's got a very big growl. And he's got big sharp teeth.

Complex language stage

Caution should be exercised when using these techniques, as they do not work with all clients. It is often preferable to use the techniques listed above under 'Linguistic stage' even with developmentally more sophisticated individuals. A possible danger of using some of the techniques listed below is that, when overused, they can change the balance of power so that the adult is the prime initiator and makes most of the decisions about what to focus on. Despite their disadvantages, these techniques can, when used skilfully, provide opportunities for facilitating and building communication. In addition, like the CFTs introduced in the linguistic stage, they can provide opportunities for modelling and eliciting a wide range of speech acts.

1 Making suggestions This technique is useful for a client who is showing poor concentration on potentially motivating toys, playing with one for only a few moments and then moving on to the next. The technique involves looking to see what the client appears most interested in and then making an oblique suggestion that requires no response from the client if she does not want to make one.

Example:
- Child: This a doll [holding doll].
- Adult: Yes. I think the doll's hungry. [Adult should not pick up the doll that the child is focusing on but, if appropriate, can pick up a second doll and act on the suggestion to give the doll food if the child fails to act.]
- Child: [Still holding the doll.]
- Adult: Dolly's eating [feeding the doll play food].

2 Reformulations Here you ask questions that involve reformulating what the child says.

Example:
- Child: He gonna fall [pointing to a toy dog balanced on top of a brick tower]!
- Adult: You think he's gonna fall, do you? I think you're right!/I don't think he is!

3 Asking yourself questions (rhetorical) This technique involves you asking yourself a question aloud so that, if clients want to, they can help you out by offering an answer to your question or they can wait to see how you answer your own question. Thus there is no pressure to answer the question. In addition there is no 'right' or 'wrong' answer to the question as there might be in a typical direct question. The benefit of using questions is that it allows the adult to present models of questions in a meaningful context and without the pressure that sometimes accompanies them.

Example:
- Child: [Playing alongside adult with toy people.]
- Adult: Is he going to fall? Is he? Is he? Is he? [Leaving space in case the child wanted to supply an 'answer', but not looking at the child expecting an answer necessarily.] Yes! He did fall!
- Child: Yes! He did and mine gonna fall now.

4 Forced alternative questions (rhetorical) This technique involves clinicians asking *themselves* forced alternative questions aloud. Clients will learn from the clinician's models and also they may well supply an answer to the clinician's question.

Example 1:
- Child: [Playing with adult with toys, but not initiating any actions with them.]
- Adult: I wonder if she wants a ride on the bus or a ride in the car.

Example 2:
- Child: [Child and adult looking at range of different coloured hats for dolls.]
- Adult: Now, do I want a red one or a blue one? I think I'll have a red one.

5 Wh- questions (rhetorical) These questions can be answered verbally or non-verbally (for example, with a shrug of the shoulders or pointing) or can be left unanswered without the risk of violating politeness principles.

Example 1:
- Adult: I wonder who knocked my tower down? [A puppet, possibly.]

Example 2:
- Adult: Where is the grandma? I can't find the grandma [making sure that the grandma figure is within easy view of the client].

6 Statements This technique involves the clinician making a statement that will typically lead to the client saying something.

Example 1:
- Adult: [Holds doll and speaks as the doll] I'm hungry/sleepy [pauses].

Example 2:
- Adult: [Holds doll/puppet and tries to get it to move a heavy bag] I need some help.

Example 3:
   Adult: [Plays with doll and then tries to put doll to bed but finds some essential item is missing] I need some blankets for my doll to go to bed.

Clinicians can demonstrate these techniques to caregivers in many different ways: with the clients themselves, showing a video tape created especially for the purpose, or through discussion and role-play with no client present. We have found that it is useful to provide the suggestions in written form, in addition to discussions and observations, as this helps caregivers to remember the details and rationales underlying the techniques.

Older Children and Interacting in Groups

Interaction styles of clinicians, caregivers and others vary across a multitude of dimensions. This diversity is part of what makes it interesting to meet new people and it would perhaps be predictable and boring (but communicatively successful) if all people adopted a similar style of interaction. Modifying aspects of one's communicative behaviour in certain ways has been shown to help clients with communication impairments. **Wood et al** (1986) demonstrated that the use of certain commonly used teaching strategies can lead to *less* learning in hearing-impaired children. For example, they found that strategies that rely heavily on enforced repetitions and two-choice questions are not successful in helping children to produce longer and more complex utterances. In contrast, adopting a style where personal contributions are made and questions are avoided while focusing on the child's theme produced more spontaneous communication. *Table 10*, based on Wood *et al*'s work, illustrates the effects of different teaching styles with hearing-impaired children.

Questions generally meet with more appropriate responses if they relate to an immediately preceding experience rather than an abstract or distant experience that may be of little current relevance to the child. It is clear that having a meaningful discussion with a group of individuals is more likely to occur if the group feel interested and motivated by the topic. It is therefore logical to ensure that the topic chosen for group discussion is one of relevance and interest to the group. Sharing experiences with a group and then discussing them is a particularly helpful way of doing this.

The clinician can set the scene for a useful discussion by telling a story, reporting on a trip, watching a TV programme first, or asking clients to introduce their own themes or to bring in interesting items from home. Wood *et al*'s findings give some guidance as to which styles may be most helpful in promoting communication with hearing-impaired children. However, professionals await further research before specific styles of interaction with pragmatically impaired individuals can be unequivocally recommended.

Modifying Clinicians' Interactive Style

We saw in the previous chapter that self-evaluation is valuable for communicative partners, including clinicians. It is an important first step if one desires to change one's style from that of a controlling teacher or clinician to that of a facilitative conversational partner. This can be done by using a video camera or audio recorder and counting the different interactive parameters that are important, such as those identified by Wood *et al*.

The second step in modifying interaction styles is to decide which aspects of your style you find are helpful for clients and which aspects you might want to try to eliminate, decrease or modify. For example, you may discover that you ask questions more frequently than is desirable. You also find that, when you do ask questions, you are able to leave an appropriate length of pause for clients to respond. In this instance you would probably decide that you wanted to reduce the proportion of questions asked but maintain the appropriate pausing after posing a question. It is probably most realistic to try to modify just one or two aspects of style at a time. Some behaviours can be modified by focusing on increasing behaviours that are incompatible with the behaviour one is wishing to diminish. For example, increasing use of pauses and silence and increasing use of comments can help a clinician who is aiming to decrease her use of 'Wh—' questions.

Making further video or audio tapes of yourself in clinical situations can help you to monitor your progress in self-training objectively. Alternatively, using a colleague to give you honest feedback, preferably with objective data recording, can be equally valuable. The interactive record (IREC) described in Chapter 6 can be a valuable tool in assisting clinicians to modify interaction style.

Teacher style	Example A = Adult, C = Child	Effect on communication
Enforced repetitions Adults ask children to repeat them	A: What are you doing? C: Playing. A: Say: "Playing with teddy." C: Playing with teddy. A: Good boy!	**Wood et al** 1986 and **McNeill** (1966) found: ▶ did not increase mean length of turn. **Wood et al** (1986) also found: ▶ children were not able to produce structures more complex than their spontaneous utterances.
Two-choice questions The adult asks the child a question that offers two choices: (i) to say yes/no; (ii) to say a word or phrase	A: Is that a big car or a little car? C: A big car. A: Yes. That's right. It *is* a big car.	**Wood et al** (1986) found: ▶ children's verbal responses were shorter than with any of the other styles; children tended to give single-word responses or non-verbal reactions; ▶ it was difficult for the teacher to know if the question had been understood as the child has at least a 50 per cent chance of getting it right by chance; ▶ children can become very passive, leaving all of the responsibility for communication with the therapist/teacher; ▶ can be useful to help a child expand a theme.
'Wh—' type questions The adult asks the child any question that involves a 'Wh—' question word such as why, what, where, when, who	A: Where is the chair? C: [Points] A: And who is sitting on the chair? C: Teddy.	**Wood et al** (1986) suggest: ▶ in excess, 'Wh—' questions are likely to inhibit children from playing an active role and taking initiative in conversation; ▶ 'wh—' questions are only likely to receive an appropriate response if the child understands the question; therefore they can be a useful diagnostic tool for monitoring comprehension; ▶ this style led to the highest incidence of repair. (See **Dillon**, 1982, for a critical overview of research in this area.)
Personal contributions The adult avoids asking questions and concentrates instead on the child's topics	A: I saw a horror movie on TV last night. C: Me too! A: I thought it was great! [Silence.] C: It scare me. Mummy scream! A: Your mummy screamed? I was scared too. C: And me scared. I like it.	**Wood et al** (1986) found: ▶ children showed more initiative and were more talkative with this style; ▶ sometimes children said more in this style than when using the phatic style (below); ▶ there can be uncomfortable silences when using this style, but children and teachers were generally able to get over the fear of silence; ▶ children are allowed more time to think of what they want to communicate with this style.
Phatics The adult tries to say nothing with any content apart from acknowledging the child's contribution. Questions are avoided.	A: You look busy. [Silence.] C: I got lots of things. A: Really. C: I got ropes here. A: I see. C: I make picture in it. T: Yes. That's great.	**Wood et al** (1986) report: ▶ the increase in mean length of utterance (MLU) can be dramatic with this style; ▶ children may begin to tell stories; ▶ it was often difficult to follow what children were communicating because they relied on gesture and mime and because they leapt from one topic to another.

Table 10 *Effectiveness of teaching strategies.*

Naturalistic Intervention

In naturalistic therapy, clinicians provide opportunities for genuine interaction. Activities, equipment and the behaviour of the clinician are, however, carefully tailored to the needs of the individual clients.

Aims of Naturalistic Therapy

Naturalistic therapy aims to give the client genuine experiences of interaction so that the following can happen:

1. knowledge of the rules of conversation and the use of language is unconsciously absorbed by the client;

2. minimal communicative attempts are recognized and rewarded by the clinician;

3. practical (non-explicit) feedback as to degrees of communicative success and failure is provided by the therapist for the client;

4. early interactive experiences which may have been missing or unsatisfactory for that particular client can be attempted in a specially enabling form;

5 the demands which the situation makes upon the immature abilities of the client are gradually increased so that discouragement is avoided and yet challenge is provided;

6 the client becomes motivated to experiment with communicative behaviours and to seek new knowledge about language and how it is used;

7 the client gains confidence as a communicator through experiencing satisfying interactions.

Benefits of the Naturalistic Approach

It is now well established that the early stages of speech and language acquisition proceed more successfully when a child's adult companions engage in plenty of contingent responding behaviour than when a directive, didactic form of interaction is used (**Cross**, 1978; **Bowerman**, 1978; **Howe**, 1981; **Wells**, 1980; **Snow**, 1979 and 1984).

Clinicians who use solely a 'teaching mode' in an attempt to accelerate young children's language learning may be misguided and are probably taking the following significant risks: (1) the child's language acquisition may be less rapid and wide-ranging than if naturalistic methods are used; (2) the language acquired may not be put to full and confident use by the child; and (3) the child's pragmatic development may lag behind the development of other language skills.

Writing specifically for clinicians, **Schiefelbusch** (1984) draws attention to **Snow's** (1984) comment that normally developing children seem to be buffered against suboptimal environments, whereas many children with disabilities require optimal social environments, in order to acquire communicative competence. The clinician's task in the latter case would be to provide some such environment at times and to help others with whom the child spends more time to do the same. Schiefelbusch then goes on to address the crucial question of what would constitute an optimum environment at various ages and stages. Clearly, once a child has become a competent communicator, optimum conditions for learning will change; for example, contingent responding no longer holds the same usefulness for developmentally older children than it did when they were younger (**Snow**, 1984, page 87).

Directive Behaviour v Contingent Responding

Environments which consist purely of directive behaviours on the part of adults constitute less than ideal conditions for infants and developmentally younger clients. Some examples of different ways of responding may make it easier to see the benefits of contingent responding.

Examples of directive behaviour on the part of an adult

Example 1:
  Adult: What have you been doing today?
  Child: Nothing.
  Adult: Nothing? Were you painting?
  Child: Yes.
  Adult: Shall we look at these pictures? Show me the pig. What does the pig say?

Example 2:
  Adult: Come in, Jenny. That's a pretty dress. Did mummy get you that dress?
  Child: Yes.
  Adult: Let's get the dolls' house cleaned up, shall we?
  Child: Yes.
  Adult: Now then, you have all the people and I'll get the other things. Good. Now what goes in the bathroom?
  Child: [Points.]
  Adult: That's the bath. Put the bath in the bathroom. Put the boy in the bath.
  Child: Boy in bath.

Example 3:
  Adult: Right, now find the cat for me.
  Child: Cat.
  Adult: What did we say about it?
  Child: The cat likes milk.

Examples of contingent responding on the part of an adult

Example 1:
  Adult: Hello David.
  Child: 'lo.
  Adult: [Silence.]
  Child: [Looks at cupboard.]
  Adult: Would you like the toys?
  Child: Toys.
  Adult: Come on, then.
  Child: [Gets toys in silence.]
  Adult: Oh, you want Mr Frog. I like Mr Frog. [Silence.]
  Child: [Makes frog jump.]
  Adult: Jump, jump, jump. Where's he going?
  Child: There.
  Adult: In the box. I see.

Example 2:
> *Child:* Dolly out.
> *Adult:* Dolly can't get out, she's stuck in the dress.
> *Child:* Dolly out.
> *Adult:* No, we'll break the dress if we pull.
> *Child:* [Reaches for doll.]
> *Adult:* I don't want to break this one. Have this one. This dress comes off. [Puts other doll out of reach.]
> *Child:* Dress off.
> *Adult:* Oh yes. What a dirty face!
> *Child:* Wash, wash.
> *Adult:* Do you want to give her a bath?
> *Child:* Bath.
> *Adult:* Come on, then.

Communication-centred contingent responding comes naturally to some individuals but for many of us it is a skilled way of interacting that has to be learnt. The reason why taking a directive approach with children is so predominant among adults may be our experiences as children within schools, our own parents' styles of interacting, teacher/clinician training and even societal expectations for adults to be 'in control' of children. Whatever the reason for the predominance of directive approaches in intervention, it is clear that communication-centred styles are of great value in working with communicatively impaired individuals. It is also clear that contingent responding styles can be learnt by people who see the value of this approach. We have discussed ways of assessing and modifying styles of interaction for both carers and clinicians in Chapters 5 and 7.

The aims of a naturalistic approach depend on the individual client's needs. Speech act facilitation will be addressed here to show clinicians how to use a naturalistic approach. The principles described apply to all other areas of pragmatic development.

Facilitating the Development of Speech Acts through Naturalistic Therapy

The ability to express communicative intents by performing primitive communicative acts is thought to develop early in life (**Halliday**, 1975; **Dore**, 1978a), becoming gradually refined and extended with maturity. In adulthood a wide and sophisticated repertoire of speech acts (for example, joking, deceiving, using sarcasm and promising) is normally available and intentions can be conveyed and understood both directly and indirectly. These acts form the basis of all communicative activity. Some clients are limited in their ability to convey communicative intents despite adequate linguistic skills. We recommend that, in view of the importance and developmental primacy of communicative acts, they should take priority in treatment planning.

Clients who seldom express communicative intents by performing speech acts or their non-verbal equivalent (pointing to comment on the existence of an object, refusing by pushing food away, reaching towards a desired object for a request and so on) benefit from the quiet, relaxed attention of a sensitive, alert and responsive communicative partner (see 'contingent responding', page 86). They are likely to have been challenged from time to time in a confrontational manner but, if this has not succeeded, it will be better for the clinician to employ a different approach. Rather than accepting responsibility for all active contributions to the interaction, the clinician can join the client and try to discover how they are feeling by *observation* rather than direct *inquiry*. For example, a client may throw blocks around aimlessly, demonstrating to the observer possible boredom, or the client may repeatedly look out of the window, perhaps demonstrating a wish to go outside. Once feelings have been identified, the client's thoughts, desires and interests can be more readily explored. Lack of communicative activity may seem to cry out for vigorous therapeutic intervention, but experience has shown that holding back while continuing to provide friendly attention can be more effective. Watching and listening quietly for minimal initiations on the part of clients is not an easy option for clinicians whose training required them to take control of therapy situations. However, this behaviour is essential with clients who are used to adopting a passive role, since there is no other effective treatment. This less directive approach stands an excellent chance of succeeding.

Two respected remedial programmes, INREAL (**Weiss**, 1981) and the **Hanen Program** (1984–1995, available from Winslow) advocate waiting for the client to take the lead. *INREAL* uses the mnemonic SOUL:

> S Silence
> O Observation
> U Understanding
> L Listening

The Hanen Program uses OWL to help 'over-eager' clinicians, parents and teachers to remember the importance of waiting:

O Observe
W Wait
L Listen

In the same vein, the Gentle Teaching approach (**Harbridge & Hobbs**, 1992) aims to remove pressure from poorly communicating students. Clinicians may also be familiar with the concept of 'Special Times' (**Pinney**, 1985; **Redwood & Bracher**, 1993). This is a similar but more regulated approach within which the client is in control of activities and the clinician is bound by certain specific rules, such as not offering interpretation. For instance, if a child were to drop baby dolls down the dolls' house chimney, the rule would discourage the speech and language clinician from commenting about the child's possible hostility to babies. The specialist play therapist, on the other hand, might do so and would have the skills to enable the child to explore and integrate hostile feelings. Two recent play therapy texts (**Newson**, 1992; **Catanach**, 1994) have helped the present authors to see clearly the implications of related professions' involvement in this type of activity. We recommend these texts, but we also wish to point out that principles used in play therapy (**Newson**, 1992) share some similarities with what we describe as naturalistic approaches. However, a relaxed, non-directive interaction with children, or older clients, for the purposes of speech and language or communication therapy does not need to focus exclusively on feelings in the way that play therapy for disturbed clients has to do. The object of such non-directive interaction is to provide the disadvantaged communicative partner with space and motivation for the expression of thoughts, feelings and wishes and thus to bring about a *meeting of minds* rather than a speech and language lesson. Paradoxically, the client's speech and language development is likely to benefit.

Goals for speech act facilitation

Initial goals for a client who has limited use of speech acts are the following:

1 caregivers and clinicians will adopt a responding role;
2 the client will explore the physical environment for sources of interest;
3 the client will observe that primitive communicative acts can be effective in that they produce an interesting or satisfying response from the clinician or caregiver;
4 the client will observe some modelled communicative acts;
5 the client will observe that there are certain 'felicity conditions' (conditions under which communicative acts are likely to be successful).

All and any stimulating and interesting materials and environments are suitable, indoors and out. Similarly, activities may comprise all and any stimulating and interesting activities enjoyed by the client. The procedure incorporates the above goals.

Goal 1: Caregivers and clinicians will adopt a responding role Because of the professional responsibility that they carry for clients' development, clinicians often find it difficult to do nothing in an interaction with a client. Despite the appearance of inactivity, however, the silence of a concerned, attentive clinician can at times provide exactly what clients need if they are to understand that their own rather inadequate communicative signals are worth persisting with and expanding. Having remained silent long enough to allow the client to attempt some form of communication (even though their intention may not be firm at this stage), the clinician provides a contingent response which encourages further experimentation on the part of the client. The importance of adopting this role needs to be explained and demonstrated to caregivers who may find it difficult to take on this role without support and encouragement. It is easy to assume that these very basic steps in communicative development have already been taken and that what the client needs is language input, which is after all the speech and language therapist's specialization. However, experience has taught us that joining the poor communicator at the stage they have reached and establishing rapport lays the best foundation for later language acquisition and use.

Goal 2: The client will explore the physical environment for sources of interest It is important for clinicians to ensure that clients are free to explore and react to the environment when they are ready to do so. They must also be given the time to do so, rather than being pressed by clinicians for a reaction. Not all clients are able to move easily enough to explore a physical environment and some environments are so familiar that exploration has ceased. In these cases the therapist imports some interesting objects, textures, tastes or events to stimulate the client's interest or even dislike.

Goal 3: The client will observe that primitive communicative acts can be effective in that they produce an interesting or satisfying response from the clinician or caregiver The clinician observes the client's behaviour with great care, responding to those behaviours which could possibly be interpreted as communicative acts. It will be useful to remember that, in order to respond contingently, it is not necessary to comply with every demand. For instance, "Oh, I see what you want. No, we mustn't touch electric plugs" can be a contingent response; so can "We don't spit it out, we say 'no'." (This would be especially helpful if the client was actually allowed to make a negative sign and have some disliked food taken away. Often unsuitable behaviours begin because a person's minimal communications have been ignored.) Clients who are not in a position to make choices or express opinions and desires, whether in a family, an institution or a clinical setting, cannot be expected to perform a wide variety of communicative acts. In those situations they will be forced to conform to the expectations of others and to confine their communications to a limited range of permitted and expected acts. In free interactions, however, it is the unexpected which generates the interest for both parties and this interest motivates further developments.

Goal 4: The client will observe some modelled communicative acts In free interaction the clinician is in a position to guess at a client's communicative intention. Sometimes it is helpful to speak client's lines so that they can know how the intention might be expressed, as in the following example. A non-verbal client with severe learning difficulties who shows understanding of simple gestures appears to want to get a drink from a table. The clinician says, "You want a drink" and makes a gesture or sign for a drink or reaches to get the drink, and then says, "Want a drink." Clinicians will also express their own communicative intentions in a form that suits the client's linguistic abilities: that is to say, one which sounds as natural as possible, but does not overtax the client's comprehension. For example, the clinician is in the home of an adult client with global dysphasia. She needs to leave and says, "I'm going home now. See you soon. Bye" and waves. Rather than saying, "It's five o'clock and I have to get back to the office, so I'd better make my farewells now. We have another appointment next week, so I'll see you on Friday." These utterances serve as models for the client in addition to demonstrating manner and timing. They also serve the purpose of showing clients how the communicative acts of other people may be interpreted.

Goal 5: The client will observe that there are certain 'felicity conditions' (conditions under which communicative acts are likely to be successful) This aim is achieved in a similar way to aim 4.

Further Development of Speech Acts

Speech acts are developed and the range of speech acts extended through further naturalistic therapy. Facilitative activities can be used in addition to naturalistic therapy when it is clear that the client is ready for learning pragmatics through the medium of narrative, drama, art, construction and craft activities. When difficulties in using speech acts are more subtle and the client's awareness of their communication skills develops, it may be valuable to investigate metapragmatic awareness training approaches. These approaches to intervention will be the focus of Chapter 9.

Summary

In this chapter we have presented what we view as some of the most fundamental methods of intervening with clients with pragmatic difficulties. We have highlighted the importance of preventive work in confronting some of the possible causes of pragmatic difficulties at their roots. This work needs to become an integral and valued aspect of the work of clinicians if progress is to be made in reducing the number of individuals experiencing pragmatic difficulties. We have presented several related ideas for training caregivers, focusing on the essential ingredients of building relationships, sharing attention and providing a responsive partner. Through the introduction of communication facilitation techniques (CFTs) we have suggested some more specific techniques that caregivers and clinicians can incorporate into their natural interactions with clients. Finally, we have discussed the benefits and principles of naturalistic approaches to intervention and presented a series of communication aims for clinicians to consider.

Recommended Reading

McLean JE & Snyder-McLean LK, *A Transactional Approach to Early Language Training*, Merrill, Columbus, Ohio, 1978.

Warren SF & Rogers-Warren AK, *Teaching Functional Language: Generalization and Maintenance of Language Skills*, Pro-Ed, Austin, Texas, 1985.

CHAPTER 9
FACILITATION & TEACHING

Introduction/*92*
Facilitating Pragmatic Development through Special Activities/*92*
    Facilitating the Development of Speech Acts/*92*
    The Influence of Activity on Elicitation of Specific Speech Acts/*93*
    Play and Role-play/*93*
    Music and Music Therapy/*94*
    Painting and Drawing/*94*
    Construction and Home Crafts/*94*
    Narrative/*94*
    Contexts for Working on Pragmatics: Play/*95*
    Contexts for Working on Pragmatics: Drama and Role-Play/*98*
    Contexts for Working on Pragmatics: Musical Activities/*100*
    Contexts for Working on Pragmatics: Drawing/*101*
    Contexts for Working on Pragmatics: Crafts, Construction and Home Skills/*103*
    Contexts for Working on Pragmatics: Narrative/*104*
Metapragmatic Awareness Training/*107*
    Teaching Metapragmatic Awareness/*107*
    Pragmatic Skills Training/*109*
    Making New Friends/*115*
    Keeping Friends/*119*
    Assertiveness Training/*121*
Direct Instruction/*122*
    Drills/*122*
    Barrier Referential Communication Games/*122*
Accepting the Difficulty and Validating the Communication Strategies/*123*
Summary/*124*
Recommended Reading/*124*

CHAPTER 9
FACILITATION & TEACHING

Introduction

This chapter will present intervention ideas that focus on using activities to promote pragmatic development or recovery. We present three main approaches: facilitating pragmatic development through special activities, metapragmatic awareness training and direct instruction. Finally, we suggest a philosophy of accepting communication difficulties in certain circumstances and promoting communicative confidence through the use of compensatory strategies.

Facilitating Pragmatic Development through Special Activities

There are many benefits to be gained from using special activities such as constructive and symbolic play, drama, narrative, art and crafts as a medium for facilitating communication development. Advantages of this approach are the following:

▶ It is possible to aim at multiple goals.
▶ Goals can be attempted in a naturalistic and motivating setting.
▶ Communication goals can be set alongside goals in other developmental domains such as fine motor co-ordination and colour concepts, reading and artwork.
▶ This approach provides many opportunities for shared experience and shared humour, which are important components of building positive relationships.
▶ The client may feel a sense of achievement at completing an art or theatre project, for example, thus improving self-esteem.
▶ The activity can provide an interesting topic of conversation for the client to share with others at a future time.
▶ Relationships can be fostered within these enjoyable interactions.
▶ Time will not be spent focusing on the client's deficits in communication, though specific deficits can be indirectly worked on.
▶ There are many opportunities for peer interactions when using these activities.

Facilitating the Development of Speech Acts

As was the case with naturalistic therapy (see previous chapter), activities that facilitate pragmatic development involve clients in a variety of absorbing activities within which they are free to explore both the activity and the relationship with the clinician. The essential difference between these two types of intervention is that, in using activities that facilitate pragmatic development, priority is given to broadening the range of comments, ideas, feelings and desires that can be conveyed and understood, and the range of types of activity is correspondingly broadened.

Methods need to be adapted to the developmental status of clients. We would not wish to 'correct' behaviours which appear faulty, but which might be seen more helpfully as developmentally appropriate. In the absence of extensive and reliable developmental data, we find it useful to tailor the individual or group treatment of pragmatic difficulties to three very broadly defined developmental levels, as follows:

Level 1: early communication   For some clients this can include a stage at which little communication is observed. It also includes the stage at which an infant, or developmentally delayed person, uses and understands combinations of non-verbal signals or sounds and single words to communicate with others.

Level 2: linguistic communication   At this stage, increasingly sophisticated verbal methods of communication are used and understood. Although some metalinguistic and metapragmatic awareness is beginning to develop, most linguistic and pragmatic knowledge is seen as being acquired unconsciously at this level.

Level 3: advanced communication   At this stage, an adult, or capable child, consciously tries to improve her communication skills. Clients at this stage can be made aware of a purpose for any suggested improvements. They can also be expected to gain metapragmatic awareness and, on the basis of this, to monitor their own performance.

It is important to realize that, within the three levels, there will be considerable fluidity. These levels are *not* scientifically established. They represent one way of selecting starting-points for the treatment of difficulties which are not yet widely researched. It is our impression that many of the problems encountered in treating pragmatic difficulties can be attributed to working at too high a developmental level for the individual client. We therefore recommend that specific pragmatic difficulties at level 1 be resolved before improvements are expected at levels 2 and 3. Similarly, treatment of a specific difficulty at level 3 is most likely to succeed if the client is already a confident communicator at level 2. Clearly it will *not* be possible to resolve *all* difficulties within one level before moving on.

Treatment approaches for level 1: early communication

- Indirect treatment (pages 8–9).
- Naturalistic methods (page 71).
- Relationship formation (page 77).
- Routines of joint attention (pages 77–8).
- Contingent responding (page 86).
- Provide stimulating materials.
- Offer verbal and non-verbal stimulation.
- Remember to leave 'space' for client to become an active participant.

Treatment approaches for level 2: linguistic communication

- Naturalistic methods.
- Provide stimulating materials.
- Provide stimulating activities.
- Give silent, encouraging attention to the client.
- Discover what is salient for the client.
- Respond contingently to the client's utterances.
- Provide good speech, language and *pragmatic* or *communicative* models.
- Offer some verbal stimulation.
- Offer some correction and information.
- Use some drills and exercises.

Treatment approaches for level 3: advanced communication

- Discuss treatment goals with the client.
- Provide information on pragmatic issues.
- Provide appropriate feedback on the client's communicative behaviour.
- Suggest realistic targets.
- Encourage metapragmatic awareness.
- Encourage self-monitoring.
- Devise exercises for specific difficulties.
- Devise aids to home practice.
- Motivate clients.

The Influence of Activity on Elicitation of Specific Speech Acts

Specific types of activity tend to elicit particular speech acts. For instance, water play seems to call forth exclamations and requests for objects; picture books elicit questions; construction tasks give rise to requests for action, and so on. We suggest that it may be valuable for the clinician to note the effect of the specific activities on individual clients.

When using activities that facilitate pragmatic development to focus on speech act development it becomes necessary to give more serious consideration to the question of whether speech acts are being performed appropriately, rather than whether they are being performed at all. If a trusting therapeutic relationship has been formed, but not in its absence, it will be possible when using activities that facilitate pragmatic development to do such things as requesting politeness markers or commenting on poor timing without endangering the communicative confidence of clients. However, some immaturities or disabilities will need to be accepted if clients' eagerness to communicate is to be preserved. This eagerness may well be a factor which promotes exploration and learning in therapy, so clinicians do well to preserve it rather than attempting to move too quickly to the more demanding metapragmatic awareness training.

Play and Role-play

It is well established that learning to play symbolically (to pretend) and to take another role are valuable activities for those with language and communication problems (**Terrell et al**, 1984; **McCune-Nicholich**, 1981; see also page 17). The extent to which these activities can be managed by those with specific pragmatic difficulties is variable. Since one is attempting something which may present special problems for a client, it may be wise to allocate blocks of time, say six weeks only, for repeated trials over a period of years. In this way maturational opportunities are not lost but time is not wasted unduly. Teaching is mainly by example, helped by such props as a well stocked toy cupboard, a dressing up box and a troupe of attractive puppets. Having an assistant model role-play with the clinician is sometimes very helpful.

More formal role-play (drama), improvization and scripted work can be helpful to clients with social difficulties and weakness in perceiving the needs of others (**Jennings**, 1986).

Music and Music Therapy

Fully trained music therapists have considerable success in working with poor communicators. There is no reason why a speech and language therapist or other professionals should not also employ recordings, songs and musical instruments in intervention. Indeed, it seems surprising that this is not done more often, since what is needed to enhance communicative competence is enjoyable mutual activity.

Painting and Drawing

Painting and drawing are favourite activities frequently used within the playgroup and nursery classroom with pre-school children. These activities can be used with all ages and can form the focus of shared discussion. They greatly assist self-expression when used sensitively. Group painting, mural making and large-scale drawings can form the basis of a co-operative group activity that may provide many opportunities for natural negotiations between peers and enjoyable interactions.

Construction and Home Crafts

Craftwork presents a valuable context for communicative instruction (**Lucas**, 1980; **Lucas Arwood**, 1991). Creative art and craft in groupwork can form the topic of conversations after the project is completed as well as providing a naturally rewarding interactive activity during the actual construction. Again groups can create a construction co-operatively or might prepare a meal together, so providing many opportunities for negotiation, shared humour and discussion.

Narrative

The ability to remember and create images and ideas is central to communicative functioning and to the individual's continuing attempt to make sense of the world. Speech and language therapy clients with semantic and pragmatic difficulties frequently appear to be having trouble with these fundamental skills. The ability to retell a simple narrative has been shown to predict recovery from or persistence of early language disorder (**Bishop & Edmundson**, 1987).

We have found that encouraging clients to involve themselves in genuinely interesting stories, whether in written, spoken, video or picture form, can lead to improvements in communicative behaviour. We would add that there is also a possibility that inner language, dialogue or thinking about life and the world in a connected manner (**Smith & Leinonen**, 1992) can also be facilitated in this way.

Encouraging clients to invent and, if writing is difficult, to dictate stories of their own can be much appreciated. It also appears to improve self-esteem and communicative confidence. It is sometimes stated that individuals with certain disorders are not capable of story work, other than in its simplest form (such as with sequence cards). However, several possibilities should be investigated before abandoning this potentially fruitful approach:

1 Allow a completely free choice of picture or story books, since the client has to be able to identify with a protagonist or to enjoy a theme in order to become involved.

2 Accept brief spells of interest at first, building these later into more sustained involvement.

3 Accept very slow and partially correct interpretations and connections at first. The child will feel encouraged if given a positive response and may become reticent if given the impression that the therapist is critical.

4 Support all spoken narratives with visual and, if possible, tactile representations. The absence of concrete reference points does appear to make it difficult for some individuals to retain, recall and connect ideas. Magnetic picture boards, model worlds, drawings and photographs can be especially useful for providing this. For much useful material on developing narrative skills see **Paul** (1992, pages 145–54).

Contexts for Working on Pragmatics: Play

Level	CONTEXT
	Clinician at Client's Home/Clinic, Clinician in Class or Group, Client in Real-life Situations (briefing for caregivers)
1	▲ Children learn to relate objects to themselves and others as a precursor to developing symbolic play. ▲ See pages 78 and 79 for interactional games with young children. ▲ Sand play, water play, finger painting and other messy play are excellent for helping children to gain confidence in their ability to manipulate different materials. They are good contexts for communication as they elicit a real need to make requests or obtain information. For example, clients may want your help in obtaining a bucket or getting some more water. They may wish to show you a pattern they have made in the sand or complain that someone has flattened their sand castle. See also Crafts, Construction and Home Skills, page 103. ▲ Gross motor play such as playing on slides, swings, roundabouts and seesaws can provide fun to share and later talk about. While using this kind of equipment, there is often a genuine need to communicate. ▲ Encourage functional use of objects such as cups, plates, spoons, forks, combs, brushes, hats, shoes, glasses, floor brushes, vacuum cleaners, cloths, blankets and crayons. Have these objects available for the child and play in parallel using modelling techniques naturalistically. For example, pick up a comb and say, "I'm going to comb my hair now" or "Shall I comb your hair now?" If clients do not do this spontaneously then you might make the request: "Please will you comb my hair now?" (giving contextual cues such as offering your hair and pointing to the comb in the child's hand). ▲ It is useful to introduce a large teddy, clown, puppet or doll early on, so that the child can spontaneously begin to relate objects to another 'animate' object. (Puppets with 'adult appeal', such as an older-looking puppet, can be chosen for adults with learning difficulties when this is felt to be more appropriate.) ▲ It is useful to have two or more different 'animate' toys around so that there are lots of possibilities for repetition when desired. For example, the client might decide to feed herself, you, the clown and the puppet. ▲ Play 'object-permanence games' (where a hidden object is searched for). This helps the client to keep an image and a name in mind. ▲ Rhymes which contain elements of play, such as 'The Wheels on the Bus', involve the group in joining in with actions.

Contexts for Working on Pragmatics: Play (continued)

Level	CONTEXT		
	Clinician at Client's Home/Clinic	**Clinician in Class or Group**	**Client in Real-life Situations (briefing for caregivers)**
2	▲ Children generally develop symbolic play (using representations of real objects to stand in their stead) without any specific encouragement from adults. When this development has not taken place at the expected time, it is essential for clinicians to encourage it, as described below. It is helpful to have stimulating materials and a comfortable space available for children to become involved in play. ▲ Allow sufficient time for children to become involved in play. The first five minutes or so will allow children to become familiar with the materials and think about what actions and events they may want the toys to be involved in. ▲ Encourage clients who are slow in their play development to use toys in different ways. This can be done by playing in parallel with the client and making toys perform different actions on different objects. For example, model your puppet saying, "I'm hungry", and then give the puppet a plastic sandwich and a cup of tea. Try not to prompt the clients to copy you all the time, but rather have faith that they will eventually copy your ideas. Allowing the client to perform actions with toys spontaneously gives a sense of achievement which builds self-esteem and self-reliance. Being instructed too often can waste this opportunity. ▲ Encourage true 'pretend play' in which the client manages without a miniature representation of a real object. For example, empty hands may contain 'eggs', or a block of wood can become a car.	▲ Use role-play games such as shop, post office, doctors and hospitals with groups of two or more children. Clinicians can provide some input *when appropriate*, but the clients need to be directing their own play to gain maximum benefit from this activity. ▲ Tell a story or show a video, then provide some stimulating props and suggest that the group re-enact it. Let the clients negotiate their own roles where this is possible. ▲ Play a 'rescue' game where a client needs rescuing by the group. ▲ If the clinician notices that clients persistently choose only one role, it may be appropriate to make a suggestion that they take a different role. ▲ Encourage co-operative play by playing garages, tea-parties, hospitals, 'superheroes', ponies, house play and playground 'miniature world play'. ▲ *Non-directive play therapy* with a clinician who focuses attention on the emotional rather than the cognitive aspect of the activity is beneficial to clients who have few opportunities to explore their own feelings and constructs. If this can be undertaken with a qualified *play therapist* who is able to make skilled interpretations, so much the better. ▲ Board games are useful activities for promoting turn taking, rule following and giving instructions. There is frequent opportunity for negotiations and explanations, as well as shared humour. Children can learn how to lose by seeing others lose 'bravely'.	▲ Children out for walks sometimes pretend that friends or animals are either with them or hiding from them. This is a sign of their developing imagination. Caregivers may need to be reassured that this behaviour is not unusual. Clients with very intense and unusual obsessions that persist over time, however, may need referral to a psychologist or psychiatrist. ▲ Imaginary friends can provide a conversational topic between caregivers and clients where personal information is shared. However, not all clients may wish to share their 'special friend'. ▲ Encourage caregivers to be accepting of children when they play with words, ideas, poetry and humour. ▲ Caregivers can gradually help clients to distinguish between reality and fantasy. ▲ 'Pretend play' with the peer group forms part of normal playground activity. Games such as 'What's the time, Mr Wolf?' or 'The farmer is in the den', as well as re-enactment of scenes from television, can help children in a number of ways. However, children with communication difficulties benefit from being shown how to join in with their peers. ▲ Structured games like I-spy, chess, noughts and crosses, hangman, *Boggle*, charades, 'I went to the market and I bought ...' can all become vehicles for pragmatic instruction and practice. ▲ Party games such as musical bumps, statues, pass the parcel, pin the tail on the pig or communicative games such as *monopoly* all help to make clients feel part of a group. However, help must be offered initially so that the person with the difficulty can cope with the game.

Contexts for Working on Pragmatics: Play (continued)

Level	CONTEXT		
	Clinician at Client's Home/Clinic	Clinician in Class or Group	Client in Real-life Situations (briefing for caregivers)
3	▶ Beyond childhood, play is channelled into various leisure activities: for instance, writing, art, reading, gardening, shopping for clothes, horse-racing, following sport, card games, board games and parties. These activities can all be used as motivating contexts for communication. ▶ Discussing fantasy in order to explore attitudes or attempt solutions to problems is helpful in several ways. Feedback allows 'reality testing'; support can be made available if necessary and the attempt to produce creative solutions can be encouraged.	▶ It is possible to structure games and exercises which *stretch the imaginative use of symbols*. For instance, group members who hold 'aces' have the privilege of speaking for twice as long as the rest. A make-believe courtroom can be set up to try people whose crimes have been reported in the newspaper. 'Identikit' pictures of 'wanted' fugitives can be constructed. A 'crown' can entitle one group member to make special decisions.	As above. Points to keep in mind: ▶ Adults do play, though many forget how to do so. ▶ Play can be free or structured and there is value in both kinds. ▶ Conventional games do not have universal appeal. ▶ True play is voluntary. ▶ Some clients, especially those with learning difficulties, may be deprived of opportunities to enjoy the types of play they like most. Also some of these clients will have a need to pass through earlier developmental stages of play in an adapted form.

Contexts for Working on Pragmatics: Drama and Role-Play

Level	CONTEXT		
	Clinician at Client's Home/Clinic	**Clinician in Class or Group**	**Client in Real-life Situations (briefing for caregivers)**
1	▲ Narrative and drama are closely related. Many of the narrative suggestions can be adapted for drama activities (pages 104–6). ▲ Like narrative, drama can develop from observing, commenting on and re-enacting simple events in the home. ▲ Encourage imitation of parents' and siblings' activities, or animals' behaviour. ▲ Demonstrate teddies, dolls and puppets interacting with one another. ▲ Use exaggerated voice and facial expressions when playing chasing games with clients who do not find this threatening. ▲ Play 'making faces': happy, sad, cross, surprised and bored. Take turns making these funny faces. ▲ Draw faces with different facial expressions onto circular cards and stick onto lolly sticks. ▲ Provide hats, shoes and other accessories. Show that you can pretend to be another character by using these with appropriate voices and mannerisms.	▲ Encourage dressing up for its own sake and as a forerunner of role-play. ▲ In groups this can progress later to interaction 'in role'. ▲ Dolls or play people can have adventures which demonstrate communication skills before clients can speak themselves. For example, a doll is going to ask for a biscuit. Help the client to advise the doll to say "Please". Or the client puts a doll in the role of 'doctor' who is going to treat another doll. The client advises the doctor to soothe the patient and explain what is about to happen. Perhaps a toy car has crashed. Someone will have to ring up and send for a breakdown vehicle. ▲ Use face paints to create different characters. Use a large mirror to show faces. ▲ Speak the lines that the client might wish to say. This will pay dividends in the future as delayed imitation begins.	▲ The drama of television provides a popular context for observing and imitating pragmatic skills. ▲ Children's programmes such as *Sesame Street* are excellent, but many adult programmes are also suitable. ▲ Imitating simple, frequently repeated sequences such as advertisements is enjoyable and can be useful (if not indulged in to excess).

Contexts for Working on Pragmatics: Drama and Role-Play (continued)

Level	CONTEXT		
	Clinician at Client's Home/Clinic	**Clinician in Class or Group**	**Client in Real-life Situations (briefing for caregivers)**
2	▲ Without a script, puppets inevitably fight. ▲ Provide puppets (glove, sock, stick, shadow, wooden spoons or paper cup pop-up puppets) with a script, or prompts, or with a definite task to perform. ▲ Manipulate the puppets to demonstrate skills or give advice to clients. ▲ Alternatively, the client can instruct and advise the puppets. ▲ Dolls, doll-house people, clothes pin dolls or puppets can act out scenes which have been worrying a client. They can show clients how to behave or can try out communication strategies on a client's behalf. ▲ The clinician and the client together can role-play a variety of interactions to fit the client's needs.	▲ Use the scope provided by groups to explore guided role-play. ▲ Allow clients to try out, select and then rehearse what they might say in particular situations. ▲ Make up plays together for actors or puppets. Children's stories such as *Goldilocks and the Three Bears*, *Red Riding Hood* and *Aladdin* can be used as a basis if necessary. This helps group cohesion. It also improves understanding of other people and their feelings and intentions if discussed sensibly. ▲ Make up dialogue to work on language form, content and use. ▲ Introduce a game of charades to a group with the emphasis on co-operation rather than competition. Modifications can be introduced, such as using prompt cards to remind a client how to structure the charade for others to interpret.	▲ Television (particularly soap operas and series), live theatre, videos and comics are sources of ideas about social behaviour and problem-solving strategies. Unfortunately, it is not yet understood what influences whether these ideas become accurate and helpful or misleading and unhelpful. ▲ Create opportunities to discuss what has been seen and what has been deduced from it. ▲ Community drama classes can be helpful. Local libraries and colleges usually have information about the availability of these classes, some of which specially welcome people with difficulties. ▲ Libraries also have, or can obtain, multiple copies of play scripts. ▲ Being in a school play can enhance language skill, communicative skill, confidence and self-esteem.
3	▲ Improvise successful and unsuccessful interactions in front of the camera and discuss appropriately. ▲ Use a video camera to give realistic feedback about a client's pragmatic strengths as well as shortcomings during real interactions. ▲ Follow this up constructively by attempting an improved version of the interaction that was videoed. ▲ Clients who can cope with video work find that it gives helpful objectivity. (See assertiveness training; giving and receiving constructive criticism, pages 121–2.) Other clients find it too threatening.	▲ As for level 2. ▲ Also provide contexts (such as play readings, video watching) for group discussion, feedback and tuition about social behaviour. ▲ Specialized *drama therapy* should be considered, especially for those clients who have socioemotional problems.	▲ As for level 2. ▲ Also reading and writing plays can be helpful in a number of ways. ▲ Amateur dramatics companies usually welcome new members who can perform to a reasonable standard or who have relevant skills to offer, such as hairdressing, electrical knowhow or costume making. This contact with the creation of imaginary worlds can be enjoyable and instructive.

Contexts for Working on Pragmatics: Musical Activities

Level	CONTEXT		
	Clinician at Client's Home/Clinic	**Clinician in Class or Group**	**Client in Real-life Situations (briefing for caregivers)**
1	▲ Use musical sounds and interesting tones of voice from an early age. ▲ Develop shared activity of banging a drum together or both shaking a tambourine or bells. Later this shared activity can be used to develop turn taking. ▲ Use a variety of lively or gentle music records, tapes and compact discs. ▲ Sing a song or rhyme leaving off the last word. (This can also be used in groups using the client's name as the word to be filled in.) ▲ Play to clients if you have an instrument. This is helpful in forming relationships and can tempt the client to join in.	▲ The whole group can enjoy listening to music together. ▲ Teach the group songs, accompanied by a guitar or a tape, or unaccompanied. ▲ Use action songs such as 'The wheels on the bus', 'Tommy Thumb', 'Heads and shoulders, knees and toes'. ▲ Gently encourage dancing to music individually and in a group if this is liked. ▲ Use musical instruments and moving to music. The interactions involved in choosing instruments and using them together helps the development of several pragmatic skills: for instance, the performance of speech acts, turn taking, negation, negotiation, non-verbal behaviours, emotional expression and responding to others.	▲ Listening to music whether 'live' or recorded is an important part of life for most people. Clinicians can make sure that this is available to clients. ▲ Libraries sometimes have a good range of music cassette tapes and video tapes suitable for pre-linguistic individuals. ▲ Singing welcome and good-bye songs in circle time at nurseries using each client's name is a good way to introduce greeting and leave taking. (For example, Hello David, Hello David, Hello David. How are you today? Good-bye David, Good-bye David, Good-bye David, we'll see you another day.) ▲ Encourage clients by example to hum and sing as they are doing other things. ▲ Recognize the significance that music holds for some people who do not speak.
2	▲ Use song and musical instruments to improve turn taking and meaning-related intonation. Try to encourage co-operation and enthusiasm in the activity rather than the singing ability of individual clients. ▲ Record sounds (or use a commercially available audio tape) and see if clients can guess what might have made the sound. ▲ Try musical activities with clients who are withdrawn. They can help them to 'blossom'. ▲ Use popular songs on tape as 'ice-breakers' and sources of enjoyment. Tapes designed for children are sadly neglected as therapy tools. They are often linguistically, rhythmically or socially useful and children of all ages and levels of ability find them attractive and memorable. Specialized *music therapy* and *dance therapy* have a great deal to offer clients with pragmatic difficulties.		▲ Some people with communication disorders are musically talented, though this can be overlooked. ▲ The opportunity to learn an instrument or to develop the voice should be available. Success in this area can raise self-esteem and indirectly affect communicative competence. ▲ Clients who are learning to play an instrument or who develop an interest in music gain an interesting topic for conversation or a compensation for silence.
3	▲ Concerts, musical events and performances can form lively and motivating topics of conversation for teenage and adult clients.	▲ Use 'old time', 'pop' and 'country' music to enliven groupwork, to awaken memory and to tempt clients to join in and sing. ▲ Music, perhaps chosen by a client, can affect the relationships and atmosphere in a group.	▲ As well as listening to music, clients can be encouraged to participate in groups, bands, choirs and so on. These activities put clients in touch with other people, while at the same time reducing the need for highly developed verbal communication.

Contexts for Working on Pragmatics: Drawing

	CONTEXT		
Level	Clinician at Client's Home/Clinic	Clinician in Class or Group	Client in Real-life Situations (briefing for caregivers)
1	▲ Feelings and ideas are shared on paper. ▲ Encourage scribbling by having a variety of drawing materials available. ▲ Take a non-directive interest so that the client enjoys your attention but does not feel pressure to follow your instructions or 'perform' for you. ▲ Provide materials and space for activities such as finger painting, dough play and collage making. ▲ Look at pictures and talk about them. Rather than repeatedly asking, "What's that?", it is helpful for the client if you say things like "I like that one"; "What a beautiful colour!"; "I think that's the daddy"; "Oh! That one's broken." Questions can be asked, of course, but it is preferable to ask open questions or questions about opinions or to think out loud. For example, "What do you think about this?" or "I wonder what's going to happen next?"	▲ Clients who are not encouraged to make a mess at home benefit from groupwork at level one. ▲ Use a *Polaroid* camera to interest the group in images of themselves and each other. Later, this can be used to good effect for many conversation starters, with, for example, photographs of events, garden produce, cars for sale, animals seen on a visit to a farm or any topical triggers of which the group has shared knowledge. ▲ Specialized *art therapy* has much to offer clients.	▲ Encourage visual awareness of community objects such as statues, billboards or displays in shops. These can provide an interesting topic of conversation and later lead to an understanding of others' likes and dislikes. ▲ Caregivers can encourage clients to make patterns on beaches or public sand-play areas and leave these for others to find. This can foster a sense of being in touch with people outside the home. ▲ Providing materials and allowing some mess does not come naturally to all caregivers and should be gently encouraged.

Contexts for Working on Pragmatics: Drawing (continued)

Level	CONTEXT		
	Clinician at Client's Home/Clinic	**Clinician in Class or Group**	**Client in Real-life Situations (briefing for caregivers)**
2	▲ Recognize representations and intentions in clients' drawings as an important stage in moving towards more confident use of picture symbols. ▲ Reward the process rather than the product. For example, you might say, "It's nice to see you really enjoying that clay", "You're using lots of colours in your picture" or "I like the way you do all different kinds of shapes with your crayons", rather than "What is it?" ▲ Discuss picture books as well as clients' work. ▲ Keep clients' work and display it to show that it is valued. ▲ Using devices to assist drawing such as stencils or Etch-a-Sketch, while not being particularly useful for developing artistic talents, can help communicative development as they often call for co-operative efforts.	▲ Use the group setting for showing, sharing and discussing work. ▲ Groups are an ideal setting for constructing collages. ▲ Use drinking straws (each member of the group having their own straw) to blow patterns into liquid paint which has been dropped onto a large sheet of paper. This can be used to facilitate turn taking, negotiation and shared humour. ▲ Display artwork within a class or work room to make the area attractive, provide conversational topics and to show that the individual's and the groups' work are valued. ▲ Picture books and artwork should be available for clients to handle and discuss. ▲ Play drawing games such as 'Pictionary,' where clients are presented with a word that they have to draw without talking.	▲ Visit art galleries, museums and exhibitions to see paintings and sculptures. ▲ Libraries, posters, community art and even graffiti can provide useful and stimulating conversational topics. ▲ Use magazines and pictures to provoke discussion. ▲ Clients' own work can be exhibited or used in newsletters and as posters. ▲ Specialized art therapy is valuable for emotionally troubled clients as well as for clients whose development is delayed. ▲ Encourage caregivers to make photographs and possibly a camera available. (Disposable ones can be affordable and convenient.)
3	As above.	As above.	▲ Encourage clients to share their work publicly through community exhibitions or by producing posters or greetings cards. ▲ Clients should be encouraged to join community classes if they find artwork appealing. This can lead to new friendships and feelings of self-esteem, provide topics of conversation and compensate for communication difficulties.

Contexts for Working on Pragmatics: Crafts, Construction and Home Skills

Level	CONTEXT
	Clinician at Client's Home/Clinic, Clinician in Class or Group, Client in Real-life Situations (briefing for caregivers)
1	▲ Assisted craftwork, building and the use of construction toys can provide satisfaction and self-esteem for clients at the pre-speech stage. ▲ Provide a 'messy area', complete with plastic sheeting or newspaper, where children are able to play with dough, sand, finger paints or jelly. Playing in this way helps clients to develop confidence and experience the joy of feeling and controlling materials. ▲ These activities also provide clinicians with contexts for encouraging communication. ▲ Simply winding up a ball of wool is an enjoyable activity that can encourage turn taking and co-operation as well as providing a topic of conversation.
2	▲ Make things with children, such as a cooker out of a cardboard box (this can later be used in symbolic activities); a mobile out of a coat hanger, string and pictures; bake cakes; candles; seasonal gifts. Communicating either verbally or non-verbally happens quite naturally while people are trying to make or mend things. The same is true of cooking, cleaning, gardening or decorating. These contexts are therefore ideal for treating pragmatic difficulties. They provide opportunities for modelling communicative behaviours and for naturalistic language instruction. ▲ Teach skills in situations where they will be of real use. This increases the likelihood of generalization. ▲ Continue assessment by observing clients' interactions in a relaxed setting when they are not being directly confronted by a demand for interaction. The genuine need to interact during joint craft activities will reveal clients' true pragmatic abilities. ▲ 'Incidental learning' also takes place within these relaxed settings where the need to interact is real. ▲ Use pasta shapes to construct a necklace with clients for themselves or a doll. To help work on turn taking you can give one child pasta tubes and the other pasta flowers. Ask for a pattern to be constructed with a repeated sequence of a tube then a flower shape. ▲ Ask each child to knit or sew one part of a small patchwork quilt for a teddy. Then have all the children contribute to sewing it together. ▲ Having several clients working on a 'knitting Nancy' (a wooden device, such as a cotton reel, with metal prongs at the top, around which wool is wound to create a knitted tube) at the same time can provide a relaxing activity that stimulates conversation and co-operation as well as a sense of achievement. ▲ Make plaster casts of hands, feet, leaves, footprints or other interesting objects. ▲ Create a calendar as a group, using *Velcro* to make interchangeable days, seasons and dates. Having a daily routine when the group consult the calendar can help clients to develop a sense of time. Giving one client the responsibility of changing the date each day can give a sense of confidence and responsibility.
3	▲ Increase feedback to clients about communicative success as well as problems. ▲ Encourage people who have had pragmatic difficulties to use other skills. This is an important part of therapy as it improves confidence and self-esteem. ▲ Encourage clients to see themselves as valuable, regardless of their communication abilities or disabilities.

Contexts for Working on Pragmatics: Narrative

Level	CONTEXT		
	Clinician at Client's Home/Clinic	**Clinician in Class or Group**	**Client in Real-life Situations (briefing for caregivers)**
1	*Foundations of narrative* ▲ Use toys to demonstrate a sequence of events such as teddy getting dressed, teddy falling off his chair and clown picking him up, toys having a tea party. ▲ Identify common events or activities which involve family, toys and pets, such as going to visit grandma, baking a cake or going to the park. Tell these events in words and/or actions (using combinations of toys, pictures and words). *Narrative proper* ▲ Read and tell short children's stories. ▲ Demonstrate with words and gestures what happened to a toy that got lost or broken, then found and mended.	▲ Choose stories to fit the comprehension and concentration levels of the group. ▲ Use objects within the story that can be shown or passed around the group. 'Props' can be used by older clients. ▲ Use actions that can be copied at appropriate points in the story. ▲ Clients who lose the thread of stories because of comprehension problems may benefit from individual treatment addressing comprehension in parallel with groupwork.	▲ Encourage caregivers to watch very simple television programmes, films and videos with the client. ▲ Emphasize the value of comment and expression of emotions during the action and of giving explanation when necessary. ▲ Tell caregivers about the helpfulness of early exposure to literacy learning through visits to the library and seeing printed material on everyday objects such as product labels. ▲ Advertisements are often in narrative form and can frequently contain humour. They provide an excellent format for working on narrative comprehension.

Contexts for Working on Pragmatics: Narrative (continued)

Level	CONTEXT		
	Clinician at Client's Home/Clinic	Clinician in Class or Group	Client in Real-life Situations (briefing for caregivers)
2	▲ Use specially selected picture stories to capture the client's interest and enjoyment: comics or heavily illustrated books which draw children into the action are very suitable. ▲ Share opinions and feelings about stories to help clients become involved: for example, "I feel sorry for that little puppy who is lost." ▲ Connect events and ideas with one another, as this is of central importance. For example, Annie throws a ball to her friend. It misses and breaks a window. The clinician can muse: "I wonder what they should do now?" Correct sequencing is of secondary importance. ▲ Ask clients to create a picture book (possibly using a scrapbook) with pictures and words that have personal meaning for them. Themes such as My family, My pets, My holiday, My toys and What I do at school may be interesting. It is important that clients have the power to choose what they do. ▲ A large client level blackboard with coloured chalks can be available to clients to draw a picture or story sequence on and then tell a story about the picture to the clinician.	▲ Teach language use within the varied contexts and vicarious experiences provided by engrossing stories. For example, a person with limited experiences can learn what sort of language to use at a party within a story about a party. ▲ Use a word processor to enhance clients' self-esteem by creating printed versions of their stories. ▲ Produce jointly created group stories, for example, by going round the group with each person contributing the next part of the story or repeating (or paraphrasing) the story so far and adding just a bit more. ▲ Make or purchase a story board (felt stuck onto a piece of hardboard). Make characters and objects by cutting out magazine pictures and sticking them onto card with felt on the back. Alternatively, *Velcro* can be used. ▲ Sharing stories in a group can bring people together in a powerful way to share and understand one another's feelings and opinions. Saving stories on audio or video tape can add an extra dimension of fun to story activities. Stories can then be demonstrated to others if desired. ▲ During circle time a 'conch' can be used to indicate whose turn it is to talk.	▲ Encourage caregivers to have television, radio and newspapers readily available and to discuss them. News stories can help to make individuals feel involved with others. Novels, short stories and poems can extend imaginative involvement. ▲ Help clients to interpret when necessary. ▲ Comics also provide useful material for sharing and discussion. ▲ Encourage caregivers to enable clients to tell their own stories in 'circle time', local newsletters and newspapers. ▲ Caregivers can help clients to form friendships by telling stories about their lives to 'penfriends' through letters or audio tapes.

Contexts for Working on Pragmatics: Narrative (continued)

Level	CONTEXT		
	Clinician at Client's Home/Clinic	Clinician in Class or Group	Client in Real-life Situations (briefing for caregivers)
3	▲ Constructing and receiving narratives challenges clients to improve their use of language, particularly at the discourse level. ▲ Use objects or pictures of characters to help clients to keep track of referents while listening to a story. ▲ Give feedback to clients when they have not made their meaning clear. ▲ Narrative also provides a valuable medium for exploring feelings or problems and possible solutions.	▲ Encourage clients to tell the stories of their lives and some of their successes and challenges. This can help them to take an objective stance in relation to themselves and others. ▲ Discuss news and stories. This gives people opportunities to extend their own experience and sympathy. It also allows them to help others to understand their point of view. ▲ Tell the group part of a story and then ask them in turn to think of different endings.	▲ Encouraging clients to write or dictate fiction can be particularly useful to certain types of client, such as those who have experienced difficult life events.

Metapragmatic Awareness Training

There are three approaches that we are going to present under the heading of metapragmatic awareness training: teaching metapragmatic awareness, pragmatic skills training and assertiveness training. Metapragmatic awareness is *conscious* knowledge of what is required in communicative interactions: for example, being consciously aware that it is necessary to take turns in a conversation, rather than simply being able to do so in a conversation; understanding humour; taking the listener's perspective; self-monitoring and understanding figurative expressions such as metaphors, similes, analogies and parodies. Teaching metapragmatic awareness to clients overlaps to a certain extent with pragmatic skills training and assertiveness training, but there are important differences between these approaches. The focus in metapragmatic awareness teaching is on thinking about the process of communication. Role-playing is of secondary importance or may not be used at all. Assertiveness training is a form of pragmatic skills training but generally focuses on more sophisticated skills than those trained in the pragmatic skills training approach. In addition, assertiveness training involves a focus on the rights of individuals, mutual respect and identifying our true goals within a communicative situation. These areas are less likely to be the focus in a pragmatic skills training approach, where the level of skill may be simpler and more emphasis is placed on practising the skill than on discussing the rights and feelings of those involved in an interaction.

Teaching Metapragmatic Awareness

Background

Metalinguistic skills are thought by many researchers (**Paul**, 1992; **Garton & Pratt**, 1989; **Chaney**, 1994) to play a role in the transition from oral language to literacy. **Paul** (1992) reports that language learning disabled students often do not progress easily from oral language to literacy without assistance. Similarly, it seems logical to us that metapragmatic skills such as awareness of turn-taking rules, thinking about what the listener might be thinking, how to give directions and how to introduce and switch topics are likely to be related not only to the client's performance in communicative situations but also to the ability to recreate imaginatively the interactive situations that form an essential part of most narrative forms, such as stories and plays.

Method

When teaching metapragmatic awareness the clinician does the following:

1. identifies specific deficits in the communicative performance of clients;
2. explains to clients why these are causing problems;
3. provides opportunities to practise;
4. gives constructive feedback on the clients' performance or on the performance of characters in plays or stories or on television.

If the client has no true disability, but is failing to perform satisfactorily for reasons such as lack of awareness, habit, lack of helpful experience or lack of confidence, improvement can be rapid. If, on the other hand, the client is unable to function in the desired manner, more basic approaches such as the pragmatic skills training approach may be needed. Some clients are not able to benefit from direct explicit instruction and can have their communicative confidence and self-esteem undermined by such attempts to create metapragmatic awareness. It is important for therapists to be able to recognize this and to have the confidence to try more subtle approaches when necessary, rather than making inappropriate demands on clients.

Early introduction to metapragmatic awareness: using puppets

An excellent method of creating metapragmatic awareness in a non-threatening manner with younger clients is to use puppets to make errors in communication and to point out the errors to the client. This removes much of the critical element from the client–therapist relationship and allows the client to become active in advising the puppet about how to behave. A good deal of pragmatic knowledge can be acquired in this way.

Teaching politeness and friendliness rules through metapragmatic awareness

It is very easy to demonstrate politeness rules through using puppets. A useful way is to have a rude puppet and two or more socially acceptable puppets. The contrast between the puppets can be exaggerated to help clients remember the importance of politeness or friendliness. It can be helpful to have children take the role of the friendly puppets and the clinician take the role of the rude puppet.

Politeness script 1

The puppets are having tea at Bob's house.

 Bob: Would anyone like a biscuit?
 Sally: [grabs one] Mine!
 Milly: Yes, please [takes one politely].
 Bob: Can you pass the milk, please?
 Sally: Get it yourself, lazy bones.
 Milly: Here you are, Bob.
 Sally: I want more tea. Get me some now!
 Bob: I'll get us all some more tea.
 Milly: Thank you, Bob. You are kind.

Politeness script 2

 Milly: Hello!
 Bob: Hi, Milly!
 Sally: Uh, oh. It's you.
 Milly: Would you like to play bikes with me?
 Bob: Yeah.
 Sally: Not really, but I've got nothing better to do so, I suppose I will.
 Milly: Could someone help me get on my bike?
 Sally: No. I'm busy.
 Bob: I'll help you Milly. There you are.
 Milly: Thank you, Bob. See you later.

Teaching figurative meanings and literal meanings through metapragmatic awareness

Puppets can also be used to help develop an understanding of the differences between figurative and literal meanings. For example, you might have two puppets who meet each other. Bert uses words figuratively but Florence does not understand because she interprets Bert's words and phrases literally. You might solicit the help of the children to help explain to Florence what Bert really means.

Figurative script

 Bert: Hi, Florence! What's new?
 Florence: Hi, Bert! What do you mean 'What's new?' I can't see anything new. I want a new bike but I haven't got one.
 Bert: No. I meant, um, I was just being friendly. That's what you say to get people to talk to you.
 Florence: Oh, I see. I brought you a present, Bert.
 Bert: You are very sweet, Florence. Thank you!
 Florence: What are you talking about Bert? I'm not a cake or a biscuit. Don't call me sweet.
 Bert: No. You don't understand. I meant that you are a sweet person. That means you are a nice person. If you don't like it, though, I won't call you sweet.
 Florence: OK.
 Bert: Well I must run. I'm snowed under at work.
 Florence: If you don't mind walking there, I'll come with you and bring some shovels to help move the snow.
 Bert: No, you didn't understand what I meant. I'm not really going to run — I just meant that I am in a hurry. There isn't any snow at work either. I just meant that I've got a lot of work to do.

Clinicians can create their own scripts to make them relevant to a particular topic, for example, or to choose expressions that are common in the client's everyday environment.

Teaching the use of socially appropriate styles through metapragmatic awareness

Puppets or play people with clear social roles, such as a teacher puppet, a baby puppet, a grandma puppet and a teenage puppet, can be used to help clients learn about the different interaction styles and use of vocabulary that are suitable with each person in different situations. The clinician can ask clients to say why a particular puppet used the wrong way of talking to the teacher, for example. It is essential to spend some time setting up the scene before introducing a script as the social appropriateness of the style adopted by any puppet will change according to the precise situation. Since one set of behaviours that might be shocking in one situation would be perfectly acceptable in another, it can be useful to have two contrasting scripts with the same puppet characters. Clinicians may also want to work on appropriate voice volume for different situations and the social differences between having a snack with friends at a burger bar compared with having a meal with parents in a restaurant. Differences in dress, 'manners', topics of conversation, vocabulary and formality are all aspects that can be concentrated on according to the clients' needs. The following examples have Sam using an appropriate style of interaction with his friend but an inappropriate style with his teacher.

Socially appropriate style script

Sam talks to his best friend in the street.

 Sam: Hi!
 Kit: What's happening?
 Sam: Nothing.
 Kit: Wanna go to the lake and do some fishing?
 Sam: No. That's boring. What about going to town and checking out that new record shop?

Kit: OK. You sure it'll be open?
Sam: Positive.
Kit: You've had it if we go all the way there for nothing!
Sam: Stop being such a pain. Be cool.

Socially inappropriate style script
Sam talks to his teacher at lunch time.
Teacher: Hello, Sam.
Sam: What's happening, Jo?
Teacher: Sam, the teachers here are called 'Mr' or 'Mrs'. We don't use our first names here.
Sam: Sorry, Mr Harvey. Say, where've you been? You look wrecked!
Teacher: I've just been in a meeting.
Sam: Great stuff.
Teacher: Would you mind taking this book to Mrs Eastwood for me?
Sam: No way!/Do it yourself./ Why don't you ask Kit to do it instead?

Pragmatic Skills Training

This section will introduce a training approach that can be of benefit to clients who are able to understand and follow role-play directions. The level of skill required is not commonly seen in children aged under three years six months, but some four-year-olds and many five-year-olds are able to participate in this kind of training.

Pragmatic skills training: teaching social effectiveness to children

Pragmatic skills training is an approach to teaching skills considered to be important for social functioning, such as making friends, following directions and offering to help someone. Several programmes exist that differ in their approaches to teaching and learning. The approach that we are going to present here is one that we have found to be useful in working with child and adolescent clients with learning difficulties. The approach incorporates ideas from several different social skills training and assertiveness programmes, including a programme entitled 'Getting along with others: teaching social effectiveness to children' (**Jackson, Jackson & Monroe**, 1983). This approach capitalizes on the beneficial aspects of behavioural techniques but manages to incorporate these into a more naturalistic group setting (**Andersen**, 1990).

It is very important to remember that *this approach will not be suitable for all clients* and may be more effective in stimulating the development of some skills than others. The therapist needs to choose the appropriate intervention method and goals for the individual client. The following questions need to be asked when considering the suitability of a social skills training group approach for an individual client:

▶ Is the client likely to benefit from a skills-based approach?
▶ Is the client likely to benefit from a group approach?
▶ What strengths and needs have been identified by the assessment?
▶ Is it possible to match the client with a group of individuals with complementary strengths and areas of need within a reasonable time period?
▶ Which skills potentially have the greatest impact on the client's communicative competence?

As with most intervention approaches, there are advantages and disadvantages of using the pragmatic skills training approach. The advantages are the following:

1 If a client has failed to learn a skill through natural interactions during the course of their everyday life then the methods of teaching may need to be changed and made simpler to learn and to use. This approach aims to do just that.
2 There are many opportunities for clients to both observe and practise skills within a semi-natural as well as within a structured situation. Groups offer a range of different communication models, with members learning from each other.
3 Groups allow for many natural opportunities for interacting with others. Interactions in one-to-one therapy can be rather artificial.
4 Multiple skills can be focused upon.
5 Skill strengths will be practised in addition to skill weaknesses. This will give opportunities to experience success within a group and to receive positive feedback.
6 There will be opportunities to observe how *not* to do various things as well as the right way to use a skill. This will provide a clear instructional method where the client is likely to remember the correct way.
7 The clinician will have many opportunities to provide a good communication model.

8   Caregivers who either observe or take part in the training can learn facilitative styles of communication from the clinician.

9   There will be many opportunities for success that will be overtly rewarded by the group. This may lead to enhanced self-esteem.

10 There will be opportunities for clients to form relationships with peers within the group. This in turn could provide more opportunities for communicative practice as well as enjoyment in the activities and a shared topic of conversation for encounters outside the group. Friendships can develop through a group as it somehow forces interaction that might otherwise not occur. This can have many 'spin-offs' for pragmatic development.

11 The positive and non-judgemental manner in which feedback is offered to clients helps preserve self-esteem even when clients are not successful in their role-play attempts.

12 Interactions with fellow group members allow for equality of status in interactions: there can be a problem with power relationships when clients view themselves as inferior in some way to the teacher.

13 The clients' individual balance of pragmatic strengths and weaknesses can be exploited for the benefit of the group.

14 Groups can be more motivating and fun for the participants.

15 In areas where resources are limited, groups can be useful in that sometimes more clients can be seen than would be seen if individual sessions were offered.

16 The groups can naturally form part of a classroom activity or a workshop session so that for the clients this can feel as if it is just part of their everyday activity.

17 Children sometimes dislike being singled out from their peers for therapy as it may draw attention to their problems, which may lead to teasing. A group setting avoids this problem and the client may indeed be afraid of missing out on the group activity.

18 Groups can be very challenging and rewarding for the teacher(s) facilitating the group.

19 Adults can find peer support within a group setting that is very different from the kind of support that a teacher or therapist is able to offer.

20 Generalization of skills can be easier from a group setting than from an individual setting as a group is more usual, particularly for school-aged children.

Disadvantages of the pragmanitc skills training approach are as follows:

1   It is time consuming to learn how to use this approach effectively.

2   Not all clients learn best in this way.

3   Shy clients can be intimidated by the role-play activities.

4   There may be personalities within the group that do not function well together.

5   There may be less individiual time for each client compared with individual direct intervention.

6   Some clients may have attention difficulties which may be exacerbated by being in a group.

7   Clients who have severely disruptive behaviours may make it very difficult for other clients to achieve much within a group setting.

8   Clients may learn bad habits from each other.

9   The clinician or teacher usually needs specialist training to facilitate a group successfully. These skills are frequently not taught at undergraduate level in speech and language therapy courses.

10 It can be more difficult for the therapist to monitor the individual progress of clients in a group setting and so only more general improvements may be noticed. Detailed observations of progress are usually only possible in individual sessions or when a group contains a scribe who observes and reports.

11 If a group member is absent, this can alter the group dynamics in a deleterious way.

12 Groups require a large room and suitable furniture that individual work does not need.

The key components with all age groups

The key components of our approach are the following:

▶ *A positive and supportive learning environment*   Praise and constructive criticism are used by clinician and group members. The participants can be taught how to give positive feedback early in the training so that all members both receive and give positive feedback during the role-plays. Teasing is forbidden. Self-esteem is nurtured.

▶ *Clients are active participants* Clients are encouraged to take responsibility for their own learning by examining why the skills are relevant for them and looking at the benefits of using these skills in their everyday lives. Both clients and clinicians are called upon to do role-plays, which makes clients become active contributors in learning, rather than passive recipients.

▶ *Skills are broken into simple steps* Each skill is segmented into manageable parts so that all clients can understand and perform each part of the skill in isolation where appropriate to aid learning, recall and practice of complex skills.

▶ *Key concepts are presented repeatedly* Skills are repeated frequently to help clients to remember important points. Clients rather than the clinician are asked to list skill segments and rationales for using skills.

▶ *Role-plays are used frequently* Structured practice in the form of simple role-plays is a key element in the training of social skills. Role-plays often create an atmosphere of togetherness and fun as well as illustrating how to perform a skill and highlighting potential pitfalls. Role-plays involving caricatures, showing how *not* to perform a skill, help understanding of the listener's perspective and add humour to the training.

▶ *Groups are formed with skill mixes* Clients' strengths and weaknesses are used to complement each other. Clients who talk too frequently may be placed in a group with clients who are poor initiators and clients who have appropriate turn-taking skills, for example. This allows clients with strengths to receive positive feedback and to feel good about some of their skills. It also allows clients to recognize poor skills in others and themselves and see how they might modify their behaviour and attitudes. However, it has often proved more effective to group shy people together and to allow talkative people to experience some competition in a noisy group.

▶ *Skills are learnt during the formal and the informal interactions in a group* Pragmatic skills training is carried out in group settings. The group serves as a natural peer group with many opportunities for informal interactions in addition to the more formal parts of the group session. Naturalistic opportunities such as having breaks for drinks, games or construction activities are used in order to maximize generalization.

▶ *Rationales* The rationale for using a skill is discussed. Clients are asked why a skill is important and what effect it may have on the listener. Only when clients are unable to think of rationales themselves will clinicians offer prompts or supply rationales. Skills learnt in isolation without understanding why they are used and the effects they may have on listeners are not so helpful. Discussing rationales helps clients to see the relevance of the training and helps to ensure that skills are learnt and used meaningfully, not just parrot style.

Structure of the training

As regards *timing*, the structure of training in social skills groups is very flexible. Some groups run on a weekly basis with an hour-long session every week for 10 to 20 weeks. Other groups are similar to a workshop where clients work intensively for two or three days for five to seven hours each day. Clinicians will want to design a structure that suits their particular situation and client group.

We have found the following useful when *preparing* for groups:

▶ Send out preparatory material to the participants or to their caregivers in advance so that they know a little of what to expect. Invite caregivers to attend if this is appropriate.

▶ Let all other fellow professionals working with your clients know of your plans to run a group and, if appropriate, invite them to join or observe the group. Possibly video-taping the group might help this to happen.

▶ Choose a location that is physically comfortable and convenient for the participants. Is there a carpeted room available? Find out where toilets are in relation to your room; consider

▶ wheelchair access if appropriate; consider how you will prepare cups of tea and snacks, whether the lighting and ambient noise level are appropriate, whether the seating is comfortable.

▶ Enlist the services of a colleague or train an assistant or caregiver to help you to run the group. Practise role-play situations beforehand so that you feel comfortable performing them in front of the group.

▶ Arrange seats so that all group members, including clinicians, are in a fully joined circle. This helps foster a sense of intimacy and encourages participation. If necessary, think about clients who would be better placed away from each other because of distracting behaviours; equally, think of clients who would serve as good role models for another client and try to have them on opposite sides of the circle.

▶ If there are two or more assistants running the group with you, it can be beneficial to have them spread out around the circle, rather than sitting next to you. This helps to distribute the focus of the group and encourages equality among group members.

▶ Choose group members carefully. Choose between three and eight children to form a group. Ideally, the individuals will not all have the same difficulties, since one of the processes of learning is imitation of others in the group. If all of the children in the group have poor eye-contact then there will be very few good peer role models for them to observe. It is also desirable that the number of children in the group who demonstrate severe behavioural difficulties (such as aggression towards others) is restricted. A group of six or eight children or adolescents with severe behavioural difficulties may well be manageable by clinicians who are very experienced and trained in handling problems of this kind, but a single child with behavioural difficulties might render a group ineffective if it is managed by an inexperienced clinician who does not have the appropriate training in working with individuals with challenging behaviours.

▶ Find out which skills are particularly relevant for your group members to acquire. This information can be gleaned from caregivers reports, clients themselves and your own assessment.

We have always found it helpful to think about the *need for group rules* prior to starting a group. This can help group members to feel comfortable as they can predict what will happen and it can forestall problem behaviours. The type of rules that may be appropriate for the group will depend on the maturity of the clients within it. Be careful not to appear patronizing when introducing ground rules with adults. If you are working with a group of six-year-old children with behavioural difficulties, more time may need to be spent talking about rules. If you are working with a group of adults who stammer, you may only need a few rules pertaining to participation and support of other group members. Where possible, it is confidence building to have the group members think of the rules that they would like to have for the group themselves. In some cases this is not possible because of the communication difficulties of the clients in the group.

Rules that we have found useful include the following:

1 Be supportive of each other.
2 No teasing or laughing at others.
3 Take responsibility for yourself (no excuses and no telling tales).
4 Keep hands and legs under control (no poking or kicking).
5 Listen to the person who is talking.
6 Participate in role-plays. (This is a useful rule for adult groups. We have found it preferable not to use this as a rule with children but rather to say, "Those children who listen well will be the first to be chosen to do a role-play", thus framing role-plays as a treat rather than a chore.)
7 Address positive feedback to the person who has done the role-play, not necessarily to the clinician.
8 Complete homework between meetings. If homework is not done then it will be completed during the break periods when others are engaging in favourite activities.
9 Allow others to have a turn at talking (don't 'hog' the floor).
10 Talk one at a time.

The *content* of the training session is flexible. We recommend the following format, as it is one we have found useful in our own work.

1 *Welcome* Clients arrive for the group and are welcomed. If this is the first session, time will be spent on introductions, ground rules and explaining the timetable and goals of the group.

2 *Introduction of the topic* Introduce the skill for the day, such as Greetings.

3 *Discussing the importance of the skill* Ask clients to tell you why it is important to greet people. Use a brainstorm approach where 'anything goes' to encourage reticent participants. For example, greeting people is important because:

- it makes people feel happy;
- it lets people know that you are there;
- it is a friendly thing to do: others will think you are friendly;
- it will make it more likely that people will greet you, which makes you feel pleased;
- if you don't greet people they may think you are unfriendly and ignore you. This may mean you won't make many friends.

4 *List the components of the skill* Ask the group to think of the behavioural components that make up a successful greeting. Prompt when appropriate and supply answers if necessary. Be sure to allow time for clients to volunteer the answers themselves. Encourage all group members to contribute. Praise all attempts, even if they are wrong. For example, a client suggests that saying 'thank you' is part of greeting someone. You might say, "That is a good idea for the next skill we are going to be taking about. It's not part of greeting usually but it *is* part of thanking someone and being polite. Well done."

It is often useful to display visually the ideas that you are hoping the client will remember, either by drawing or by writing. However, the clarity that this offers has to be balanced against the inconvenience of moving out of the group circle over to the display. One method we have found especially convenient with a relatively small group of four to six clients is to use a small wipe board or chalk board that you can hold on your lap or place on a small table at your side for all the group to see. You might write:

The components of a greeting are:

- Use a pleasant face — have a smiling face.
- Use a pleasant voice — use the right volume and intonation.
- Look at the person.
- Say 'Hello' (and their name if appropriate).

5 *Model the wrong way to do it* With your assistant, model greeting someone the wrong way. One way of doing this would be to whisper "Hello" without looking at the other person. Another way might be to say "Hello" loudly and aggressively with a frown on your face, getting too close to the other person. It can be helpful to choose the wrong way to do it with reference to your knowledge of how certain members of your group make greetings inappropriately. It is possible to ask clients to volunteer to role-play how to do a skill the wrong way, but there are certain risks involved: they may do it the right way, they may think that group members are laughing at them if the role-play is humorous; they may find it difficult to think of an example unless you supply a script or a list of possibilities. We have generally found it preferable for the clinician and assistant to carry out this role-play. (If you are unable to enlist the help of an assistant then it is possible to ask a client to help you. Alternatively, use a video that you have made especially to illustrate a skill, or even tell a brief story to introduce the topics.)

6 *Ask for feedback from the group* After the role-play, ask for feedback about what the participants did. Ask why it was the wrong way to make a greeting and ask how you think the listener might have felt to be greeted in that manner. Use the opportunity to repeat the key features of making a greeting and the effect that it has on the listener and speaker. Ensure that you praise participants for giving feedback as much as for the quality of the feedback given.

7 *Model the right way to do it* With your assistant, model greeting someone the right way. Exaggerate (if appropriate) the important features of greeting someone, so that these are easily perceived and recalled (see components of a greeting under **4** above).

8 *Clients practise role-plays* Choose clients or ask for volunteers to role-play the correct way to greet someone. Ask clients to tell the group (or if necessary remind the clients) of the features of making a greeting the right way. Set the scene for the clients briefly, then let them start the role-play. For example, you might say, "You knock on Gill's door. She answers the door and you greet her." Make your example and wording appropriate to the client who is doing the role-play.

9 *Feedback from group* Praise the clients for their participation as well as for their actual performance. Ask the clients who participated what they thought about the role-play. This gives them a chance to explain what went wrong, rather than have someone else point it out to them. Be specific in your praise. For example, instead of saying, "That was a good role-play" say, "I liked the way you gave Gill a big smile when you greeted her. You looked really friendly." Ask group members to give positive feedback first. Ensure that they stick to the ground rules that you have set about how to give positive feedback. Ask for suggestions for improvement also.

10 *Problems* Practising skills through role-play avoids many of the problems that are involved in using those skills in the real world. It can be useful to help clients to think of possible problems in using each skill, how they might feel when this happens and what they would do about it. For example, a client may learn to perform a greeting perfectly. When he attempts to use the skill with the school secretary, instead of responding with a pleasant greeting in return she might say, "Not now. I'm too busy." Unless clients are prepared for the harsh realities of life they may stop using what they have learnt. In addition to discussing a range of possible problems for each target skill, it can be useful to do a role-play to practise how to deal with the problem.

11 *Time to practise in a more natural setting* During the session ensure that there is a break or a change of activity so that clients have an opportunity to practise skills that they have learnt during the session. Good activities include snack time, especially where clients are given the responsibility of preparing and sharing out drinks and biscuits for the group. Other activities may include free play for child clients or card games or discussion for adults.

12 *Homework* It is useful to have some homework planned for the clients to complete prior to the next session. This can act as a link between the clinician and the caregivers and encourage them to assist the client with working on the target skills. We have found it useful to keep homework brief so that it gets done. It is useful to incorporate a component of practice of a skill that has been worked on during that session. Topics for homework assignments include:

▶ Practise greeting three different people. Write down their names if you know them and write down what you said to them.

▶ Write down three reasons why it is useful to be able to greet people.

▶ Write down four things that you need to remember when making a greeting.

Homework is, of course, adapted to suit different client groups. Clients with reading and writing difficulties can carry out homework using audio recording.

Specific pragmatic skill format

On the following pages we describe some of the most frequently used pragmatic skills which are presented in a format that clinicians can use as guidelines in intervention. Clinicians can use this format to generate their own ideas for skills that are especially pertinent to the client group they are working with.

Making New Friends

1 Introducing Yourself

Importance	Components	Wrong Way	Right Way	Problems	Homework
▲ Lets other people know your name. ▲ People may like you because you are friendly. ▲ People may want to talk to you. ▲ If you don't introduce yourself you may be ignored.	1 Friendly face. 2 Friendly voice. 3 Make eye-contact. 4 Say: "Hello. My name is Pete" (optional). 5 You can also say: "What's your name?" or "I live in London."	Pete and Sue are at a party. Sue looks at her feet as she moves towards Pete and says: "I like you." Pete moves away.	Pete and Sue are at a party. Sue looks at Pete and smiles as she moves towards him and says: "Hello. My name is Sue."	▲ The other person says: "Go away." ▲ Another person interrupts you as you are in the middle of introducing yourself. ▲ The other person says: "I've already met you."	1 Introduce yourself to three different people. 2 Write down four reasons for introducing yourself.* 3 Write down the parts of introducing yourself. 4 Watch a TV programme and watch how people introduce themselves. 5 Think of situations where it might not be appropriate to introduce yourself.

2 Starting a Conversation (one way to make friends)

Importance	Components	Wrong Way	Right Way	Problems	Homework
▲ You will be able to tell people about yourself. ▲ You will be able to hear about other people's interests. ▲ People may like you because you are friendly. ▲ If you don't start conversations you may be ignored.	1 Friendly face. 2 Friendly voice. 3 Make eye-contact. 4 Say: "Hello. My name is Pete" (if you don't already know the person). 5 Ask questions of the other person. 6 Tell things about yourself.	Jane and Chris are at class. Jane looks at Chris, frowns at him and says: "What do you think you're doing in here? This isn't your class." Chris leaves the classroom.	Jane and Chris are at class. Jane looks at Chris, smiles at him and says: "Hello. My name is Jane. Are you new here?" Chris says: "Yes. This is my first day. By the way, I'm Chris."	▲ The other person ignores you. ▲ The other person replies, but you don't understand what they said. ▲ The other person says: "Would you like to meet my friends? They are new too."	▲ Start a conversation with three different people. ▲ Write down four reasons for starting a conversation. ▲ Write down how to start a conversation. ▲ Watch a TV programme and watch how different people start conversations. ▲ Think of situations where it might be difficult to start a conversation.

* Homework tasks for any of these social skills can be adapted for clients who have difficulty writing, for example by using drawings to illustrate social interactions, using multiple choice questions in simple written form or in the form of pictures or recording homework on an audio-cassette tape.

Making New Friends (continued)

3 Joining in a Conversation

Importance	Components	Wrong Way	Right Way	Problems	Homework
▲ People will want to listen to you if you are good at joining in conversations. ▲ People may like you because you are friendly. ▲ Joining in conversations is a good way to get to know other people. ▲ If you don't join in conversations you may be ignored.	1 Listen to the conversation to know what the topic is. 2 Think about what to say. 3 Wait for a pause in the conversation. 4 Use a friendly face and voice. 5 Look at the people's eyes. 6 Say something on the topic. 7 Ask a question relating to the topic.	Sam joins a group of people talking about Christmas shopping. He doesn't wait for a pause and says: "I am going to put up a really big Christmas stocking." The other people wonder why he interrupted them, ignore him and carry on their discussion.	Sam joins a group of people talking about Christmas shopping. One of the group says: "I'm going to go Christmas shopping next Saturday with my brother." Sam waits for a pause, looks at the group and says: "I'm going on Saturday too. It's going to be very busy." Someone else says that they are going shopping on Monday and the group continue their chat.	▲ The other people in the group say: "You are not one of our friends." ▲ Another person interrupts you as you are in the middle of joining the conversation. ▲ You join the group and realize they are talking about a TV programme that you have never heard of before. ▲ You want to join the group but are worried that people won't understand you.	1 Practise joining conversations on two different occasions. 2 Write down four reasons for joining in a conversation. 3 Write down the parts of joining a conversation. 4 Watch TV programmes to see how people join in conversations. 5 When might it not be appropriate to join in a conversation? 6 Listen (unobtrusively) to conversations in libraries or on buses, and write down five different topics of conversation that you have overheard.

4 Saying Just the Right Amount (so that people won't get bored with you)

Importance	Components	Wrong Way	Right Way	Problems	Homework
▲ People will enjoy spending time with you. ▲ People will want to hear what you have to say. ▲ What you say will be interesting and new. ▲ If you say too much people may avoid you or feel bored by you.	1 Friendly face and voice. 2 Look for subtle or obvious signs of boredom (yawning, looking away, looking at a clock, ignoring you). 3 Listen to others. 4 Let others have a turn at talking. 5 Don't talk too much.	Fritz sees Jo running towards the bus stop. F: Hi! How are you? J: OK. I'm late for my bus. F: I caught a bus this morning and it was late. It made me late. I'll use my bike next time. Have you got a bike? J: No. Sorry, got to go. F: My bike is red and it's very new…	Fritz sees Jo running towards the bus stop. F: Hi! How are you? J: OK. I'm late for my bus. F: Don't let me keep you. See you tomorrow. Bye! J: Bye! Let's have a coffee tomorrow at break. I'd like to have a chat. F: Yeah, great. See you.	▲ You are very upset about a shopkeeper who was rude to you. You have tried to talk to people about it but after about 15 minutes they leave. ▲ Your friend talks about a soap opera that bores you. ▲ You begin telling someone about your favourite hobby and they look bored.	1 Practise saying just the right amount with three different people. 2 Write down four reasons for using the right amount of words. 3 Write down how to use the right amount of words. 4 Watch a TV programme and watch how people take short and long turns in talking. 5 Write down a list of five things that you find boring. 6 Ask friends what they do when someone bores them.

Making New Friends (continued)

5 Listening to Others

Importance	Components	Wrong Way	Right Way	Problems	Homework
▲ People may like you more if you are interested in them. ▲ If you listen well, you will understand people better. ▲ If you don't listen, people may not enjoy talking with you. ▲ If you don't listen, you may miss out on important or useful information.	1 Face the speaker and give eye-contact. 2 Concentrate on speakers and remember what they say. 3 Try not to interrupt or switch topics. 4 Show the speaker you are interested by your facial expression. 5 Make brief comments when appropriate, such as "Really?", 'Mm', "Yes."	Richard and Simon are at a party. Richard glances around the room. S: I think I'd better go home now. R: Where are you going? S: Cambridge. R: Why Cambridge? S: That's where I live. R: Oh, really? That's nice. Have a good journey to … em … now where was it you said you were going?	Richard and Simon are at a party. Richard looks directly at Simon. S: I think I'd better go home now. R: You said you lived in Cambridge, so you've got a long journey ahead of you. S: Yes, it takes an hour or so from here. R: Have a good trip home.	▲ You can't hear what the other person is saying. ▲ Another person interrupts you as you are in the middle of listening to someone. ▲ The other person says, "Am I boring you?" ▲ You are tired and are finding it difficult to concentrate on your teacher. You are worried he may have noticed. ▲ You listen well, but the other person doesn't give you a chance to talk.	1 Have a conversation with three different people. Try to listen hard to what they say. 2 Write down four reasons for listening to others. 3 Write down the parts of listening to others. 4 Watch a TV programme and watch how people show that they are good listeners or that they are not listening. 5 Ask friends and family how they remember what others say to them.

6 Being Sensitive to the Feelings of Others (people get fed up with those who brag)

Importance	Components	Wrong Way	Right Way	Problems	Homework
▲ People may find it annoying if you boast about your achievements a lot. ▲ People may enjoy being with you if you share the pleasure of your achievements with them but don't brag about them. ▲ Others may like it if you notice their achievements rather than focusing on your own.	1 If something nice happens to you, or if you win something, tell close friends how you feel. But tell them only once. 2 Try not to mention it to those who did not win and who may be wishing that they had. 3 Thank people who congratulate you. 4 Thank people who supported you and helped you to win or gave you a gift. 5 Remember how it feels to lose.	Gill just won a prize for swimming. Howard is feeling sad that he lost. G: Look at my prize everyone! I won the race! I beat everyone. I am the greatest. H: Well done, Gill. G: You lost, Howard. I knew I could beat you. Everyone knew I would win. I bet you thought you might win. H: You weren't the only winner today, you know. G: You're jealous because I'm the best swimmer in the world.	Gill just won a prize for swimming. Howard is feeling sad that he lost. G: I won the race! I'm so happy. H: Well done, Gill. G: Thanks! I didn't think I could do it. All that practice we did together really helped me. I am grateful to you. I hope you win the backstroke. H: You deserved to win. G: Thank you. Our team is doing so well. I'm very pleased.	▲ You have just got a new video/car that all your friends want. You are dying to tell them about it. ▲ Your basketball team wins a game in which you scored the winning goal. The coach praises everyone but doesn't say anything to you about your goal. ▲ Your friend is bragging about how popular she is at her new school. ▲ You have a new girlfriend. Your best friend likes her too and may be envious, but you still want to tell him.	1 Write down three reasons for being modest rather than bragging. 2 Write down what to remember when trying to be modest and not brag. 3 Tell someone about something nice that happened to you or a gift that you received. Were you able to tell them modestly, without bragging? 4 Write down how you feel when someone starts to brag to you. How do you deal with them?

Making New Friends (continued)

7 Offering to Help (it feels nice to help others when they need us)

Importance	Components	Wrong Way	Right Way	Problems	Homework
▲ People may like you more if you offer to help them. ▲ It feels nice to help others when they need us. ▲ If you ever need help yourself, people will be more likely to help you. ▲ If you don't help, people may think you are an unhelpful person.	1 Use a pleasant face and voice. 2 Look for something you can do to help someone, or make sure you notice when someone needs help. 3 Ask if you can help. 4 If the person says "yes" then do it.	Rick's grandmother is tired but she has run out of milk and needs to walk to the shops to get some more. Rick is sitting down, reading a newspaper. G: Oh dear. I need some more milk. I'm so tired but I had better go to the shops. R: It's very cold outside. I'm glad I don't have to go to the shops.	Rick's grandmother is tired but she has run out of milk and needs to walk to the shops to get some more. Rick notices that she needs help, smiles and says: "Don't worry, I can nip down to the shops for you and buy some milk." Rick goes to the shop right away and buys the milk.	▲ You just offered to help someone and they ignored you. ▲ You offer to help your mother and she says, "It's about time you did something to help around here; and when you've finished that, I've got a few more things for you to do." ▲ You help someone and they don't say "Thank you." ▲ You help someone to move some fragile lights and accidentally break one. ▲ You offer to help your friend but she says: "It's OK. You look busy too."	1 Offer to help three different people. What happens? 2 Write down four reasons for offering to help others. 3 Write down the parts of offering to help others. 4 Think of 10 chores that you could offer to do around the house or in your class. Write them down and offer to do them over the next week. 5 Ask friends and family how they feel if someone offers to help them. 6 Think of three situations when you might not offer to help someone.

8 Asking for Help (you may be very glad you did; don't do it too often, though)

Importance	Components	Wrong Way	Right Way	Problems	Homework
▲ You may need help to get you out of an emergency or a difficult situation. ▲ People may enjoy being able to help you because it may make them feel useful. ▲ It helps to make friends when not done too often. ▲ People will be more likely to accept your offer of help if you also allow them to help you.	1 Use a pleasant face and voice. 2 Find someone who doesn't look too busy. 3 Use politeness words such as "please" and "Would you mind ….?" 4 Remember to say, "Thank you" to whoever helps you. 5 If someone says "No", remember they may well have a good reason and that you are asking for a favour. Stay polite and ask someone else. 6 In an emergency, shout, "help!"	Keiren and his dad are playing with toys. K: Get my car from behind the cupboard. D: I don't like being ordered around. K: I said get it. I need it now. [Starts crying.] D: That's a bit silly Keiren, crying over a car. I'm going to leave you to calm down. When you've calmed down we can play with the toys again and you could ask me to help you with getting that car.	Keiren and his dad are playing with toys. K: Could you please get my car from behind the cupboard, Dad? D: Yes. I'll try. [Reaches behind the cupboard and retrieves the lost car.] K: Thank you.	▲ You have just helped your sister to carry her heavy bags. You ask her to help you to fix your computer and she refuses. ▲ Someone offers to help you carry a tray of cups but they trip and break some of them. ▲ A man falls down the stairs at the railway station and it looks like he has hurt himself badly. You don't know first aid. ▲ A stranger offers to give you a lift home.	1 Write down three reasons for asking others for help. 2 Write down what to remember when asking someone for help. 3 Ask someone to help you with something and write down what happened. 4 Write down how you feel when you help someone else.

Keeping Friends

1 Saying Nice Things to People

Importance	Components	Wrong Way	Right Way	Problems	Homework
▲ Helps to keep friends. ▲ People may like you because you are friendly. ▲ Puts others in a good mood. ▲ You may find that people start to say nice things to you, too.	1 Friendly face and voice. 2 Think of something nice to say about the person. (About the way they look or something they have done.) 3 Look at the person. 4 Say something nice.	Harry and Pete see each other waiting for a bus. H: Hi, Pete. P: Hi. H: You've got a dirty stain on your shirt. Didn't you wash it? P: Oh dear. It's my best shirt. H: Apart from that you look OK. Don't worry.	Harry and Pete see each other waiting for a bus. H: Hi, Pete. P: Hi. H: I like your shirt, Pete. It looks great. Are you going anywhere special? P: Thanks. Yes, I'm going to a concert tonight.	▲ You pay your friend a compliment and he rejects it, saying, "Oh no, these shoes are awful." ▲ You pay a compliment and the other person starts to brag. ▲ Someone pays you a compliment and you feel embarrassed. ▲ You tell your friend how good she is at being on time and she says, "Oh, don't be silly. I wish you were good at that."	1 Say something nice to three different people. 2 Write down four reasons for saying something nice to someone. 3 Write down how to say something nice to someone. 4 Watch a video and see how people say nice things to each other. What things do they compliment? 5 Think about three people and write down five things that you like about each of them.

2 Showing an Interest in Others

Importance	Components	Wrong Way	Right Way	Problems	Homework
▲ You will find out about people, which can be interesting and enjoyable. ▲ You will be able to hear about other people's interests. ▲ People may like you because you are friendly. ▲ If you don't show an interest in others, they may ignore you.	1 Friendly face and voice. 2 Make eye-contact. 3 Ask how the person is. 4 Ask what the person has been doing. 5 Listen to what the other person says. 6 Make comments and contributions when appropriate.	Ursula and Wendy bump into each other while shopping at the supermarket. They haven't seen each other for several months. U: Hi, Wendy. W: Hi. U: I'd better go. W: Yes. Bye.	Ursula and Wendy bump into each other while shopping at the supermarket. They haven't seen each other for several months. U: Hi, Wendy. W: Hi. U: How are you? W: Fine. U: I haven't seen you for ages. What have you been doing? W: Oh, I've been working very hard at my new job. U: What new job?	▲ The other person ignores you. ▲ You ask how the other person is and she spends the next 10 minutes telling you about her illnesses. ▲ You ask what other people have been doing and they reply: "Nothing." ▲ Someone new asks how you are and you feel terrible. ▲ Someone asks what you have been doing and you can't remember.	1 Start a conversation with three different people and show an interest in them. 2 Write down four reasons for showing an interest in others. 3 Write down six things to do when showing an interest in others. 4 Listen to the radio and see how interviewers show an interest in the people they interview. 5 Think of things that you have done over the last week that may be of interest to others.

Keeping Friends (continued)

3 Asking, not Telling

Importance	Components	Wrong Way	Right Way	Problems	Homework
▲ It is more polite to ask people to do things than to tell them. ▲ People may like you more if you ask not tell. ▲ People are more likely to do what you want if you ask rather than tell. ▲ Telling is bossy and people do not like bossiness.	1 Keep a friendly face and voice. 2 Keep calm. 3 Use politeness words such as "please" and "Would you mind…?" 4 If someone is doing something that you do not like, ask them to change what they are doing. 5 Give a reason for your request. 6 Thank the person for following your request.	Kim is playing at Roy's house. Roy has made a building out of bricks. R: Don't touch my model. K: But I want to play with the bricks, too. R: Get lost. It's mine. Don't come anywhere near it or I'll tell my mum.	Kim is playing at Roy's house. He has made a building out of bricks. R: Please could you play with these bricks over here, Kim, because I'm building a hospital with those. K: OK. I don't mind. R: Thank you. You can play with the hospital when it's finished if you want to. K: Yes. Maybe I will.	▲ You ask a boy to move so you can get past. He says, "No." ▲ You ask a friend not to smoke when he sits near you but he laughs at you. ▲ You ask your tutors to call you Chris not Chrissie but they always forget. ▲ You ask some young children to be quiet but they just shout louder. ▲ Someone asks you to move your car. You don't want to because you are busy.	1 Ask five people to tell you the time and to direct you to the train station. Write down what happened. 2 Write down four reasons for asking, not telling. 3 Write down how to ask, not tell. 4 Watch TV programmes to see how people ask others to do things. 5 Think how you feel when told to do something rather than asked. Write down how you feel.

4 Keeping a Secret

Importance	Components	Wrong Way	Right Way	Problems	Homework
▲ Friends like to feel sure that they can trust you. ▲ It can be exciting to be trusted with a secret. ▲ Telling the secret may hurt someone who is not supposed to hear it or spoil a nice surprise. ▲ You can feel safe about telling friends your secrets if you trust each other.	If someone tells you a secret: 1 Remember that it is a secret and don't tell anyone. 2 If someone asks you to reveal a secret then tell them politely that you cannot and change the subject right away. 3 If you accidentally tell a secret, make sure you tell your friend and apologize. 4 If you know you cannot remember to keep a secret then tell your friends not to tell you theirs.	Charlie has just told Frances what he has bought for Justin's birthday present. Justin approaches Frances later. J: I'd love to know what Charlie has got for my birthday. F: I know what he's got for you. It's a secret. J: Go on, tell me, please. F: It's very nice. J: I'm dying to find out. Please tell me. F: OK. But don't tell Charlie that I told you. It's a fishing rod. J: I'll go and thank him.	Charlie has just told Frances what he has bought for Justin's birthday present. Justin approaches Frances later. J: I'd love to know what Charlie has got me for my birthday. F: I'm sure it's something nice. Do you want to play cards? J: OK.	▲ A friend tries again and again to get you to tell a secret. You think that she will not give up until you tell her. ▲ An adult frightens you and tells you not to tell anyone else or they will hurt you. ▲ You tell a friend about a surprise party for your mother and realize that she has overheard you. ▲ You overhear a friend telling another friend a secret that she promised she would tell no-one.	1 Practise keeping secrets by remembering unimportant things that your friends tell you and making sure that you don't tell anyone about them. 2 Write down four reasons for keeping secrets. 3 Write down how to keep a secret. 4 Think of three things that you would not like anyone to know about at the moment. 5 Think of ways of telling friends that it is important that they keep a secret for you.

Assertiveness Training

Assertiveness training aims to change individuals' behaviours and beliefs so that they are better able to express their needs, desires and opinions to others and to respond appropriately to the behaviour of others.

Teaching techniques

Assertiveness training has many similarities with pragmatic skills training in that role-play is used extensively; reasons for using assertiveness skills are discussed by group members and clients give feedback to each other. Assertiveness training usually uses role-play where the participants practise the skills being acquired. The role-play is repeated several times until the participant feels more confident while using the particular assertiveness skill.

Assertiveness training involves changing one's beliefs about oneself and about social interaction, as well as learning new behaviours. Much effort is directed towards changing the participants' long-held beliefs about rights and responsibilities and increasing their confidence in themselves. The way that this is done is often by group discussion and by the group facilitator giving exercises to participants to complete in pairs or small groups. For example, participants might be asked to share ideas to help increase confidence; they might be asked to share 10 communication situations that they find most difficult and 10 that they find relatively easy.

Content of assertiveness training

The areas of skill taught in an assertiveness training course can be designed to fit the particular client group's needs. In many mainstream and commercially run courses there are skill areas that recur, including the following:

- making a request to another person;
- saying "no" to a request;
- negotiating a compromise;
- giving and receiving praise and compliments;
- giving and receiving criticism constructively;
- offering to help someone;
- accepting an offer of help;
- making a complaint.

In successfully performing each skill the person is encouraged to think about:

- the person's own rights within the situation;
- the rights of the other people involved in the situation;
- the emotions being experienced during the situation by all concerned;
- what the person, or possibly both people, *really* want from a particular situation.

Success has been reported with diverse client groups. For example, **Van Hasselt** (1985) demonstrated an improvement in eye gaze, posture, voice tone and requests to others for behavioural change in a group of four visually handicapped adolescents. **Hersen & Bellack** (1976) have demonstrated improvements in the skills of schizophrenic clients following assertiveness training. **Michelson *et al*** (1983a) reported that a systematic programme of assertiveness training with child psychiatric outpatients was effective in improving their social skills. Many people without serious pragmatic impairments take courses in assertiveness training and find their lives become easier when they use some of the principles advocated within the assertiveness model. We think that assertiveness training is appropriate for anyone who has difficulty in expressing their desires or beliefs to others openly. See **Jeffers** (1995) for an interesting approach to changing attitudes and beliefs as well as actions to improve relationships. This can include clinicians who find it difficult to request the resources they need to offer a satisfactory service to clients and their families. Equally, assertiveness training can be useful for spouses or parents who find it difficult to make requests of other family members in an appropriate manner.

Assertiveness training can be of benefit to a range of clients and age groups, especially those who show a developing awareness of and desire to change problem areas in their communication. Assertiveness training is probably most suitable for clients from the ages of nine or ten upwards who have low self-esteem, or who tend to be reticent, aggressive or manipulative in their interactions. However, it will be obvious that many individuals with even mild communication difficulties as well as caregivers and professionals who occasionally find it difficult to express their needs or views may benefit from assertiveness training provided by a qualified tutor. Certainly, no clinician who has not participated in a basic course should attempt to use this approach with clients. Simply reading about the techniques does not prepare one for the emotions that can be evoked in training groups.

As regards teaching schedules, assertiveness is usually taught in small groups of between four and 15 people and is often spread over several days, weeks or months, depending on the needs of clients. There is sometimes a follow-up session several weeks later to help the participants to evaluate any changes that they have made and to work on any areas that they are still finding particularly difficult.

An example of the way one particular skill could be taught with an assertiveness perspective is making a request to someone. First, the following beliefs are expressed, aloud or to oneself:

▶ I have a right to feel whatever feelings I have.

▶ I have a right to express my feelings.

▶ I have the right to equal treatment, though not necessarily a right to dominate.

▶ Others have the right to be heard and to put forward their point of view.

Next, assertive behaviours are adopted:

▶ assertive but relaxed stance;
▶ open body posture;
▶ clear audible voice;
▶ head up (but not too high);
▶ neutral facial expression;
▶ continuous eye-contact;
▶ right situation chosen;
▶ simple language;
▶ reason given, explaining what effect it has on you and how you feel;
▶ sanction explained, if necessary;
▶ use of a special technique, such as the 'broken record' technique (where one repeats a request firmly and calmly as many times as is appropriate);
▶ thanking the person if they comply.

Role-play with the group watching, ready to offer constructive criticism. Role-play with a partner playing the role of a specific person, perhaps demonstrating a variety of different reactions. Repeat the role-play several times so that it begins to feel natural.

Readers who are interested in this approach for working with colleagues, caregivers or clients are recommended to attend an assertiveness course themselves and, if they would like to make assertiveness training an important part of their work, we would recommend that they become assertiveness trainers by taking a trainers' course such as those run by the Redwood Group or the University of Surrey. Although there are many books that can be used to try to acquire assertiveness skills (for example, **Stubbs**, 1986; **Beck & Beck**, 1992; **Dixon**, 1982; **Holland & Ward**, 1990) it seems probable to us that role-playing a variety of behaviours within the context of several hypothetical situations is necessary to reap the full benefits of this approach. The value of thinking about assertive behaviours separately from assertive beliefs is probably limited.

Direct Instruction

Although direct instruction is a form of meta-linguistic awareness training we are treating it separately as it is a method that is very commonly used with both adult and child clients within clinical settings. The most common form of direct instruction is the use of drills. Some direct instruction can be done through the use of games such as referential communication games.

Drills

Drills are universally used by speech and language therapy departments and there is an abundance of creative resource books available to clinicians (**Cooke & Williams**, 1985; **Watt**, 1994; **Toomey**, 1994a; **Paul**, 1992; **Blank & Marquis**, 1992; **Kamholz Schuller & Diamond Seraydarian**, 1992; **Bernarding**, 1992; **Marquis & Lewis**, 1992; **Marquis**, 1992; **Brooks**, 1992; **Odom & McConnell**, 1992). For this reason, and because we feel that drills, though useful, are frequently overused with clients with communication difficulties, we have chosen not to include drill activities in this book.

Barrier Referential Communication Games

These games involve two (or sometimes more) individuals each manipulating an arrangement of objects or pictures or creating a drawing or construction. Neither individual can see the other person's array because there is a barrier between the participants, or they are telephoning one another. One individual generally gives instructions to the second individual to create a pattern from blocks, cards or other objects that is identical to that of the first individual. The purposes of such games are as follow:

▶ To help clients to learn how to give and follow instructions. Clients learn what helps make an instruction successful and why some instructions are inadequate for the listener.
▶ To help clients to learn that others need to be given adequate and precise information.
▶ To develop awareness that others have minds similar to our own.
▶ To help clients learn how to ask for and give clarifications.
▶ To encourage smooth turn taking.
▶ To develop awareness of the appropriateness of different question types.

The games proceed as follows:

1. The clinician will choose toys, pictures, blocks or shapes suited to the client's age and interests. The size and number of materials will be dictated by the developmental level of the participants.
2. The materials on one side of the barrier will be arranged in a pattern (the complexity of the pattern will depend on the skill level of the participants and the goals of the session). The materials on the other side of the barrier will be exactly the same, but will not be placed in any special way.
3. The partner with the special arrangement will give instructions to the second person so that they can create an identical array. (A variation of this can be to have the second person ask questions of the partner with the special arrangement to discover what to do with the materials.)
4. The clinician can be one of the participants or can be an observer. If the clinician is an observer it can be useful at times to point out to each partner whether or not their instruction or question was adequate for the listener's needs and for the completion of the task.
5. The task ends when the second partner thinks that a satisfactory replica has been created. The barrier can be removed at this stage and differences between the patterns can be corrected.
6. The clinician can ask questions of the participants such as "Why do you think Yvonne put all of the red blocks here rather than the green ones?", hoping to elicit insights as to the inadequacy of a message. For example, a client might respond: "Because I said, 'Move the blocks' and I should have said, 'Move the green blocks.' I didn't explain it enough." If further explanation is needed, the clinician can say: "What would you do if I said 'Move the blocks'? Would you know whether to move the green ones or the red ones?" Questioning like this, done sparingly and sensitively and in good humour, can help clients to gain awareness of the adequacy and inadequacy of messages.

A variation on this game that can be great fun for young and old clients alike is the commercially produced game called 'Guess Who?' (1987). In this game there are about 30 different faces. The idea is for each partner to guess which face the other person has chosen as their target face. They do this by asking questions such as: "Has your face got a big nose?" If the partner answers "Yes" then all the faces with small noses can be eliminated from the search. The game ends when each partner has successfully guessed the other's target face.

Games such as 'Twenty Questions' can stimulate the same awareness of the importance of being precise in answering and asking questions. Variations on this exercise are phoning descriptions of robbers to the police or practising 'mail order' telephone calls with two identical catalogues. A wealth of barrier games can be found in **Marquis** (1992) and **Eberhardt, Deal & Hanuscin** (1992).

Accepting the Difficulty and Validating the Communication Strategies

It is possible to emphasize the need for improved communicative *performance* at the expense of communicative *confidence*. When a client is barely capable of improved performance or when progress is slow, it can be more beneficial to convey a sense of personal acceptance and appreciation. It may be helpful to both caregiver and client to accept the communication difficulty and validate compensatory communicative strategies that the client uses. This can raise a client's self-esteem, motivate a client to experiment or, in some cases, possibly facilitate language acquisition. Even though some communicative strategies can appear problematic, for instance the use of shortened, telegrammatic or non-verbal methods of communicating, they may succeed in getting the client's message across. Successful strategies could be preferable from the client's point of view to laboured and difficult 'improved' utterances.

The same can be said for accepting and validating the developmental stage at which clients find themselves. For example, we have found that people who overinitiate (**Adams & Bishop**, 1989), or who ask endless questions in the way that small children do, outgrow these stages as their communicative competence and self-esteem increase.

The task of the clinician is, first, to provide the client with opportunities to become confident, and then gently to discourage those strategies which are not successful and those immature behaviours which are inappropriately retained (for instance, sleeve pulling to gain attention or filling spaces with stereotyped utterances). Advising relatives and associates along the lines described above can often have a beneficial effect. Clinicians working with children will have had plenty of opportunity to observe that this is the case. Those working with adults may wish to consult **Lesser & Milroy** (1993, pages 288–330).

Summary

This chapter has presented further intervention ideas for clinicians and caregivers. Activities can form a convenient as well as an enjoyable medium for facilitating pragmatic development. Whereas this chapter has focused on the activities that can be used to facilitate pragmatic skill and knowledge for a range of individuals, Chapter 10 will focus on specific pragmatic difficulties and specific client groups, along with suggestions for the most appropriate intervention approaches.

Recommended Reading

Brinton B & Fujiki M, *Conversational Management with Language-Impaired Children: Pragmatic Assessment and Intervention*, Aspen, Rockville, Maryland, 1989.

Dinkmeyer D & McKay GD, *The Parent's Handbook: Systematic Training for Effective Parenting,* American Guidance Service, Circle Pines, Minnesota, 1989.

King CA & Kirschenbaum DS, *Helping Young Children Develop Social Skills: The Social Growth Program,* Brooks/Cole Publishing, Belmont, California, 1992.

Leonard LB, Wilcox J, Fulmer K & Davis A, Understanding Indirect Requests: An Investigation of Children's Comprehension of Pragmatic Meanings, *Journal of Speech and Hearing Research* 21, pp528–37, 1978.

MacDonald JD, *Environmental Language Inventory: A Semantic-Based Assessment and Treatment Model for Generalized Communication*, Merrill, Columbus, Ohio, 1978.

Phillips D, *How to Give Your Child a Great Self-Image*, Plume, New York, 1991.

Varni JW & Corwin DG, *Growing Up Great: Positive Solutions for Raising Confident, Self-Assured Children,* Berkley Books, New York, 1996.

Weybright G & Rosenthal Tanzer J, *Putting it into Words: An Introduction to Indirect Language Stimulation,* Communication Skill Builders, Tucson, Arizona, 1986.

CHAPTER 10
SPECIFIC CLIENT GROUPS & SPECIFIC PRAGMATIC DIFFICULTIES

Introduction/*126*
Application of Pragmatics to Intervention with Specific Client Groups/*126*
    Non-Communication in Childhood/*126*
    Delayed and Disordered Speech and Language Development, Articulatory Problems and Delays /*126*
    Phonological Delay and Disorder/*126*
    Syntactic Delays and Disorders/*126*
    Dysfluency/*127*
    Voice Problems/*127*
    Loss of Previously Intact Speech and Language/*127*
Treatment Suggestions for Specific Pragmatic Difficulties/*127*
    Possible Causes/*128*
    Specific Deficits/*129*
Summary & Concluding Remarks/*133*
Recommended Reading/*134*

Chapter 10
SPECIFIC CLIENT GROUPS & SPECIFIC PRAGMATIC DIFFICULTIES

Introduction

In this chapter we present treatment suggestions firstly for specific client groups and secondly for specific pragmatic difficulties.

Application of Pragmatics to Intervention with Specific Client Groups

Non-Communication in Childhood

Keep in mind that pragmatic development takes place before and concurrently with other aspects of development such as phonological, syntactic and semantic development. This means that clinicians should attend to pragmatic development first and continue to attend to it, rather than postponing communicative interactive intervention until after attempts at speech and language remediation.

Delayed and Disordered Speech and Language Development, Articulatory Problems and Delays

Attend not only to easy and developmentally early sounds, but to those which will prove particularly useful to the child. Teach sounds by combining auditory, visual and tactile approaches within contexts in which they are noticeable or useful, rather than hoping for later generalization from meaningless exercises. These do have their place, however, as practice vehicles, where continuous speech is poorly articulated and unclear. Motivate the client to pay special attention to clear, intelligible delivery through games, stories and exercises where intelligibility matters, such as 'Crime Report', 'Cliff Hangers', jokes and 'mail order' games where the client is involved in using speech and language to achieve clearly defined objectives such as placing an order for a specific piece of equipment or helping imaginary detectives to solve a crime.

Accept some problems in speech and language in order to maintain communicative confidence.

Include pragmatics in initial and ongoing assessments.

Phonological Delay and Disorder

Attend particularly to communicative confidence building, pragmatic and semantic knowledge, syntactic knowledge and motivation to communicate before expecting improved performance in any area. If, and only if, pragmatic abilities are satisfactory up to the point where intelligibility gets in the way, begin work on phonological knowledge and awareness as a whole. Do this through rhymes, songs, stories, minimal pair games and funny examples of sounds changing meanings. Amplification through an auditory trainer or 'sound mirror' has been found to be very helpful as a means of clarifying knowledge of phonology, even for children without known hearing loss. This has to be used with care and for short periods only. Remember that, for children in the early stages of development, most linguistic knowledge is unconscious. Cultivating metalinguistic awareness is helpful to some, but this approach is unsuitable for most very young children. However, once the child has become an eager and successful non-verbal communicator, some improvement in phonological performance can be casually suggested. Doing this within meaningful and personally significant contexts has been found to aid the generalization of newly learned productive skills.

It is well known that visual and tactile approaches, and especially the link to literacy, can be helpful to those children who find particular difficulty with auditory learning. These visual approaches can also be employed in meaningful contexts as an aid to generalization.

Syntactic Delays and Disorders

It will be helpful to keep in mind four clinical rules:

1. Children must be eager and successful communicators if they are to be motivated to acquire and use language.
2. Failure and correction breed struggle; success breeds success. Therefore respond to children's poor attempts at communication with enthusiasm. Correction and improvement come later, by which time the child should be confident and eager to learn.

Usually a spontaneous burst of syntactic development occurs in children who gain communicative confidence and who therefore wish to perform speech acts more efficiently.

3 A wide variety of interesting communicative contexts promotes wide-ranging language acquisition and use.

4. When it is thought appropriate to teach syntax directly, that is when the child has improved pragmatically and when spontaneous improvement is slow despite encouragement to communicate, bear in mind the advice of **Leonard & Fey** (1991, page 352): 'Of those grammatical problems exhibited by the child, choose for intervention one that seems to be hindering the development of some pragmatic skill.' This need not conflict with the need to choose developmentally appropriate syntactic structures (**Crystal, Fletcher & Garman,** 1976) if a little extra thought is given to combining the two requirements.

Dysfluency

Attend first to communicative confidence and self-esteem through non-verbal means such as play, drawing, writing and 'free stammering'. Teach control techniques, if necessary, within personally relevant contexts such as a favourite story, directions to (real) destinations, communication about favourite places and pastimes or client-initiated topics. We find that this greatly assists generalization of controlled speech. Allow clients to share invention and selection of assignments for the same reason. Whether control techniques or free stammering are advocated, it is essential for the client to experience being in control of some interactions and having to consider the communicative partner in other interactions. Older clients benefit from work on metapragmatic awareness.

Voice Problems

Again the issues of metapragmatic awareness and generalization of skills are important. Clients benefit from understanding the range of possibilities for voice use and the effect their own voice use can have on other people and on interactions. New skills seem to be more readily generalized if taught and practised within meaningful contexts as well as (rather than instead of) in repetitive routines. Giving real-life examples of the way more appropriate voice use can improve interactions has been found useful.

Loss of Previously Intact Speech and Language

The addition of pragmatic requirements to a previously well established repertoire of treatment measures can present clinicians with problems concerning the best use of professional time. On the other hand, when combined with specific speech or language therapy, work on pragmatics can yield some of the most encouraging results in treatment effectiveness terms. We suggest that pragmatic assessment will yield much of the information that is needed to establish the value of therapy with this client group. **Lesser & Milroy** (1993) suggest, when writing about dysphasia, that teaching relatives to recognize and validate communication strategies rather than demand normal communicative behaviour can be highly beneficial.

Treatment Suggestions for Specific Pragmatic Difficulties

A list of the specific difficulties which have been mentioned in the literature dealing with pragmatic dysfunction appears in Chapter 4. We have made a preliminary attempt to divide this long list into categories. We have also tried to separate pragmatic difficulties from some of their possible underlying causes whereas, in the literature, these are lumped confusingly together. Research is needed to clarify these matters and to evaluate treatment methods.

In treating pragmatic difficulties, the most successful approach has been to combine attention to clients' behaviour with attention to factors which underlie the behaviour. Scientifically, there is too much uncertainty as to the real causes of pragmatic difficulty to allow firm statements about underlying factors to be made. Clinically, however, it is possible to allow for this uncertainty by approaching treatment planning in a spirit of inquiry. *Begin with the assumption that a client has certain pragmatic abilities which are not being used.* Provide experiences of respectful and facilitative interaction and observe the client carefully. Do not make the assumption that the client's family or institution has already provided encouraging and facilitative conditions. This is unwise for two reasons: first, there are many normal and caring environments where this is not done to the extent which individual clients need; and second, unhelpful environments are unfortunately more common than is generally supposed (see page 39).

Factors other than the environment will of course be considered by clinicians during this exploratory treatment. If no improvement is noted after a period of exposure to facilitative interaction, say six sessions, factors other than the environment should begin to take precedence in treatment planning. Fortunately, no harm is likely to result if clinicians search experimentally for the most helpful approach to a client's pragmatic difficulties. The problem of time allocation is controlled by limiting the duration of experimental therapy. Below are some suggestions on how to proceed when certain of the factors mentioned in the pragmatics literature are thought to underlie a particular client's difficulties. We have grouped the factors in one way here, though other conceptual frameworks could be seen as equally valid.

Possible Causes

Neurological and psychiatric disorders

These need to be identified so that clients and their families receive all possible assistance and advice. It is our impression that, while people with serious disorders of this kind are, inevitably, recognized and referred to the proper consultants, those with milder neurological and psychiatric conditions are not. It is not practical, or even desirable, to refer every client with pragmatic difficulties to colleagues, but a multidisciplinary approach of some kind is called for because of the extent to which neurological, cognitive, psychiatric and communicative disorders overlap. (See Chapter 4.)

Environmental factors

These may in some cases play an important part in the causing or perpetuation of pragmatic difficulties. For both children and adults, such factors range from simple lack of the opportunity to learn and experiment, to unhelpful styles of interaction in a family or institution, to actual maltreatment of various kinds (**Smith & Leinonen,** 1992, page 228; **Law & Conway**, 1991 and 1992). There is a good deal that speech and language clinicians can do, through indirect treatment, to improve clients' communicative environments. Caregivers may require information, advice and demonstration concerning clients' communicative needs. Support and encouragement for caregivers can also contribute significantly to the well-being of clients, since positive and confident individuals usually treat those in their care with more consideration than do those who are distressed.

Clinicians also have to remember that, if they are in doubt as to the safety or suitability of a client's environment, they are obliged to confer with specially delegated colleagues on the matter of protection. It is unfortunately easy to assume, when caregivers behave in a socially acceptable way and show reasonable concern for a client with communication difficulties, that neglect, excessive punishment and mental or physical abuse are out of the question. What has to be borne in mind is that communication difficulties, particularly pragmatic ones, can sometimes result from inappropriate care. Also caregivers, or others in the environment with the opportunity to do so, have been known to take advantage of a person's inability to report their actions. A useful step is to acknowledge the *possibility* that behaviour problems or communicative abnormalities *could* result from unhappiness and stress, rather than from wilfulness or 'disorder' in the client.

Immaturity

As a factor underlying pragmatic difficulty, immaturity is not yet well understood. It is clearly possible for clients to be pragmatically immature, just as they may be immature in other areas of development. As in the case of immature phonology or syntax, it appears to be essential to avoid pressurizing individuals to produce types of performance which are beyond their current capability. It has also been observed clinically that it is beneficial to allow individuals to pass through developmental stages rather than expecting certain stages to be 'skipped' as no longer appropriate to the client's age. It appears that only by completing early developmental stages can individuals gain sufficient mastery and confidence to perform satisfactorily at later stages. Treatments may well be unsuccessful because they ignore the need to encourage clients to acquire the *foundations of communicative competence* before demanding refinements. For instance, a person who has recently become developmentally ready to play imaginatively may need to do this for a while before being expected to imagine what a communicative partner thinks or feels. A further example might be that of a person who dominates interactions or asks frequent questions in the way that young children do. Such a person might need to pass through this stage before being expected to interact in a more considerate way. It would be a mistake, however, to carry a policy of waiting for developmental readiness too far by expecting too little of clients.

Personality factors

Personality factors can sometimes interfere with pragmatic performance. Rather than expecting too fundamental a change, clinicians usually work 'with the grain of the wood', as it were. A fundamental clinical skill lies in validating who and what a person is, while at the same time helping that person to modify certain inappropriate behaviours and beliefs. For example, one might respect a shy client's wish for security and reasonable privacy while, at the same time, refusing to collude with the same client's tendency towards social withdrawal.

Specific Deficits

Social or emotional factors

Social or emotional problems may be the result of constitutional disability, as in the case of autism, for example, or may result from circumstances which impinge on communicative skills, such as frightening experiences resulting in lack of trust. Many speech and language clinicians are skilled in dealing with the latter type of problem and will be able to offer counselling when this is needed by clients with pragmatic difficulties. Clients can also benefit when relatives, teachers or nursing staff can also be offered support, a listening ear or advice. Counsellors or psychologists, however, can be more helpful than speech and language clinicians when social or emotional problems of a serious nature underlie pragmatic difficulties. A multidisciplinary approach is likely to be the most successful.

Low involvement with other people sometimes appears to underlie poor pragmatic performance. Relationship building (page 77) can be helpful in leading such individuals out of isolation. This is especially successful when people who will be able to offer a long-term commitment to the client can be drawn into the client–therapist relationship at an early stage. When this is not feasible, it is important not to encourage overdependence on the therapist. On the other hand, it is worth remembering that, once a person has experienced one rewarding relationship, they may well seek others.

Low involvement with *tasks* can also lead to poor pragmatic performance. When this is the case, clinicians have a choice: either to use indirect motivators and exhortation to increase the client's conscientiousness or to devise more motivating and developmentally appropriate tasks. For example, a young child might be prepared to work hard at explaining to an incompetent puppet how to perform a certain manoeuvre or an older person might describe an item carefully when pretending to order it from a mail order catalogue on the telephone, whereas neither would become seriously involved with these same tasks if they were presented in the context of picture cues.

Lack of confidence is the single greatest obstacle to adequate communication. Confident individuals with serious speech and language problems can be seen to communicate well. On the other hand, clients who doubt their ability to understand what other people are trying to convey and who doubt whether their own contributions to the interaction will be appreciated by others can be poor communicators despite relatively intact speech and language abilities. For this reason it is imperative to cultivate clients' confidence at the same time as working on their skills — even *before* working on their skills in some cases. Simple methods of increasing communicative confidence are usually effective. The most obvious step is to accept whatever clients are able to manage in the way of expression eagerly and without criticism, making every effort to understand what is intended. At the same time it is important to make one's own contributions intelligible by tailoring them to the known abilities of the client. Utterances that are sufficiently loud, slow, clear, simple and relevant, from clients' points of view, encourage them to think of themselves as competent receivers of spoken language or signing.

Speech and language clinicians are, by nature of their training, good at using these ways of increasing clients' confidence. They are also good at introducing correction in an unthreatening manner so as not to undermine confidence. What clinicians could do to build communicative confidence even more would be to spend more time communicating with clients on the client's own terms, rather than prematurely introducing teaching and correction. This applies especially to some dysphasic clients, to young children in the early stages of language development and to clients with learning difficulties. It applies to many clients whose difficulties are principally pragmatic and whose need for confidence building can be overlooked by therapists who are excessively keen to remove problematic behaviours. The *feeling of being able* to perform certain functions appears to be as important as possessing the ability itself. Indeed, relatives and associates have sometimes been astonished to discover how efficiently clients can communicate, given the right circumstances. Success of this kind tends to 'snowball', leading to further improvements; therefore it is an excellent use of clinical time to make sure that it is brought about.

Low self-esteem is closely linked to the issue of communicative confidence. Feeling able to use the means of communication is not especially helpful if one thinks one has nothing of value to say. Similarly, it is not useful unless one also feels entitled to express opinions, requests and so on. With this in mind, and with the intention of bringing about general improvement in clients' lives and behaviour, clinicians traditionally try to improve self-esteem. What is not always recognized is the possibility that certain kinds of pragmatic shortcoming are as likely to be related to low self-esteem as they are to disability. Take, for example, the apparent inability to make requests for clarification and to repair breakdowns in interaction. One is unlikely to monitor interactions for communication breakdowns or to attempt to repair these if one's expectation of success is low. Also people who think that they are not intelligent may be unlikely to keep a careful check on their understanding of what is being said or to request clarification when it is necessary. To label such people as deficient in the ability to clarify and repair on the basis of their failure to demonstrate these skills would be a mistake.

Another mistake that is sometimes made is to label disruptive and abrasive people too readily as having a high opinion of themselves. While it is possible for that to be the case, such people may well be suffering from quite the opposite view. Once self-esteem is raised, behaviour often improves.

Perhaps the most effective step that clinicians can take with regard to self-esteem is to designate it as a treatment objective. Once it is clear to clinicians and administrators that improvements in the way clients see themselves are to be seen as equal in value to improvements in skill, it becomes possible to prioritize either skills or self-concept appropriately.

Methods of enhancing self-esteem include the following:

- ▶ Giving undivided attention in reasonable amounts, even if the client is not talking. Understanding that the pejorative appellation 'attention-seeking' can be applied to clients in a way that damages their self-esteem further. A more helpful term is **'attention-needing'** (**Mosley,** 1994).
- ▶ Listening to people, valuing their expression of opinions or feelings and treating them respectfully regardless of age, speech and language ability or intellectual status. This can be done for clients without necessarily agreeing with or indulging them unduly. It is relevant in this context to note that the National Society for the Prevention of Cruelty to Children (UK) has pointed out that, unfortunately, many professionals dealing with children are not accustomed to listening to them respectfully.
- ▶ Remembering what people have said.
- ▶ Showing people that they have been thought about in their absence.
- ▶ Asking people's advice in problem-solving situations, or getting incompetent puppets to ask for their advice.
- ▶ Thanking people and showing appreciation.
- ▶ Providing opportunities for success by devising achievable targets. Providing encouraging feedback, especially providing permanent, visual, take-away evidence of success. The latter is routinely made available for children but its value is sometimes forgotten by clinicians working with adults.
- ▶ Encouraging clients to evaluate their own performance rather than relying entirely on a clinician's judgement.
- ▶ Giving praise not only for achievement but for personal qualities. Providing permanent, visual information about a person's strong points, in addition to spoken encouragement. This may take the form of a picture of an apple tree on which each fruit represents one quality the client possesses. Care needs to be taken, however, in the process of giving praise, as a patronizing attitude on the part of the praise giver can undermine self-esteem in the receiver rather than enhancing it.
- ▶ Experimenting with alternative methods of revealing the client's abilities. Computer work has been strikingly successful in this way with some pragmatically impaired clients.

- Providing honest information about problem behaviours in a respectful and supportive way and expecting the client to set goals jointly with the clinician.
- Helping clients to find or set up small support groups and putting them in touch with national support groups.
- Putting clients in touch with assertiveness trainers, or providing this type of training for groups of clients.
- Giving reasonable responsibility and encouraging independence. Other ideas and references can be found in **Mosley** (1994).

Defensiveness as an underlying factor in pragmatic difficulty may show itself in inappropriate or nonsensical utterances; repeated stereotypes such as "See you later", "I can't", or "No way"; 'opting-out' replies to questions such as "Don't know" or monosyllabic replies; or in muttered and evasive responses to questions. Usually, these less than satisfactory contributions occur when a person has been 'put on the spot' by a communicative partner who either feels entitled to do this or who has not realized how confrontational they appear. Within relaxed, undemanding interactions the more competent partner responds sensitively to the less competent one so that the need for defensive behaviour does not arise. **McTear** (1985a) suggested that clinicians might consider engaging in this type of interaction more frequently with their pragmatically failing clients. If they do not do so it may possibly be due to the pressure they feel to *teach* clients something measurable in order to justify their professional involvement. We strongly recommend that the therapeutic effect of more relaxed interactions is evaluated, since it may well be found that more benefit derives from less teaching.

Factors in the self

Weak sense of self is seen by some authorities (**Jordan & Powell,** 1990) as a fundamental problem for autistic children. Other people with pragmatic difficulties may possibly share this problem to a lesser extent (**Dickinson,** 1996; **Stenhouse,** 1994). Jordan & Powell recommend that, for these clients, attention should be focused on the person and the person's experience of learning or achieving, rather than upon tasks themselves. Very task-centred clinicians sometimes find this a difficult switch to make, but it is worth investigating since it can be effective.

Some clients have ***weak integrative ability.*** The various types of knowledge and skill that are needed for successful communicative performance have to be integrated if a person is to interact successfully with other people. The best way we know of helping clients to learn how to integrate is to engage them in real, spontaneous, unpredictable and interesting interactions. These need to take place within dependable, supportive relationships. Teaching separate skills and items of knowledge is valuable but, if their integration and use are left to chance or addressed as an afterthought, some clients will fail to benefit.

Weak inner coherence might be said to exist in those clients with pragmatic difficulties who give the impression of failing to relate the isolated experiences of their lives to one another and failing to arrive at their own integrated view of matters. **Stott** (1966) described similar problems of what he called 'temporal integration' in children. The concept of inner coherence deserves investigation. In the meantime, speech and language clinicians have a contribution to make in describing clients' difficulties with the integration of information. Furthermore, it is possible to help people with poor integrative ability to have more confidence in their ability to make sense of some of their experiences and to relate items of information to one another. This can be done through story telling and story dictation, the discussion of stories and television, event planning, letter writing, problem solving, animal care, health education and general discussion. Some clients find it particularly helpful to receive visual back-up of the information which they need to integrate.

Cognitive factors

Slow cognitive or linguistic processing may affect both the production and reception of language. As far as we are aware, this is difficult to influence by therapy. There is, however, a good deal to be gained by intervention. Clients' self-esteem can be raised if they are persuaded that, despite slowness, they have a right to be heard and to participate in conversations. Once clients' expectations are raised, some communicative partners will begin to treat them more considerately. Listeners may have to be alerted to the fact that silence on the part of a client does not necessarily mean that they have nothing to contribute. Intervention aims to break the cycle of failure in which the client becomes discouraged because there is never enough time allowed for effective participation in interactions. It should be demonstrated, possibly by video tape, that the client can make valid contributions when interacting with an informed partner, for instance a clinician. It should also be explained that some, apparently eccentric, replies to questions are likely to be replies to a question that was asked *before* the one to which a reply is currently expected.

Linguistic deficit, especially semantic deficit, can contribute to pragmatic failure by making it appear that a person is unable or unwilling to respond appropriately to what others say. Irrelevant or apparently evasive replies to questions, for instance, may well result from failure to comprehend the question correctly. Appropriate initiations can also be affected by linguistic deficit, since clients are likely to restrict their initiations to those for which they already have the necessary linguistic skills. This might account for features such as excessive use of question forms. **Leonard & Fey** (1991) suggest that, when identifying targets for language remediation, clinicians would do well to select those skills which were found to be disabling the client pragmatically.

Rigidity of thought and concept boundaries is difficult to influence fundamentally. However, helping clients to feel secure within an accepting relationship can sometimes lead to more self-acceptance and flexibility on their part. This, in turn, can allow them to explore a wider range of conceptual possibilities and to abandon the need for absolute certainty which supports their rigidity.

Some speech and language therapists claim to have been successful in teaching organizational principles to *disorganized* clients and motivating them to put these to day-to-day use. A great deal has been written about attention disorders such as distractibility and obsessional attention in children. Much of this work has appeared in the *Journal of the Association for Child Psychology and Psychiatry*. In addition, a widely used text (**Cooper, Moodley & Reynell,** 1978) discusses developmental stages of attention control, together with methods of helping children through those stages. In the UK, speech and language clinicians using the latter's well researched treatment approach have helped a great many child clients to control their attention and to divide it between an activity and an adult instructor. The children then become able to benefit from their time in school to an extent that would not otherwise have been possible.

From the point of view of clinicians wishing to facilitate pragmatic development, however, 'attention control' presents a challenge. While the ability to attend appropriately is crucial for the educational future of any child, too great a willingness to have one's attention directed and controlled by others can militate against full personal involvement in the learning process. Passivity on the part of child clients does not help them to learn to perform a wide variety of speech acts or to experiment with speech and language skills. When an adult controls a child's attention, rather than helping the child to take an interest in activities, ideas and people, an educational opportunity is being lost. What is needed is careful tailoring of the treatment approach to the individual client's needs.

Treatment for those whose attention is obsessive is not well understood as far as we are aware. However, we have met individuals who claim to have been able to reduce this problem by gaining insight and objectivity.

Creative factors

Weak imaginative ability is hypothesized in some clients with pragmatic difficulties. While it would be difficult to prove whether imaginative ability is absent or simply not used, the important question is whether or not imaginative activity can be stimulated. In some individuals it is certainly possible to introduce the notion of 'pretending' and to suggest intriguing 'pretend play' scenarios, or, for older clients, narrative themes. The presence of an interested and co-operative companion (the clinician) does seem to help some clients to explore some of the possibilities of the imagination in a way that they would not do on their own.

Weak or absent 'theory of mind' (page 23) sometimes appears to be strengthened by demonstration, discussion and explanation concerning other people's mental processes. It is not easy to be certain whether apparent improvements are attributable to changes in the way clients imagine other peoples' thoughts or to their having decided to behave 'as if' other people had certain, specific thoughts. In real life it probably does matter which of these is the case; however, any type of gain may possibly be worthwhile from the point of view of clients who find social relationships baffling and from the point of view of their families.

Poor empathy with others may be related to theory of mind and to shortcomings of the imagination, or to social or emotional factors. It seems possible that the ability to empathize develops as a result of experiencing close relationships with others who are themselves empathic and that deprivation of these experiences can result in lack of empathy. Observation suggests, however, that some individuals are more naturally empathic than others. Supportive relationships, together with explanation to the client, do appear to improve this ability. Narratives, drama, television, films and newspapers provide suitable contexts for discussing and practising empathy. Specific exercises can also be fairly easily devised. Imagining what other people feel is likely to depend, to some extent, on past experience. This would normally include visual information about their feelings. In current situations one also relies, to some extent, on feedback from others, including visual feedback. Thus a difficulty with interpreting facial expression (prosopagnosia) might contribute to poor empathizing ability and might be compensated for by verbal explanation.

Memory or access deficits

Memory problems which appear to underlie many pragmatic difficulties can sometimes be alleviated by providing visual cues. Clients are taught to keep the visual reminders with them and to refer to them as often as necessary. Research into the relationship between memory problems and pragmatic difficulty could have valuable clinical applications.

Word-finding difficulty can underlie pragmatic difficulties. A client may be well aware of how to perform various communicative functions but may not be able to retrieve the necessary words at the right moment for neurological reasons. Useful discussion of how this problem can be addressed can be found in **Smedley** (1989) and **Hyde-Wright** (1993).

Discourse tracking difficulty, indicated by confusions and inconsistencies, could reflect cognitive deficit, problems of memory, problems of concentration or language disability. It can be difficult for clinicians to be certain which of these is affecting a particular client most strongly. It has been found helpful to encourage clients to focus on the content and intention of what has been written or said using visual cues and prompts.

Knowledge deficits

Lack of world knowledge or social knowledge may be due to lack of experience or to a failure to absorb information with the casual ease which characterizes most people's acquisition of world knowledge. In either case, education and therapy together hold the key to improvement. For some clients social skills training is particularly suitable.

Lack of specific pragmatic knowledge and skill may be the real explanation for pragmatic difficulties, but we hope to have shown above that other possible explanations can provide indications for effective therapy. Direct instruction, demonstration and explanations of the way in which communication works, is sometimes appropriate therapy for clients who have deficits in specific pragmatic knowledge and skill (see pages 72–3). For example, the clinician might explain: "People expect you to look at them when you speak", or "You need to explain who you're talking about, not just say 'he shouted', because I don't know who 'he' is."

Many clients also benefit from greatly increased exposure to interactive situations with facilitative partners. Balancing the need for exposure to facilitative interactions with the need for direct instruction is not a straightforward matter in remedial settings where direct instruction is traditionally expected. We would like to urge clinicians to investigate this matter further since our own results from interaction-based therapy have been encouraging. **Linguistic knowledge,** as distinct from linguistic skill, can be deficient and should be improved by ensuring that clients receive adequate amounts of input of a type which they find interesting and at a speed which they can process. Experimenting with input in different modalities and through different media can make an important contribution to the improvement of some clients.

Summary and Concluding Remarks

We have presented a wide range of different approaches to pragmatic intervention, based on our own clinical experience and our reading of research into pragmatic development and impairment. Research data as to the relative effectiveness of each approach for different client groups are lacking. However, we hope that, through using these approaches with a variety of different clients, clinicians will be able to expand their available repertoire of strategies and increase the likelihood of providing effective intervention. As more clinicians are given the time to keep records of specific approaches used, and incorporate these into research projects, our knowledge base will be improved. Then, perhaps, we will be able more confidently to recommend particular approaches for specific difficulties.

Offering intervention to clients with pragmatic difficulties is not yet a matter of applying proven techniques to bring about predictable results. It is currently a matter of using available information to devise approaches which stand a reasonable chance of improving the lives of clients and their families. We have been able to present some relevant information and to describe intervention approaches which have been successful for some clients. Our hope is that, as clinicians gain experience in working with clients with pragmatic difficulties, more certainty will develop. Scientific investigation into pragmatic difficulties and their causes should ultimately provide reliable methods of helping individuals whose lives and relationships are made difficult by problems with the pragmatics of communication.

Recommended Reading

Cole ML & Cole JT, *Effective Intervention with the Language-Impaired Child,* 2nd edn, Aspen, Rockville, Maryland, 1989.

Fey ME, *Language Intervention with Young Children,* College-Hill, Boston, Mass, 1986.

Gallagher TM (ed), *Pragmatics of Language: Clinical Practice Issues,* Singular Publishing, San Diego, 1991.

Keogh WJ & Reichle J, 'Communication Intervention for the "Difficult to Teach" Severely Handicapped', Warren SF & Rogers-Warren AK, *Teaching Functional Language: Generalization and Maintenance of Language Skills,* Pro-Ed, Austin, Texas, 1985.

Appendix I
ANNOTATED BIBLIOGRAPHY

This brief review of most of the currently available literature concerned with identification of semantic and pragmatic difficulties is included for three reasons: first, it may be of interest to clinicians and researchers; second, the long list in Chapter 4 of features said to be found in 'semantic–pragmatic disorder' originated in the works described here; third, we hope the review may serve to clarify what has unfortunately become a confusing amalgam of observations and concepts from differing disciplines by identifying the sources of these ideas.

Aarons & Gittens (1990 and 1993), as autism advisers to The Royal College of Speech and Language Therapists (UK), comment on the existence of pragmatic difficulties within autism. Their view is that, particularly at the upper end of the autistic ability scale, people may be unhelpfully diagnosed as having a 'semantic–pragmatic language disorder' when in fact their disability extends beyond the sphere of language. In these circumstances, they argue, individuals will be deprived of the considerable support and assistance available through the National Autistic Society and will receive only partially appropriate therapy and teaching. Aarons and Gittens suggest that both parents and professionals view a diagnosis of autism with a degree of dread which renders them unwilling to investigate the condition with an open mind. Certainly, it is noticeable that individuals diagnosed as having Asperger's syndrome (a milder condition related to autism) evoke some of the descriptions of semantic–pragmatic disorder which can be found in the literature (cf **Bishop**, 1989).

It has been our experience that people who have difficulty with the semantic and/or pragmatic aspects of language may not exhibit social impairment, but that, when they do, a diagnosis of autism or Asperger's syndrome, or even referral to a setting in which such a diagnosis could be expected, is sometimes resisted.
Powell & Jordan (1993) have also drawn attention to the importance of accurate diagnosis for educational purposes. They point out that teaching strategies which might otherwise be appropriate are likely to be completely unsuitable in the presence of autism, where the child's greatest need is to become aware of herself as a learner.

Speech and language clinicians perhaps fear that people who carry a diagnosis of autism or Asperger's syndrome will be excluded from appropriate educational opportunities to integrate with more 'normal' peers and receive language tuition. Nevertheless, they do need to be fully aware of how well the more able autistic person can function, so that problems in diagnosis can be minimized for the sake of clients and their families.

Abbeduto & Rosenberg (1987), take an integrative view of communicative functioning, discuss the types of knowledge which have to be integrate (linguistic/world/social) for adequate pragmatic performance. In connection with what they termed 'mental retardation', they examine the following:

- turn taking;
- recognition of obligations established by illocutionary acts;
- fulfilment of such obligations;
- active participation in conversation;
- co-ordination of propositional content with contextual information.

These authors recognize that a variety of factors, including environmental and cognitive ones, will shape a person's ability to perform these functions.

Adams & Bishop (1989), in what they describe as 'a necessary first step' towards more rigorous classification, find that children identified as semantic–pragmatic disordered tend to violate turn-taking rules and to fail to establish referents when using pronouns. However, the one 'stable and abnormal conversational characteristic' which emerges in these particular children is excessive initiation (page 238). This is in contrast to other studies which have mentioned unwillingness to initiate. One possible explanation is that these children were functioning at a very immature level in this respect; another is that overinitiation is a defensive or mild autistic feature not present in all people with semantic and pragmatic difficulty.

Beveridge & Conti-Ramsden (1987) provide an accessible account of what they term 'conversational disability'. They explain that many language-disabled children have difficulty in performing speech acts and that some conversationally disabled people have additional difficulties in meeting the demands of particular interactive contexts. For example, they may say things which seem irrelevant, inappropriate or unclear; their introduction and maintenance of topics is inadequate; they may appear shy, withdrawn and talk little; pauses may be unusually long; they may provide minimal responses and not follow their conversational partner's line of reasoning; their range of speech acts may be limited; there can be over-literalness and thus difficulty with inferencing and with joking.

Bishop (1989), in a special issue of the *British Journal of Disorders of Communication* devoted to autism, addresses the problem of whether a child whose communication skills are poor is likely to be diagnosed differently by different professions. The paper is an important one and should preferably be studied in the original. Dealing with the term 'semantic–pragmatic disorder' Bishop suggests that, while **Rapin & Allen** (1983) accept the possibility that people who are autistic may also exhibit the 'semantic–pragmatic deficit syndrome', it may be preferable to employ the term 'specific semantic–pragmatic disorder' when one needs to signify that a person exhibiting a cluster of problems in the areas of pragmatics and semantics is *not* autistic. There are those who find this policy objectionable on the grounds that, if some autistic traits are present, it is better to acknowledge these so that the seriousness of a person's disability is not minimized (**Aarons & Gittens,** 1990 and 1993).

Bishop & Adams (1989) examine the way in which judgements of appropriateness or inappropriateness in conversation are made, a theme pursued by **Smith & Leinonen** (1992).

Bishop & Adams (1992) investigate the inferential comprehension of a group of 61 school children with specific language impairment (SLI) some of whom fit the clinical picture of semantic–pragmatic disorder. The latter were expected to perform less well than other children in answering questions about a short story when inferences had to be made to arrive at the answer. In fact all SLI children had difficulty in answering questions about stories as compared to normal children. However, neither they nor the subgroup of children with semantic and pragmatic difficulties did significantly worse when the answer required inferential activity, although there was some differential effect. This result could possibly be explained by heterogeneity even within the subgroup. Many clinicians will know some children who appear to experience serious difficulty with inferential reasoning, while also knowing others who do not, despite a diagnosis of semantic–pragmatic disorder.

Browning (1987) presents an account of her son's struggle with language disability. Rereading this illuminating biography reveals that what was regarded as a case of developmental dysphasia in fact presented multiple problems of a semantic and pragmatic nature. Clinicians will, in all probability, recall other similar cases.

Byers-Brown & Edwards (1989) In order to avoid confusion we should like to draw attention to the fact that two sections in this volume deal with semantic–pragmatic problems, mentioning many of the characteristics included in this review. It will be apparent that the children they describe are rather more pervasively disabled than those discussed by the majority of the other authors mentioned. This will be of interest to clinicians working with severely handicapped populations.

Conti-Ramsden in **Mogford-Bevan & Sadler** (1991) compares three methods of studying what she terms pragmatic disabilities: (1) case studies, (2) group design studies and (3) group comparison studies. Children who have these disabilities, she explains, have difficulty in recognizing and satisfying the social rules which demand that language fits the social context in which it is used. The children have difficulty in school, in making friends and in coping with everyday social interaction. Conti-Ramsden's comments on the methods of studying these children conclude with the observation that, whatever method is employed, the studies will only be as adequate as the theory of pragmatic competence which underlies them. Such theories she regards as in need of refinement.

The proceedings of the conference on Child Language Disorders, Roros, Norway, 1990 (published by the Norwegian Centre for Child Research, Report No 24, Trondeim, 1991) include six papers concerning semantic, pragmatic and interaction issues.

Conti-Ramsden & Gunn (1986) present a single case of a child with 'conversational disability', one purpose of which is to highlight the value of longitudinal studies. This particular child demonstrated some, but not all, of the features mentioned by other writers in this field. The authors ask whether this will usually be the case; whether therapy affects the presentation of the disorder; and whether the presenting picture will vary reliably over time.

Donahue (1987) considers carefully the question of how far learning-disabled children's language development and pragmatic competence are related, but comes to no conclusion. The importance of her paper lies in the way it focuses attention on the underlying nature of pragmatic difficulties, rather than their superficial presentation.

Fey & Leonard (**Prutting & Kirchner,** 1983) look at the conversational performance of language-impaired children. They tentatively identified the following patterns: (1) unresponsiveness and poor conversational participation; (2) responsive but non-assertive and limited participation; and (3) socially normal but linguistically impaired conversational performance. One problem with these descriptive categories is that it is not really known what normal conversation-initiating and responding behaviour is. It seems likely that expectations will vary according to such factors as the developmental age of the child, cultural, subcultural and situational conventions, and the role relationship between participants.

Friel-Patti & Conti-Ramsden (1984) point out that language-disordered children can exhibit a variety of pragmatic difficulties which may well persist throughout the school years. These authors do not use a catch-all diagnostic term, but their paper is an important one, of interest to any clinician working with impaired pragmatic performance.

Gallagher (1991) in an edited volume gathers together many of the foremost American authors currently working in the field of pragmatics. A fairly detailed review of this important volume can be found in the *European Journal of Disorders of Communication* 28(1), pp112–6, 1993.

Gravell & France (1991) contain much relevant material under the heading of communication and its breakdown (in psychiatric populations).

Hassibi & Breuer (1980) stress the need to distinguish between psychotic and language-disordered children. It should be noted, however, that when they wrote, the following features were regarded as possibly psychotic:

- speech low in communicative value because the needs of the listener are disregarded;
- lack of appreciation that words and syntax must have shared meanings in order to be understood;
- use of pronouns without provision of the referent;
- neologisms;
- word order problems;
- wandering attention;
- introduction of unrelated element connected with interior rather than shared themes.

Hyde-Wright & Cray in **Mogford-Bevan & Sadler** (1991) provide the following list of broad characteristics of children at a special school who are said to have semantic–pragmatic disorder: they fail to respond in an appropriate manner to either the linguistic or the social demands of situations; conversation may break down as they fail to see what is relevant; they show poor integration between content and use of language; comprehension is more impaired than expression; concept formation is poor and rigid; they cannot use language as an anchor to reality, failing to correlate the language they hear with their experiences in the real world.

Joanette & Brownell (1990) provide an edited volume containing 11 chapters which deal with issues related to discourse and pragmatic abilities in brain-damaged people.

Johnson (1990) shares with readers his subjective experience of right hemisphere stroke with its attendant pragmatic difficulties. He stresses the opinion of his neurologist that it is the brain's inability to function as a whole, rather than its loss of specific areas, which gives rise to the impairment.

Johnston (1985) explores possible differences between deficits in social cognition and 'true pragmatic disorder' (page 90).

Lucas (1980) discusses semantic and pragmatic language disorders, indicating that she considers the two to be closely linked. Under the heading of 'semantic disorders', she mentions inadequate acquisition of the perceptual and functional characteristics of objects, actions and events, together with an inability to relate these to the lexicon, failure to acquire the semantic rules underlying speech acts, auditory misperception, off-target responding, tangentiality, syntactic errors, 'semantic word errors', word-finding problems, neologisms, problems in identifying topics and referents, echolalia and verbal perseveration. Pragmatic problems described by Lucas include the following:

▶ failure to solve situational problems verbally;
▶ failure to initiate;
▶ provision of inadequate paralinguistic cues for the listener;
▶ inability to specify referents;
▶ use of inappropriate prosodic and paralinguistic behaviours;
▶ failure to use questions and requests;
▶ unco-operative behaviour;
▶ overall inability to convey intents by the performance of communicative acts;
▶ problems with time and space.

Lucas Arwood (1983) elaborates further on these themes, though in a less accessible style. **Lucas Arwood** (1991) is the useful second edition of **Lucas** (1980).

McTear (1989) reports on a single case of 'pragmatic disorder'. This 10-year-old boy, who had received treatment for an 'articulation problem' but whose syntax was normal, demonstrated over-loud speech, occasional problems with the perception of cause and effect and with temporal sequencing, poor eye-contact and listener orientation. He physically separated himself from groups. There were perceptual and motor abnormalities. Imagination appeared to be restricted. Also noted were literal interpretation, minimal conversational contributions, failure to use ellipsis, poor inferencing, failure to take his partner's knowledge into account, frequent use of "I don't know" and difficulty in making factual and especially causal information clear. McTear hazards some suggestions as to the possible underlying causes of the problems: deficiencies in handling and integrating information, uncertainty of the knowledge possessed by others, overuse of coping strategies and shortage of non-threatening experiences within which coping strategies might not be needed.

McTear in **Mogford-Bevan & Sadler** (1991) examines the nature of what he chooses to call 'conversational disability'. Usefully he outlines and discusses the following subtypes: (1) problems due to linguistic impairment; (2) problems involving conversational rules; (3) cognitive deficits affecting the use of language; (4) sociocognitive deficiencies; and (5) affective and emotional difficulties.

McTear & Conti-Ramsden (1992) provide a detailed examination of issues in childhood pragmatic disability, including development, alternative explanations of the presenting difficulties, assessment, research directions and treatment possibilities.

Mogford-Bevan & Sadler (1991) in introducing a short, accessible but well informed volume dealing with semantic and pragmatic difficulties, explain that semantic and pragmatic problems are not necessarily related and that there is no particular reason for thinking that word-finding difficulties represent a distinctive feature of semantic and pragmatic disorder, as has sometimes been claimed. After some useful discussion, they conclude that the term 'semantic–pragmatic' is not really justified. However, they view discussion of terminology as possibly less valuable than attempts to understand how to help the children concerned.

Morris-Smith (1989) states that many children with what she terms 'high-level language disorder' (possibly synonymous with semantic–pragmatic disorder) had, in the past, been wrongly diagnosed as behaviourally disturbed. Because of superficially adequate linguistic performance and certain masking strategies, diagnosis is difficult. Attention was drawn to the following possible markers for high-level language disorder: pedantic speech, 'chunked' borrowed phrases, repetitive stock-response formats including clichés, poor auditory short-term memory and discrimination, idiosyncratic interpretations, tangential remarks, associative thinking, word-finding difficulties and paraphasia.

Prutting & Kirchner (1983) identify three broad types of pragmatic difficulty in language-disordered children: (1) lack of sensitivity to various dimensions of the social context; (2) normal social sensitivity with poor conversational performance due to linguistic difficulties at the discourse level; and (3) cognitive impairment giving rise to limited comprehension, poor topic maintenance, lack of referential specificity and inappropriate lexical choices.

Rapin & Allen (1983) identify six subcategories of developmental language disorder (DLD), two of which involve pragmatic problems. These are the 'syntactic–pragmatic' and the 'semantic–pragmatic' syndromes. These can perhaps be seen as simplified but potentially helpful labels. By the time **Rapin** (1987) delivered her own and **Allen's** revised thoughts on this categorization it appears to us that discussion of the true complexity of relationships between one type of language disability and another, plus the relationship between these and psychosis and autism, was being attempted. In the circumstances it is not surprising that a somewhat confusing picture emerged or that less experienced professionals subsequently sought to resimplify the concepts of what were now called the 'lexical–syntactic deficit syndrome' and the 'semantic–pragmatic deficit syndrome'. Clinically, it was noted that clients exhibited difficulties of a pragmatic nature and these clients were then labelled as having 'semantic–pragmatic disorder'. For details of Rapin and Allen's description, we refer readers to the original papers, but it should be noted here that a key concern for them was that children with language disabilities were at risk of the potentially unhelpful diagnosis of 'psychosis' if the nature of their difficulties could not be explained.

Sahlén & Nettelbladt (1993) provide thorough descriptions of two children said to have semantic–pragmatic disorder, arguing that the pragmatic difficulties of the children are most probably secondary to their semantic/conceptual deficits, since their pragmatic behaviour becomes relatively normal when adequate contextual cues are available. The purposes of the study are to take a neurolinguistic and interactional perspective in describing the children, to consider possible underlying mechanisms of the disorder and to examine the relationship between semantics and pragmatics. Difficulties noted include echolalia, tangentiality, topic switching, failure to understand 'wh—' questions and requests for clarification, poor recognition of emotional prosody, poor narrative skill, word-finding difficulty, imprecision, overuse of deixis, inappropriateness, verbosity, egocentricity, confusion and opting out of interactions. Other difficulties are also discussed in these very thorough studies.

Smedley (1989) in a paper based, not on scientific investigation but on considerable personal experience of children whose problems are described as 'semantic–pragmatic', discusses a considerable number of their difficulties. Somewhat to our surprise, he claims that 'symptom' clusters are shared by all the children varying only 'in degree'. The children attend a special junior school for children with speech and language problems and can therefore be assumed to be in serious difficulties. The main characteristics of their disorder were mazes (word-search behaviours such as false starts, hesitations and circumlocution), literal paraphasia, semantics paraphasia, substitutions, neologisms (all the above due to word-finding difficulty), literalness, poor narrative skills, multiple comprehension problems, syntactic difficulties with complex constructions, poor inferencing, absence of referents, problems with 'given' and 'new' distinctions, and immature temporal and spatial language. Such a list raises a multitude of questions which the original article does attempt to answer. Few of Smedley's hypotheses have since been discussed in the literature.

Smith & Leinonen (1992) present a theoretical account of pragmatic function and dysfunction applicable to both children and adults, together with a discussion of issues in assessment and treatment, brief case studies and some discussion of administrative issues in creating services for people with pragmatic difficulties.

Spence *et al* (1989), writing from the perspective of a special senior school for language-disordered children, describe what they take to be the strategies used by seven children in the face of 'high-level semantic difficulties'. Some of the strategies affect pragmatic performance. Superficially, these children used language correctly, but *concealment strategies* were noted, such as controlling the conversation, supposedly in order to avoid problem areas, reluctance to admit poor comprehension, reluctance to correct mistakes, self-distraction, impulsive responding and acceptance of nonsensical interaction. It was appreciated by the writers that some of the above strategies would be unnecessary if the children's disabilities were perceived and allowed for in the outside world. Their confidence and self-image were found to be very poor and their expectation that their environment would make sense was low.

The disabilities noted were as follows:
- excessive time needed for correct interpretation of what was said;
- auditory imprecision;
- lack of appreciation of word boundaries;
- over- and underextension of concepts;
- failure to make use of non-verbal information;
- lack of appreciation of gestalt (our interpretation);
- poor integration of information;
- poor revision skills;
- rigidity;
- short-term memory problems;
- poor monitoring;
- weak temporal and spatial concepts;
- lack of organization.

The authors conclude by stressing the present lack of understanding of the fundamental causes of such difficulties. They comment that the children described might be referred to as 'semantic–pragmatic' disordered children by other authors. Finally they make a plea for further investigation of these types of problem.

Weintraub & Mesulam (1983) suggest that children whose right cerebral hemisphere has been damaged will have difficulty with the development of such skills as speech act comprehension, comprehension of non-literal meanings, appreciation of metaphor and humour, and use of appropriate paralinguistic behaviour.

Wolff & McGuire (1995) re-examine the concept of 'schizoid personality' in the light of current thinking on Asperger's syndrome, to which it is related. 'Semantic–pragmatic disorder' is also mentioned. Clinicians with an interest in the notion of an 'autistic continuum' or 'autistic spectrum disorders' will find this paper interesting.

APPENDIX II
CLIENT-CENTRED ASSESSMENT

Name	Date
Contact Details	DOB

	Question	Comment
1	Do you like talking to people?	
2	Is it nice to be with other people?	
3	Who do you like talking to best?	
4	There are always some people who are not so easy to talk to. Are there any awkward people for you?	
5	Have you got some friends? Do you want to tell me about your friends? Do you go out together, or what?	
6	What are your interests and hobbies? Would you like to tell me about some of these?	
7	How do you get on with making new friends?	
8	If we think of a typical week in your life, where would you go? Who would you talk to?	
9	How do you get on with your family? Tell me about them. Who helps you?	
10	What do you think about school/work/training centre? Do you like the holidays best or the term/work time best? Why is that?	
11	What about the people you go to school/work with?	

© *Andersen-Wood & Smith, 1997. You may photocopy this page for administrative use only.*

12	Has anyone ever said anything about the way you talk to them?	
13	Is it easy to get people to understand what you want to say? What do you do about it when	
14	people don't understand what you're getting at?	
15	Do some people get upset about things you say?	
16	What do you think about that?	
17	Do you always understand what other people mean?	
18	What do you do when you don't understand something? Is that OK?	
19	Are other people nice about it when you don't understand them?	
20	Do you know what my job is? Do you know about the sort of thing I can help you with?	
21	Are there any things you would like to know about speech and language therapy?	
22	Are there any special things you would like to learn in therapy?	
23	Is there anything you would like to change about your conversations with other people?	
24	Would you like to learn some ways of getting on well with people?	
25	Are you willing to try some new things, like using a video camera?	
26	Would you like to bring anyone to class with you?	

© Andersen-Wood & Smith, 1997. You may photocopy this page for administrative use only.

Use of the Client-Centred Assessment

The questionnaire could be used informally as part of an initial interview (adapted to the linguistic and cognitive level of the individual client). One way of introducing the questionnaire is by saying "I'd like to ask you some questions today so that I can get to know you better. You may want to ask me questions as well."

The clinician may choose to fill in the questionnaire in the client's presence. Alternatively, the questions can be memorized and simply used as a guide for a very informal discussion and completed when the client has left, so that the process of writing down the client's responses does not interfere with getting to know them and encouraging them to feel at ease. However, it is good practice to inform the client that you will write down some notes to help you to think about the possible options for intervention.

An Alternative Questionnaire

Some clients find it easier to talk about themselves by completing ready-made sentences, such as the following:

My friends are called …
We like to be together when we …
The trouble with making friends is …
I wish people would …
I like talking to people who …
Things I hate are …
My friends like to …
My parents want me to …
I wish my family would …
The worst thing about talking to people is …
I like to …
Sometimes I want to …
It makes me unhappy when …
I'm good at …
People sometimes …
In therapy time I want to …
In therapy time I'd like to learn …
I wish people wouldn't …
I wish I didn't have to …
If I could have three wishes, I'd wish …

APPENDIX III
CHILD INFORMATION SHEET

To get to know your child better it would be helpful if you told me about his/her everyday activities, likes and dislikes and people he/she comes into contact with.

About My Child		
Name	Completed by	
DOB	Date completed	
Brothers and sisters	Name	Age
Friends	Name	Age
Favourite relatives	Name	Relationship
Pets	Name	Type
Favourite activities and toys		
Favourite books		
Favourite video or TV programmes		
Favourite songs		
Favourite places		
Favourite things to eat		
Favourite topics of conversation		
Particularly disliked activities or objects		
Attending any play group/nursery	Name	When
Attending any community activities, eg. scouts/church	Activity	When
Recent family events such as parties/holidays/visits	Event	When
Anything else you think may be useful to help me get to know your child		

© Andersen-Wood & Smith, 1997. You may photocopy this page for administrative use only.

APPENDIX IV
CLIENT INFORMATION SHEET

To get to know you better, it would be helpful if you told me about your family, friends, work activities, likes and dislikes.

\	Client Information	
Name	Completed by	
DOB	Date completed	
Spouse	Name	Age (optional)
Children		
Grandchildren		
Brothers/sisters		
Parents		
Other favourite relatives		
Friends		
Pets		Type
Current/past occupation(s)		
Favourite activities and hobbies		
Favourite books and magazines		
Favourite video or TV and radio programmes		
Favourite songs/plays		
Favourite places/holidays		
Favourite things to eat and drink		
Usual mode of transport		
Favourite topics of conversation		
Particularly disliked activities or people		
Attending any community activities	Activity	When
Recent family events	Event	When
Anything else you think may be useful to help me get to know you		

© Andersen-Wood & Smith, 1997. You may photocopy this page for administrative use only.

BIBLIOGRAPHY

Aarons M & Gittens T, 'What is the True Essence of Autism?', *Speech Therapy in Practice* 5(8), 1990.

Aarons M & Gittens T, *The Handbook of Autism: a guide for parents and professionals*, Routledge, London, 1991.

Aarons M & Gittens T, *The Autistic Continuum*, NFER-Nelson, 1992.

Aarons M & Gittens T, 'Semantic Pragmatic Disorder (Or a Little Bit Autistic?)', *Bulletin of the College of Speech & Language Therapists* 494, 1993.

Abbeduto L & Rosenburg S, 'Linguistic Communication and Mental Retardation', Rosenberg S (ed), *Advances in Applied Psycholinguistics* 1, Cambridge University Press, Cambridge, 1987.

Adams C & Bishop DVM, 'Conversational Characteristics of Children with Semantic–Pragmatic Disorder: Exchange Structure, Turntaking, Repairs and Cohesion', *British Journal of Disorders of Communication* 24(3), pp211–39, 1989.

Aicardi J 'Diseases of the Nervous System in Childhood', *Clinics in Developmental Medicine*, pp115–118, 1992.

Ainsworth MDS, Bell SM & Stayton DJ, 'Infant Mother Attachment and Social Development: Socialization as a Product of Reciprocal Responsiveness to Signals', Richards MPM (ed), *The Integration of a Child into a Social World,* Cambridge University Press, Cambridge, 1974.

Andersen L, 'Fathers and Mothers: A Case Study of Interaction Style Differences', Poster presented at American Speech and Hearing Association Annual Convention, Atlanta, 1989.

Andersen L, 'Social Skills Training: A Speech-Language Clinician's Approach', Poster presented at conference on learning difficulties, London, 1990.

Andersen L, Rutter M, Dunn J, O'Connor T, Castle J, Bredenkaup D & Groothues C, 'Communication Skills in Romanian and UK Adopted Children at Four Years', Paper presented at the International Symposium in Study of Behavioural Development, Quebec City, Canada, 1996.

Andersen-Wood L, 'Speech Pathology in Romania: A Training and Intervention Product', Poster presented at the American Speech Language and Hearing Convention, San Antonio, 1992.

Austin JL, *How to Do Things With Words*, 2nd edn, Oxford University Press, Oxford, 1963.

Baginsky M, *Vocational Education Opportunities for Students with Speech and Language Impairments*, NFER-Nelson, Slough, 1991.

Baltax CAM, 'Pragmatic Deficits and Psychiatric Disorders in Children and Adolescents', International Pragmatics Conference, University of Barcelona, 1990.

Baltax CAM & Simmons JQ, 'Pragmatic Deficits in Emotionally Disturbed Children and Adolescents', Schiefelbusch RL & Lloyd LL (eds), *Language Perspectives: Acquisition, Retardation and Intervention*, pp223–24, Pro-Ed, Austin, Texas, 1988.

Baron-Cohen S, 'Do People with Autism Understand what Causes Emotion?', *Child Development* 62(2), pp385–95, 1991.

Baron-Cohen S & Bolton P, *Autism: The Facts,* Oxford University Press, Oxford, 1993.

Baron-Cohen S, Lesley AM & Frith U, 'Does the Autistic Child Have a Theory of Mind?', *Cognition* 21, pp37–46, 1985.

Bates E, 'Acquisition of Pragmatic Competence', *Journal of Child Language* 1(2), pp277–81, 1974.

Bates E, *Language in Context: The Acquisition of Pragmatics,* Academic Press, New York, 1976a.

Bates E, 'Pragmatics and Sociolinguistics in Child Language', Morehead D and Morehead A (eds), *Normal and Deficient Child Language,* University Park Press, Baltimore, 1976b.

Bateson MC, 'Mother Infant Exchanges: The Epigenesis of Conversational Interaction', Aaronson D & Reiber RW (eds), *Developmental Psycholinguistics and Communication Disorders* 18, pp103–13, New York Academy of Sciences, New York, 1975.

Beck K & Beck K, *Assertiveness at Work,* McGraw Hill, Maidenhead, 1992.

Becker JA, 'Implications of Ethology for the Study of Pragmatic Development', Kuczaj SA, *Discourse Development: Progress in Cognitive Development Research,* Springer-Verlag, New York, 1984.

Becker JA, 'Processes in the Acquisition of Pragmatic Competence', Conti-Ramsden G & Snow CE (eds), *Children's Language* 17, Lawrence Erlbaum Associates, Hillsdale, New Jersey, 1990.

Belkin A, 'Facilitating Language in Emotionally Handicapped Children', Winitz H (ed), *Treating Language Disorders: for Clinicians by Clinicians*, University Park Press, Baltimore, 1983.

Bernarding MB, *Exploring Pragmatic Language: Games for Practice,* Communication Skill Builders, Tucson, Arizona, 1992.

Berry MF, *Teaching Linguistically Handicapped Children*, Prentice-Hall, Englewood Cliffs, NJ, 1980.

Beveridge M & Conti-Ramsden G, *Children with Language Disabilities*, Open University Press, Milton Keynes, 1987.

Bishop DVM, 'Comprehension of Spoken, Written and Signed Sentences in Childhood Language Disorders', *Journal of Child Psychology and Psychiatry* 23(1), pp1–20, 1982.

Bishop DVM, *Test for the Reception of Grammar*, NFER-Nelson, Windsor, 1983.

Bishop DVM, 'The Concept of Comprehension in Language Disorders', *Proceedings of First International Symposium on Specific Speech and Language Disorders in Children,* AFASIC (Association for All Speech Impaired Children), London, 1987.

Bishop DVM, 'Autism, Asperger's Syndrome and Semantic-Pragmatic Disorder: Where are the Boundaries?', *British Journal of Disorders of Communication* 24(2), pp107–21, 1989.

Bishop DVM & Adams C, 'Conversational Characteristics of Children with Semantic–Pragmatic Disorders 11: What Features Lead to Judgements of Inappropriacy?', *British Journal of Disorders of Communication* 24(3), pp241–63, 1989.

Bishop DVM & Adams C, 'What do Referential Communication Tasks Measure? A Study of Children with Specific Language Impairment', *Applied Psycholinguistics* 12(2), pp199–215, 1991.

Bishop DVM & Adams C, 'Comprehension Problems in Children with Special Language Impairment: Literal and Inferential Meaning', *Journal of Speech & Hearing Research* 35(1), pp119–29, 1992.

Bishop DVM & Edmundson A, 'Language Impaired 4-Year-Olds: Distinguishing Transient from Persistent Impairment', *Journal of Speech and Hearing Disorders* 52(2), pp156–73, 1987.

Blank M & Marquis MA, *Directing Discourse: 80 Situations for Teaching Meaningful Conversation to Children*, Communication Skill Builders, Tucson, Arizona, 1987.

Blank M & Marquis MA, *Directing Discourse:* Communication Skill Builders, Tucson, Arizona, 1992.

Blomert L, Koster C, van Mier H & Kean ML, 'Verbal Communication Abilities of Aphasic Patients: the Everyday Language Test', *Aphasiology* 1(6), pp463–74, 1987.

Bloom K, Russell A & Wassenberg K, 'Turn taking Affects the Quality of Infant Vocalizations', *Journal of Child Language* 14(2), pp211–27, 1987.

Bloom L, *Language Development: Form and Function in Emerging Grammars*, MIT Press, Cambridge, Mass, 1970.

Bloom L & Lahey M, *Language Development and Language Disorders,* Wiley, New York, 1978.

Bloom L, Rocissano L & Hood L, 'Adult-Child Discourse: Developmental Interaction between Information Processing and Linguistic Knowledge', *Cognitive Psychology* 8(4), pp521–52, 1976.

Blum-Kulka S & Snow CE, 'Developing Autonomy for Tellers, Tales and Telling in Family Narrative Events', *Journal of Narrative & Life History* 2(3), pp187–217, 1992.

Blurton-Jones N, 'Characteristics of Ethological Studies of Human Behaviour', Blurton-Jones (ed), *Ethological Studies of Child Behaviour,* Cambridge University Press, Cambridge, 1972.

Boehm A, *Boehm Test of Basic Concepts,* Psychological Corporation, New York, 1971.

Booth Johnston E, Derickson Weinrich B & Randolph Johnson A, *A Sourcebook of Pragmatic Activities: Theory and Intervention for Language Therapy (PK6)*, Communication Skill Builders, Tucson, Arizona, 1984.

Boucher J, 'The Theory of Mind Hypothesis of Autism: Explanation, Evidence and Assessment', *British Journal of Disorders of Communication* 24(2), pp181–98, 1989.

Bowerman M, 'Semantic and Syntactic Development: A Review of What, When and How in Language Acquisition', Schiefelbusch R (ed), *Bases of Language Intervention*, University Park Press, Baltimore, 1978.

Brazelton TB, 'Joint Regulation of Neonate-Parent Behaviour', Tronick EZ, *Social Interchange in Infancy: Affect, Cognition and Communication,* University Park Press, Baltimore, 1982.

Brinton B & Fujiki M, 'Development of Topic Manipulation Skills in Discourse', *Journal of Speech & Hearing Research* 27, pp350–8, 1984.

Brinton B & Fujiki M, *Conversational Management with Language-Impaired Children: Pragmatic Assessment and Intervention,* Aspen, Rockville, Maryland, 1989.

Brooks AR, *Structured Role Play: Therapy Activities for School and Home,* Communication Skill Builders, Tucson, Arizona, 1992.

Brown G & Yule G, *Discourse Analysis,* Cambridge University Press, Cambridge, 1983.

Brown R, *A First Language: The Early Stages,* Harvard University Press, Cambridge, Mass, 1973.

Browning E, *I Can't See What You're Saying,* Angel Press, East Wittering, Sussex, 1987.

Bruner JS, 'The Ontogenesis of Speech Acts, *Journal of Child Language* 2(1), pp1–19, 1975.

Bruner JS, 'Learning the Mother Tongue', *Human Nature* 1, pp42–9, 1978.

Bruner JS, 'The Social Context of Language Acquisition', *Language & Communication* 1, pp155–78, 1981.

Bruner JS, 'The Formats of Language Acquisition', *American Journal of Semiotics* 1, pp1–16, 1982.

Bruner JS, *Child's Talk*, Norton, New York, 1983.

Bruner JS, *Actual Minds, Possible Worlds,* Harvard University Press, Cambridge, Mass, 1986.

Bryan KL, 'Assessment of Language Disorders After Right Hemisphere Damage', *British Journal of Disorders of Communication* 23(2), pp111–25, 1988.

Bryan KL, *The Right Hemisphere Language Battery,* 2nd edn, Whurr, London, 1994.

Buhai Haas C, *Look at Me: Creative Learning Activities for Babies and Toddlers,* Chicago Review Press, Chicago, 1987.

Byers-Brown B & Edwards M, *Developmental Disorders of Language,* Whurr, London, 1989.

Calculator SN & Bedrosian JL (eds), *Communication Assessment and Intervention for Adults with Mental Retardation,* College-Hill, Boston, 1988.

Cantwell DP & Baker L, 'Interrelationship of Communication, Learning and Psychiatric Disorders in Children', Simon CS (ed), *Communication Skills and Classroom Success: Assessment of Language-Learning Disabled Students,* Taylor & Francis, Basingstoke, 1985.

Carlomagno S, *Pragmatic Approaches to Aphasia Therapy,* Whurr, London, 1994.

Catanach A, *Play Therapy: Where the Sky Meets the Underworld,* Jessica Kingsley, London, 1994.

Chaney C, 'Language Development, Metalinguistic Awareness and Emergent Literacy Skills of 3-year-old Children in Relation to Social Class', *Applied Psycholinguistics* 15(3), pp371–94, 1994.

Channel 4, *The Colour Me Loud Guide: Everything You Wanted to Know About Joining a People First Group,* Mental Health Media, 356 Holloway Rd, London, 1994.

Chapman R, 'Exploring Children's Communicative Intents', Miller JF (ed), *Assessing Language Production in Children: Experimental Procedures,* pp111–36, Arnold, London, 1981.

Chomsky N, *Aspects of the Theory of Syntax,* MIT Press, Cambridge, Mass, 1965.

Christie P, Newson E, Newson J & Prevezer W, 'An Interactive Approach to Language and Communication for Non-Speaking Children', Lane DA & Miller A (eds), *Child and Adolescent Therapy: A Handbook,* Open University Press, Buckingham, 1992.

Clancy P 'The Acquisition of Communicative Style in Japanese', Schieffelin B & Ochs (eds), *Language Socialisation Across Cultures,* Cambridge University Press, Cambridge, 1986.

Code C, *Language, Aphasia and the Right Hemisphere,* Wiley, Chichester, 1987.

Coggins TE & Carpenter RL, 'The Communicative Intention Inventory: a System for Observing and Coding Children's Early Intentional Communication', *Applied Psycholinguistics* 2(3), pp235–52, 1981.

Cole ML & Cole JT, *Effective Intervention with the Language-Impaired Child,* 2nd edn, Aspen, Rockville, Maryland, 1989.

Collis GM & Schaffer HR, 'Synchronization of Visual Attention in Mother-infant Pairs', *Journal of Child Psychology and Psychiatry and Allied Disciplines* 16(4), pp315–20, 1975.

Colmar S & Wheldal K, 'Behavioural Language Teaching: Using Natural Language Environment', *Child Language Teaching and Therapy* 1(2), pp199–216, 1985.

Connard PA, *The Preverbal Assessment-Intervention Profile,* Pro-Ed, Texas, 1984.

Conti-Ramsden G, 'How Can We Study Pragmatic Disabilities?' Mogford-Bevan K & Sadler J, *Child Language Disability Vol 2: Semantic and Pragmatic Difficulties,* Multilingual Matters, Clevedon, 1991.

Conti-Ramsden G & Gunn M, 'The Development of Conversational Disability: a Case Study', *British Journal of Disorders of Communication* 21(3), pp339–52, 1986.

Cooke J & Williams D, *Working with Children's Language,* Winslow Press, Bicester, 1985.

Cooper J, Moodley M & Reynell J, *Helping Language Development,* Arnold, London, 1978.

Corsaro WA, 'Young Children's Conception of Status and Role', *Sociology of Education* 52(1), pp46–59, 1979.

Corsaro WA, 'The Development of Social Cognition in Pre-school Children: Implications for Language Learning', *Topics in Language Disorders* 2(1), pp77–95, 1981.

Coultard M, *An Introduction to Discourse Analysis,* 2nd edn, Longman, London, 1985.

Coupe J & Porter J, *The Education of Children with Severe Learning Difficulties: Bridging the Gap Between Theory and Practice.* Available from the Mellands School, Manchester.

Coupe J & Golbart J, *Communication Before Speech,* David Fulton, London, in press.

Coupe J, Barton L, Barber M, Collins L, Levy D & Murphy D, *Affective Communication Assessment,* Manchester University Press, Manchester, 1985.

Cox M, *The Child's Point of View,* 2nd edn, Harvester, New York, 1991.

Crago MB & Cole EB, 'Using Ethnography to Bring Children's Communicative and Cultural Worlds into Focus' Gallagher TM, *Pragmatics of Language: Clinical Practice Issues,* Chapman & Hall, London, 1991.

Craig HK, 'Applications of Pragmatic Language Models for Intervention', Gallagher TM & Prutting CA (eds), *Pragmatic Assessment and Intervention Issues in Language,* College-Hill, San Diego, 1983.

Craig HK, 'Pragmatic Characteristics of the Child with Specific Language Impairment: An Interactive Perspective', Gallagher TM (ed), *Pragmatics of Language: Clinical Practice Issues,* Singular Publishing, San Diego, 1991.

Crockford C & Lesser R, 'Assessing Functional Communication in Aphasia: Clinical Utility and Time Demands of Three Methods, *European Journal of Disorders of Communication* 29(2), pp165–182, 1994.

Cross T, 'Motherese and its Association with Syntactic Acquisition in Young Children',

Waterson N & Snow C (eds), *The Development of Communication*, Wiley, London, 1978.

Crystal D, *Profiling Linguistic Disability*, Arnold, London, 1982.

Crystal D, 'Towards a "Bucket" Theory of Language Disability: Taking Account of Interaction Between Linguistic Levels', *Clinical Linguistics & Phonetics* 1(1), pp7–22, 1987.

Crystal D, 'Postilion Sentences', *Child Language Teaching and Therapy* 11(1), pp79–90, 1995.

Crystal D, Fletcher P & Garman M, *The Grammatical Analysis of Language Disability*, Arnold, London, 1976.

Culloden M, Hyde-Wright S & Shipman A, 'Non-Syntactic Features of "Semantic–Pragmatic" Disorders', *Advances in Working with Language Disordered Children*, ICAN, London, 1986.

Cutting J, *The Right Cerebral Hemisphere and Psychiatric Disorders*, Oxford University Press, Oxford, 1990.

Damico J, 'Clinical Discourse Analysis: a Functional Approach to Language Assessment', Simon CS (ed), *Communication Skills and Classroom Success: Assessment of Language-Learning Disabled Students*, Taylor & Francis, Basingstoke, 1985.

Davies S, Bishop D, Manstead ASR & Tantam D, 'Face Perception in Children with Autism and Asperger's Syndrome', *Journal of Child Psychology and Psychiatry* 35(6), pp1033–57, 1994.

Davis G & Wilcox M, 'Incorporating Parameters of Natural Conversation in Aphasia Treatment,' Chapey R (ed), *Language Intervention Strategies in Adult Aphasia*, Williams & Wilkins, Baltimore, 1981.

Davis GA & Wilcox MJ, *Adult Aphasia Rehabilitation: Applied Pragmatics*, NFER-Nelson, Windsor, 1985.

de Beaugrand R & Dressler W, *Introduction to Text Linguistics*, Longman, London, 1981.

Deffebach KP & Adamson LB, 'Teaching Referential and Social-Regulative Words to Toddlers: Mothers' Use of Metalingual Language', *First Language* 14(42.3), pp249–61, 1994.

DeHart G & Maratsos M, 'Children's Acquisition of Presuppositional Usages', Schiefelbusch RL & Pickar J (eds), *The Acquisition of Communicative Competence*, pp237–93, University Park Press, Baltimore, 1984.

Department of Health, *Children and Young People on Child Protection Registers: Year Ending 31 March 1996*, Department of Health, England, 1997.

DesLauriers AM & Carlson CF, *Your Child is Asleep: Early Infantile Autism: Etiology, Treatment, Parental Influences*, Dorsey Press, Homewood, Illinois, 1969.

Dewart H, 'Investigating Comprehension of Syntax', Grundy K (ed), *Linguistics in Clinical Practice*, Taylor & Francis, London, 1995.

Dewart H & Summers S, *The Pragmatics Profile of Communication Skills in Childhood*, NFER-Nelson, Windsor, 1995.

Dewart H & Summers S, *The Pragmatics Profile of Everyday Communication Skills in Adults*, NFER-Nelson, Windsor, 1997.

Dickinson C, *Effective Learning Activities*, Network Educational Press, Stafford, 1996.

Dik SC, *Functional Grammar*, North Holland, Amsterdam, 1978.

Dillon JT, 'The Multidisciplinary Study of Questioning', *Journal of Educational Psychology* 74(2), pp147–65, 1982.

Dinkmeyer D & McKay GD, *The Parent's Handbook: Systematic Training for Effective Parenting*, American Guidance Service, Circle Pines, Minnesota, 1989.

Dixon A, *A Woman in Your Own Right*, Quartet, London, 1982.

Donahue M, 'Interaction Between Linguistic and Pragmatic Development in Learning-Disabled Children: Three Views of the State of the Union', Rosenberg S (ed), *Advances in Applied Psycholinguistics* 1, Cambridge University Press, Cambridge, 1987.

Donahue-Kilburg G, *Family-Centred Early Intervention for Communication Disorders Prevention and Treatment*, Aspen, Maryland, 1992.

Dore J, 'Holophrases, Speech Acts and Language Universals', *Journal of Child Language* 2(1), pp21–40, 1975.

Dore J, 'Conditions for the Acquisition of Speech Acts', Markova I (ed), *The Social Context of Language*, Wiley & Sons, Chichester, 1978a.

Dore J, 'Requestive Systems in Nursery School Conversations: Analysis of Talk in its Social Context' Cambell R & Smith P (eds), *Recent Advances in the Psychology of Language: Language Development and Mother-Child Interaction*, Plenum Press, New York, pp271–92, 1978b.

Dore J, 'Variation in Pre-School Children's Conversational Performance', Nelson K (ed), *Children's Language* 1, pp397–444, Wiley, New York, 1978c.

Dore J, 'Conversation and Pre-School Language Development', Fletcher P & Garman M (eds), *Language Acquisition,* Cambridge University Press, Cambridge, 1979a.

Dore J, 'Conversational Acts and the Acquisition of Language', Ochs E & Schieffelin BB (eds), *Developmental Pragmatics*, Academic Press, New York, 1979b.

Dunn J, *Young Children's Close Relationships: Beyond Attachment*, Sage, London, 1993.

Dunn K & Kendrick C, 'The Speech of Two and Three Year Olds to Infant Siblings: Baby Talk and the Context of Communication', *Journal of Child Language* 9(3), pp579–95, 1982.

Dunn LM, *Peabody Picture Vocabulary Test*, American Guidance Service, 1965.

Dunn LM & Dunn LM, *The British Picture*

Dunn LM, Whetton C & Pintilre D, *Vocabulary Scale – Long Form,* NFER-Nelson, Windsor, Berks, 1982.

Dunn LM, Whetton C & Pintilre D, *British Picture Vocabulary Scale,* NFER-Nelson, Windsor, 1982.

Eberhardt Deal J & Hanuscin L, *Barrier Games for Better Communication,* Communication Skill Builders, Tucson, Arizona, 1992.

Edelman G, *PACE: Promoting Aphasics' Communicative Effectiveness,* Winslow Press, Bicester, 1987.

Elder JH, 'In Home Communication Intervention Training for Parents of Multiply Handicapped Children', *Scholarly Inquiry for Nursing Practice* 9(1), pp71–92, 1995.

Ellis AW & Young AW, *Human Cognitive Neuropsychology,* Lawrence Erlbaum, London, 1988.

Ellis R & Wells G, 'Enabling Factors in Adult–Child Discourse', *First Language* 1(1), pp46–62, 1980.

Erber B, 'Conversation as Therapy for Older Adults in Residential Care: the Case for Intervention', *European Journal of Disorders of Communication* 29(3), pp269–78, 1994.

Ervin-Tripp S, 'Children's Verbal Turn-Taking' Ochs E & Schieffelin BB (eds), *Developmental Pragmatics,* pp391–429, Academic Press, New York, 1979.

Ervin-Tripp S, Guo J & Lampert M, 'Politeness and Persuasion in Children's Control Acts', *Journal of Pragmatics* 14(2), pp307–31, 1990.

Evans D & Williams C, *Let's Explore Science: Sound and Music,* Dorling Kindersley, London, 1993.

Faerch C & Kasper G, 'Pragmatic Knowledge: Rules and Procedures', *Applied Linguistics* 5(3), pp214–25, 1984.

Farrar MJ, 'Discourse and the Acquisition of Grammatical Morphemes', *Journal of Child Language* 17, pp607–24, 1990.

Feldman CF, Bruner J, Renderer B & Spitzer S, 'Narrative Comprehension', Britton BK & Pellegrini AD (eds), *Narrative Thought and Narrative Language,* pp1–78, Lawrence Erlbaum Associates, Hillsdale, New Jersey, 1990.

Fey ME, *Language Intervention with Young Children,* College-Hill, Boston, Mass, 1986.

Fey ME & Leonard LB, 'Pragmatic Skills of Children with Specific Language Impairment', Gallagher TM & Prutting CA (eds), *Pragmatic Assessment and Intervention Issues in Language,* College-Hill, San Diego, 1983.

Fisher JJ, *Toys to Grow With: Hundreds of Play Ideas for Babies and Toddlers,* Collins, London, 1988.

Fogel A, 'Temporal Organization in Mother-Infant Face-to-Face Interaction' Schaffer HR (ed), *Studies in Mother-Infant Interaction,* pp119–52, Academic Press, New York, 1977.

Fogel A, *Developing Through Relationships: Origins of Communication,* Harvester Wheatsheaf, Hemel Hempstead, 1993.

Fogel A & Thelen E, 'Development of Early Expressive and Communicative Action: Reinterpreting the Evidence from a Dynamic Systems Perspective', *Developmental Psychology* 23, pp747–61, 1987.

Foster SH, 'Interpreting Child Discourse', French P & MacLure M (eds), *Adult-Child Conversation,* pp268–86, Croom Helm, London, 1981.

Foster SH, *The Communicative Competence of Young Children: A Modular Approach,* Longman, New York, 1990.

Friel-Patti S & Conti-Ramsden G, 'Discourse Development in Atypical Language Learners', Kuczaj SA (ed), *Discourse Development: Progress in Cognitive Development Research,* Springer-Verlag, New York, 1984.

Frith U, *Autism: Explaining the Enigma,* Blackwell, Oxford, 1989.

Frith U, *Autism & Asperger Syndrome,* Cambridge University Press, Cambridge, 1991.

Furrow P, Nelson K & Benedict H, 'Mothers' Speech to Children and Syntactic Development: Some Simple Relationships', *Journal of Child Language* 6, pp423–42, 1979.

Gaag van der A, *The Communication Assessment Profile for Adults with Mental Handicap,* Speech Profiles Ltd, London, 1988.

Gallagher TM, 'Revision Behaviours in the Speech of Normal Children Developing Language', *Journal of Speech & Hearing Research* 20, pp303–18, 1977.

Gallagher TM, 'Pre-Assessment: A Procedure for Accommodating Language Use Variability', Gallagher TM & Prutting CA (eds), *Pragmatic Assessment and Intervention Issues in Language,* College-Hill, San Diego, 1983.

Gallagher TM (ed), *Pragmatics of Language: Clinical Practice Issues,* Singular Publishing Co, San Diego, 1991.

Gallagher TM & Craig HK, 'An Investigation of Overlap in Children's Speech', *Journal of Psycholinguistic Research* 11(1), pp63–75, 1982.

Gallagher TM & Prutting CA (eds), *Pragmatic Assessment and Intervention Issues in Language,* College-Hill, San Diego, 1983.

Garton A & Pratt C, *Learning to be Literate: The Development of Spoken and Written Language,* Blackwell, Oxford, 1989.

Garton AF, 'The Production of "This" and "That" by Young Children', *First Language* 6, pp29-39, 1986.

Garvey C, 'The Contingent Query: A Dependent Act in Conversation', Lewis M & Rosenblum LA (eds), *Interaction Conversation and the Development of Language,* Wiley, New York, 1977.

Garvie E, *Story as Vehicle,* Multilingual Matters, Clevedon, 1990.

Gee R, *Entertaining and Educating Young Children,* Usbourne Publishing Ltd, London, 1986.

Golinkoff R, Hirsh–Pasek K, Cauley K &

Gordon L, 'The Eyes Have It: Lexical and Syntactic Comprehension in a New Paradigm', *Journal of Child Language* 14, pp23–45, 1987.

Gould J, 'The Lowe and Costello Symbolic Play Test in Socially Impaired Children', *Journal of Autism and Development Disorders* 16(2), pp199–213, 1986.

Grandin T & Scariano M, *Emergence Labelled Autistic*, Costello, Tunbridge Wells, 1986.

Gravell R & France J, *Speech and Communication Problems in Psychiatry*, Chapman & Hall, London, 1991.

Green G, 'Communication in Aphasia Therapy: Some Procedures and Issues Involved', *British Journal of Disorders of Communication* 9(1), pp35–46, 1984.

Green K & Rees R, 'Intervention with Deaf Children Requires a Pragmatic Approach', *Human Communication* 1(3), pp20–23, 1992.

Grice P, 'Logic & Conversation', Cole P & Morgan J (eds), *Syntax and Semantics III: Speech Acts*, Academic Press, New York, 1975.

Grice P, 'Further Notes on Logic and Conversation', Cole P (ed), *Syntax and Semantics: 9 Pragmatics*, Academic Press, New York, 1978.

Guess Who?, MB Games, Milton-Bradley Ltd, Waterford, Ireland, 1987.

Guralnick MJ & Paul-Brown D, 'Peer Related Communicative Competence of Pre-School Children: Developmental and Adaptive Characteristics', *Journal of Speech & Hearing Research* 32(4), pp930–43, 1989.

Gutfreund M, *Bristol Language Development Scales*, NFER-Nelson, Windsor, 1989.

Halliday MAK, *Learning How to Mean*, Arnold, London, 1975.

Halliday MAK, *Language as Social Semiotic*, Arnold, London, 1978.

Halliday MAK & Hasan R, *Cohesion in English*, Longman, London, 1976.

Hanen Program, Canada, available from Winslow Press, Bicester.

Hannon KE & Thompson MA, *Life Skills Workshop: An Active Program for Real Life Problem Solving*, Lingui Systems, Illinois, 1992.

Happe FGE, 'An Advanced Test of Theory of Mind: Understanding of Story Characters, Thoughts and Feelings by Able, Autistic, Mentally Handicapped and Normal Children and Adults', *Journal of Autism and Developmental Disorders* 24(2), pp129–54, 1994.

Harbridge E & Hobbs D, *Learning Together: How Gentle Teaching Helps People with Challenging Behaviours,* Hexagon Publishing, Croydon, 1992.

Hargrove PM & McGarr NS, *Prosody Management of Communication Disorders*, Singular Publishing Group, San Diego, 1994.

Harris PL, *Children and Emotion: The Development of Psychological Understanding*, Blackwell, Oxford, 1989.

Hassibi M & Breuer H Jnr, *Disordered Thinking and Communication in Children*, Plenum Press, New York, 1980.

Hawkins P, 'Discourse Aphasia', Grunwell P & James A (eds), *The Functional Evaluation of Language Disorders*, Croom Helm, London, 1989.

Hersen M & Bellack AS, 'A Multiple Baseline Analysis of Social Skills Training in Chronic Schizophrenics', *Journal of Applied Behaviour Analysis* 9(3), pp239–45, 1976.

Hess JH, Wagner M, DeWald G & Conn P, 'Conversation Skill Intervention Programme for Adolescents with Learning Disabilities', *Child Language Teaching and Therapy* 9(1), 1993.

Heublein EA & Bate CP, 'Procedures for a Descriptive Analysis of Intention', *Seminars in Speech and Language* 9(1), pp37–44, 1988.

Hobbs J, 'Topic Drift', Dorval B (ed), *Conversational Organization and its Development,* Ablex, Norwood, New Jersey, 1990.

Hoff-Ginsberg E, 'Some Contributions of Mothers' Speech to their Children's Syntactic Growth', *Journal of Child Language* 12, pp367–85, 1985.

Hoff-Ginsberg E, 'Function and Structure in Maternal Speech: Their Relation to the Child's Development of Syntax', *Development Psychology* 22, pp155–63, 1986.

Holland AL, *Communicative Abilities in Daily Living*, University Park Press, Baltimore, 1980.

Holland S & Ward C, *Assertiveness: A Practical Approach*, Winslow Press, Bicester, 1990.

Holt J, *How Children Fail*, Penguin, Harmondsworth, 1982.

Holt J, *How Children Learn*, Penguin, Harmondsworth, 1984.

Howard S, Hartley J & Muller D, 'The Changing Face of Child Language Assessment 1985–1995', *Child Language Teaching & Therapy* 11(1), pp7–22, 1995.

Howe CJ, *Acquiring Language in a Conversational Context*, Academic Press, London, 1981.

Howlin P, 'Asperger's Syndrome – Does it Exist and What Can be Done About it?', *Proceedings of the First International Symposium, Specific Speech and Language Disorders in Children, University of Reading*, AFASIC, London, 1987.

Howlin P, 'Changing Approaches to Communication Training with Autistic Children', *British Journal of Disorders of Communication* 24(2), pp151–68, 1989.

Howlin P, 'Problems of Diagnosis', Paper given at Asperger's Syndrome course, Inge Wakehurst Trust, 1991.

Hughes DL, *Language Treatment and Generalisation*, Taylor & Francis, London, 1985.

Hulit LM & Howard MR, *Born to Talk: An Introduction to Speech & Language Development,* MacMillan, New York, 1993.

Hutchings S, Comins J & Offiler J, *The Social Skills Handbook,* Winslow Press, Bicester, 1991.

Hyde-Wright S, 'Teaching Word Finding Strategies to Severely Language Impaired Children', *European Journal of Disorders of Communication* 28(2), pp165–75, 1993.

Hyde-Wright S & Cray B, 'A Teacher's and A Speech Therapist's Approach to Management', Mogford-Bevan K & Sadler J, *Child Language Disability 2: Semantic and Pragmatic Difficulties,* Multilingual Matters, Clevedon, 1991.

Hymes D, 'On Communicative Competence', Pride JB & Holmes J (eds), *Sociolinguistics,* Penguin, London, 1972.

Jackson NF, Jackson DA & Monroe C, *Getting Along with Others: Teaching Social Effectiveness to Children,* Research Press, Champaign, Illinois, 1983.

James SL, 'Effects of Listener Age and Situation on the Politeness of Children's Directives', *Journal of Psycholinguistic Research* 7, pp307–17, 1978.

James SL, *Normal Language Acquisition,* Pro-Ed, Austin, Texas, 1990.

Jeffers S, *Dare to Connect: How to Create Confidence, Trust and Loving Relationships,* Piatkus, London, 1995.

Jennings S, *Creative Drama in Groupwork,* Winslow Press, Bicester, 1986.

Joanette Y & Brownell HH, *Discourse Ability and Brain Damage,* Springer-Verlag, New York, 1990.

Johnson KL & Heinze BA, *Hickory Dickory Talk,* Lingui Systems, East Moline, 1990.

Johnson M, *Functional Communication in the Classroom: A Handbook for Teachers and Therapists of Language Impaired Children,* Department of Psychology and Speech Pathology, Manchester Metropolitan University, 1992.

Johnston EB, 'Communication Abilities Test', unpublished Doctoral thesis, University of Cincinnati, 1980.

Johnston EB, Weinrich BD & Johnson AR, *A Sourcebook of Pragmatic Activities: Theory and Intervention for Language Therapy (Pk6),* Communication Skill Builders, Tucson, Arizona, 1984.

Johnston EB, Weinrich BD & Johnson AR, *A Sourcebook of Pragmatic Activities: Theory and Intervention for Language Therapy (7–12),* Communication Skill Builders, Tucson, Arizona, 1985.

Johnston JR, 'The Discourse Symptoms of Developmental Disorders', Dijk TA van (ed), *Handbook of Discourse Analysis Vol 3,* Academic Press, London, 1985.

Jolliffe T, Lansdown R & Robinson C, 'Autism: a Personal Account', *Communication* 26(3), 1992.

Jones S, Smedley M & Jennings M, 'Case Study: a Child with a High Level Language Disorder Characterised by Syntactic, Semantic and Pragmatic Difficulties', *Advances in Working with Language Disordered Children,* ICAN, London, 1986.

Jordan R & Powell S, *The Special Curricular Needs of Autistic Children: Learning and Thinking Skills,* Association of Heads and Teachers of Adults and Children with Autism, 1990.

Jordan R & Powell S, *Understanding and Teaching Children with Autism,* Wiley, Chichester, 1995.

Kamholz Schuller J & Diamond Seraydarian F, *Step by Step,* Communication Skill Builders, Tueson, Arizona, 1992.

Kay J, Lesser R & Coltheart M, *PALPA: Psycholinguistic Assessments of Language Processing in Aphasia,* Lawrence Erlbaum, Hove, 1992.

Kaye K, *The Mental and Social Life of Babies: How Parents Create Persons,* Methuen, London, 1982.

Kaye K & Charney R, 'How Mothers Maintain Dialogue with 2-year-olds', Olson DR (ed), *The Social Foundations of Language and Thought,* Norton, New York, 1980.

Keenan EO & Klein E, 'Coherency in Children's Discourse', *Journal of Psycholinguistic Research* 4(4), pp365–80, 1975.

Kemper S, 'The Development of Narrative Skills: Explanations and Entertainments' Kuczaj S, *Discourse Development: Progress in Cognitive Development Research,* Springer-Verlag, New York, 1984.

Keogh WJ & Reichle J, 'Communication Intervention for the "Difficult to Teach" Severely Handicapped', Warren SF & Rogers-Warren AK, *Teaching Functional Language: Generalization and Maintenance of Language Skills,* Pro-Ed, Austin, Texas, 1985.

Kiernan C & Reid B, *Pre-Verbal Communication Schedule,* NFER-Nelson, London, 1987.

King CA & Kirschenbaum DS, *Helping Young Children Develop Social Skills: The Social Growth Program,* Brooks/Cole Publishing, Belmont, Califorina, 1992.

King F, 'Assessment of Pragmatic Skills', *Child Language Teaching and Therapy* 5(2), pp191–201, 1989.

Kirchner DM & Prutting CA, 'Pragmatic Criteria for Communicative Competence', *Seminars in Speech and Language* 10(1), pp42–50, 1989.

Klein H, 'The Assessment and Management of Some Persisting Language Difficulties in the Learning Disabled', Snowling MJ (ed), *Children's Written Language Difficulties,* pp59–79, NFER-Nelson, Slough, 1985.

Krauss RM & Glucksberg S, 'Social and Nonsocial Speech,' *Scientific American* 236(2), pp100–5, 1977.

Kuczaj S, *Discourse Development: Progress in Cognitive Development Research,* Springer-Verlag, New York, 1984.

Lakoff R, 'The Logic of Politeness: Or Minding Your Ps and Qs', Papers from the Ninth Regional Meeting of the Chicago Linguistic Society, University of Chicago, Chicago, 1973.

Landells J, 'Assessment of Semantics', Grundy K (ed), *Linguistics in Clinical Practice,* Taylor & Francis, London, 1995.

Law J (ed), *The Early Identification of Language Impairment in Children,* Chapman & Hall, London, 1992.

Law J & Conway J, *The Effect of Abuse and Neglect on the Development of Children's Communication,* AFASIC, London, 1991.

Law J & Conway J, 'Treatment of Abused and Neglected Children: The Role of Speech and Language Therapists', *Bulletin of the College of Speech and Language Therapists* 487, pp8–9, 1992.

Leech GN, *Principles of Pragmatics,* Longman, London, 1982.

Leinonen E, 'Functional Considerations in Phonological Assessment of Child Speech', Yavas M (ed), *Phonological Disorders in Children: Theory Research and Practice,* Routledge, London, 1991.

Leinonen E, 'Children's Pragmatic Difficulties: Problems with Context Analysis', *Finnish Journal of Logopediatrics & Phoniatrics* 15(3&4), pp87–96, 1995.

Leinonen E & Letts C, 'Referential Communication Task: Comparison of Children with Semantic Pragmatic Difficulties with Age Matched Control Children', Child Language Seminar, Manchester University, 1991.

Leinonen E & Letts C, 'Referential Communication Skills in Normal and Pragmatically Impaired Children', Second AFASIC symposium, Specific Speech and Language Disorders in Children, Harrogate, 1992.

Leinonen E & Letts C, 'Why Pragmatic Impairment? A Case Study', European Research Symposium on Child Language Disorders, University of Amsterdam, 1994.

Leinonen E & Smith BR, 'It Takes at Least Two to Tango: Understanding Children's Communicative Success and Failure', Child Language Seminar, Hatfield Polytechnic, 1989.

Leinonen E & Smith BR, 'Appropriacy Judgements and Pragmatic Performance', *European Journal of Disorders of Communication* 29(1), pp77–84, 1994.

Leith WR, *Handbook of Clinical Methods in Communication Disorders,* NFER-Nelson Windsor, 1984.

Leonard LB, 'Facilitating Linguistic Skills in Children with Specific Language Impairment', *Applied Psycholinguistics* 2(2), pp89–118, 1981.

Leonard LB & Fey ME, 'Facilitating Grammatical Development: The Contribution of Pragmatics', Gallagher TM (ed), *Pragmatics of Language: Clinical Practice Issues,* Chapman & Hall, London, 1991.

Leonard LB, Wilcox J, Fulmer K & Davis A, 'Understanding Indirect Requests: An Investigation of Children's Comprehension of Pragmatic Meanings', *Journal of Speech & Hearing Research* 21, pp528–37, 1978.

Lesser R & Milroy L, 'Two Frontiers in Aphasia Therapy', *Bulletin of the College of Speech Therapists* 420, pp1–4, 1987.

Lesser R & Milroy L, *Linguistics and Aphasia: Psycholinguistic and Pragmatic Aspects of Intervention,* Longman, London, 1993.

Letts C, 'Linguistic Interaction in the Clinic, How do Therapists Do Therapy?', *Child Language Teaching and Therapy* 1(3), pp321–31, 1985.

Letts C, 'Exploring Therapy and Classroom Interactions', Grunwell P & James A (eds), *The Functional Evaluation of Language Disorders,* Croom Helm, London, 1989.

Levinson SC, *Pragmatics,* Cambridge University Press, Cambridge, 1983.

Lingui Systems Employees, *The Achiev (sic) Organizer Lesson Plans,* Lingui Systems, Illinois, 1990.

Lomas J, Pickard L, Bester S, Elbard H, Finlayson A & Zoghaib C, 'The Communicative Effectiveness Index: Communication Measure for Adult Aphasia', *Journal of Speech and Hearing Disorders* 54(1), pp113–24, 1989.

Longacre RE, 'The Paragraph as a Grammatical Unit', Givon T (ed), *On Understanding Grammar,* Academic Press, New York, 1979.

Lowe M, 'Trends in the Development of Representational Play in Infants from One to Three Years: An Observational Study', *Journal of Child Psychology and Psychiatry and Allied Disciplines* 16(1), pp33–47, 1975.

Lucas EV, *Semantic and Pragmatic Disorders: Assessment and Remediation,* Aspen, Rockville, 1980.

Lucas Arwood EV, *Pragmatism: Theory and Application,* Aspen, Rockville, 1983.

Lucas Arwood EV, *Semantic and Pragmatic Language Disorders,* 2nd edn, Aspen, Gaithersburg, 1991.

Lund NJ & Duchan JF, *Assessing Children's Language in Naturalistic Contexts,* Prentice-Hall, Englewood Cliffs, NJ, 1983.

Lynch C & Cooper J, *Early Communication Skills,* Winslow Press Ltd, Bicester, 1991.

MacDonald JD, *Environmental Language Inventory: A Semantic-Based Assessment and Treatment Model for Generalized Communication,* Merrill, Columbus, Ohio, 1978.

MacDonald JD, 'Language through Conversation: A Model for Intervention with

Language-Delayed Persons', Warren SF & Warren AK, *Teaching Functional Language*, Pro-Ed, Austin, Texas, 1985.

MacDonald JD & Gillette Y, *Ecological Communication System*, Harcourt Brace Jovanovich Inc, San Antonio, 1986.

MacDonald JD & Gillette Y, 'Communicating Partners: A Conversational Model for Building Parent-Child Relationships with Handicapped Children', Marfo K (ed), *Parent-Child Interaction and Development Disabilities: Theory Research and Intervention*, Praeger Publishers, New York, 1988.

Mackay G & Dunn W, *Early Communication Skills*, Routledge, London, 1989.

MacLaughlin ML, *Conversation: How Talk is Organized*, Sage Publications, New York, 1984.

MacWhinney B, 'Constraints on Learning as Default Assumptions: Comments on Merriman's and Bowman's "The Mutual Exclusivity Bias in Children's Word Learning"', *Developmental Review* 11(2), pp192–4, 1991.

Matson JL & Ollendick TH, *Enhancing Children's Social Skills: Assessment and Training*, Pergamon Press, New York, 1990.

McCrea Cochrane R, 'Language and the Atmosphere of Delight', Winitz H (ed), *Treating Language Disorders: For Clinicians by Clinicians*, pp143–62, University Park Press, Baltimore, 1983.

McCune-Nicholich L, 'The Cognitive Bases of Relational Words in the Single Word Period', *Journal of Child Language* 8, pp15–34, 1981.

McDevitt TM & Ford M, *Processes in Young Children's Communicative Functioning and Development*, Lawrence Erlbaum Associates, Hillsdale, New Jersey, 1987.

McLean JE & Snyder-McLean L, *A Transactional Approach to Early Language Training*, Merrill, Columbus, Ohio, 1978.

McLean JE & Snyder-McLean L, 'Application of Pragmatics to Severely Mentally Retarded Children and Youth', Schiefelbusch RL & Lloyd LL (eds), *Language Perspectives: Acquisition Retardation and Intervention*, Pro-Ed, Texas, 1988.

McNeill D, 'Developmental Psycholinguistics', Smith F & Muller GA (eds), *The Genesis of Language*, pp15–84, MIT Press, Cambridge, Mass, 1966.

McTear M, 'Structure and Process in Children's Conversational Development', Kuczaj SA (ed), *Discourse Development: Progress in Cognitive Development Research*, Springer-Verlag, New York, 1984.

McTear M, *Children's Conversation*, Blackwells, Oxford, 1985a.

McTear M, 'Pragmatic Disorders: A Question of Direction', *British Journal of Disorders of Communication* 20(2), pp119–27, 1985b.

McTear M, 'Pragmatic Disorders: A Case Study of Conversational Disability', *British Journal of Disorders of Communication* 20(2), pp129–42, 1985c.

McTear M, 'Is There Such a Thing as Conversational Disability?' Mogford-Bevan K & Sadler J (eds), *Child Language Disability 2: Semantic & Pragmatic Difficulties*, Multilingual Matters, Clevedon, 1991.

McTear M & Conti-Ramsden G, 'Assessment of Pragmatics', Grundy K (ed), *Linguistics in Clinical Practice*, Taylor & Francis, London, 1992a.

McTear M & Conti-Ramsden G, *Pragmatic Disability in Children*, Whurr, London, 1992b.

Marquis MA, *Creatures and Critters: Barrier Games for Referential Communication*, Communication Skill Builders, Tucson, Arizona, 1992.

Marquis MA & Lewis NP, *Familiar Actions and Objects: A Go-Fish Card Game for Early Development*, Communication Skill Builders, Tucson, Arizona, 1992.

Matterson E, *Play with a Purpose for Under-Sevens*, Penguin, London, 1989.

Menyuk P, Liebergott JW & Schultz MC, *Early Language Development in Full-Term and Premature Infants*, Lawrence Erlbaum Associates, Hillsdale, New Jersey, 1995.

Mey JL, *Pragmatics: An Introduction*, Blackwell, Oxford, 1994a.

Mey JL, 'How to Do Good Things With Words: A Social Pragmatics for Survival', *Pragmatics* 4(2), pp239–63, 1994b.

Michelson L, Mannarino AP, Marchione K, Stern M, Figueroa J & Beck S, 'A Comparative Outcome Study of Behavioural Social Skills Training, Interpersonal Problem Solving and Non-Directive Control Treatments with Child Psychiatric Outpatients: Process, Outcome and Generalization Effects', *Behaviour Research and Therapy* 21, pp545–56, 1983a.

Michelson L, Sugai DP, Wood RP & Kazain AE, *Social Skills Assessment and Training with Children: An Empirically-Based Handbook*, Plenum Press, New York, 1983b.

Miller GA, *Spontaneous Apprentices: Children and Language*, The Seabury Press, New York, 1977.

Miller JF, Chapman R, Branston M & Reichle J, 'Language Comprehension in Sensory Stages 5 and 6', *Journal of Speech and Hearing Research* 23, pp284–311, 1980.

Miller N, 'Strategies of Language Use in Assessment and Therapy for Acquired Dysphasia', Grunwell P & James A (eds), *The Functional Evaluation of Language Disorders*, Croom Helm, London, 1989.

Milroy L & Perkins L, 'Repair Strategies in Aphasic Discourse: Towards a Collaborative Model', *Clinical Linguistics and Phonetics* 6(1), pp27–40, 1992.

Mogford-Bevan K & Sadler J (eds), *Child Language Disability Vol 2: Semantic and Pragmatic Difficulties*, Multilingual Matters, Clevedon, 1991.

Morris C, 'Signs, Language and Behavior',

Morris-Smith J, *Speech Therapy in Practice* 5(7), 1989.

Morris-Smith C, 'How to Diagnose the Child with HLLD', *Speech Therapy in Practice* 5(7), p15, 1989.

Mosley J, 'An Evaluative Account of the Working of a Dramatherapy Peer Support Group within a Comprehensive School', *Support for Learning* 6(4), pp156–64, 1994a.

Mosley J, 'Developing Self-Esteem', *Special Children* 74 (Back to Basics 12), 1994b.

Muma JR, 'Speech and Language Pathology: Emerging Clinical Expertise in Language', Gallagher TM & Prutting CA (eds), *Pragmatic Assessment and Intervention Issues in Language*, College-Hill, San Diego, 1983.

Myers Pease D, Berko-Gleason J & Pan BA, 'Learning the Meaning of Words: Semantic Development and Beyond', Berko-Gleason J (ed), *The Development of Language*, MacMillan, New York, 1993.

National Oracy Project, *'Talk' Documents*, National Curriculum Council, London, 1991–1993.

Nelson K, *Making Sense: The Acquisition of Shared Meaning*, Academic Press, London, 1985.

Nelson K, *Narratives from the Crib*, Harvard University Press, Cambridge, Mass, 1989.

Newson E, 'The Barefoot Play Therapist: Adapting Skills for a Time of Need', Lane DA & Miller A (eds), *Child and Adolescent Therapy, a Handbook*, Open University Press, Milton Keynes, 1992.

Nicolski L, Harryman E & Kresheck J, *Terminology of Communication Disorders: Speech-Language-Hearing*, 3rd edn, Williams & Wilkins, Baltimore, 1989.

Nind M & Hewett D, *Access to Communication: Developing the Basics of Communication with People with Severe Learning Difficulties through Intensive Interaction*, David Fulton, 1994.

Ninio A & Bruner JS, 'The Achievements and Antecedents of Labelling', *Journal of Child Language* 5, pp1–15, 1978.

Ochs E & Schieffelin BB (eds), *Developmental Pragmatics*, Academic Press, New York, 1979.

Odom S & McConnell S, *Play Time/Social Time: Organizing Your Classroom to Build Interaction Skills*, Communication Skill Builders, Tucson, Arizona, 1992.

Owens RE, *Language Development: An Introduction*, MacMillan, New York, 1992.

Panagos JM, Bobkoff K & Scott CM, 'Discourse Analysis of Language Intervention', *Child Language Teaching and Therapy* 2(2), pp211–29, 1986.

Panagos JM, Bobkoff-Katz K, Kovarskey D & Paul R, *Pragmatic Activities for Language Intervention: Semantics, Syntax and Emerging Language*, Communication Skill Builders, Tucson, 1992.

Paul R, 'Comprehension Strategies: Interactions between World Knowledge and the Development of Sentence Comprehension', *Topics in Language Disorders* 10(3), pp63–75, 1990.

Paul R, *Pragmatic Activities for Language Intervention: Semantics, Syntax and Emerging Literacy,* Communication Skill Builders, Tucson, Arizona, 1992.

Paul R & Shiffer S, 'Communicative Intentions in Normal and Late Talking Toddlers', *Applied Psycholinguistics* 12(4), pp419–31, 1991.

Paul R & Smith RL, 'Narrative Skills in 4-year-olds with Normal, Impaired and Late Developing Language', *Journal of Speech & Hearing Research* 36(3), pp592–8, 1993.

Peery JC & Stern DN, 'Gaze Duration Frequency Distributions during Mother-infant Interaction', *Journal of Genetic Psychology* 129(1), pp45–55, 1976.

Pellegrini AD, *Applied Child Study: A Developmental Approach,* Lawrence Erlbaum Associates, Hillsdale, New Jersey, 1987.

Penn C, 'The Profiling of Syntax and Pragmatics in Aphasia', *Clinical Linguistics and Phonetics* 2(3), pp179–207, 1988.

People First, *Oi! It's My Assessment, Why Not Listen to Me?*, People First, London, 1991.

Pevner ZS, *Communication Workshop*, Lingui Systems, Illinois, 1986.

Phillips D, *How to Give Your Child a Great Self-Image,* Plume, New York, 1991.

Piaget J, *The Language and Thought of the Child*, The World Publishing Co, Cleveland, Ohio, 1955. (Originally published in French, 1923.)

Pine JM, 'The Language of Primary Caregivers', Gallaway C & Richards BJ (eds), *Input and Interaction in Language Acquisition,* Cambridge University Press, Cambridge, 1994.

Pinney R, *Children's Hours: Special Times for Listening to Children,* Spider Web, 1985.

Powell S & Jordan R, 'Being Subjective About Autistic Thinking and Learning to Learn', *Educational Psychology* 13(3–4), pp359–70, 1993.

Prelock PA, 'The Non-Verbal Component of Clinical Lessons', *Child Language Teaching and Therapy* 4(3), pp278–96, 1988.

Prinz P & Weiner F, *The Pragmatics Screening Test,* The Psychological Corporation, Ohio, 1987.

Prutting CA, 'Pragmatics as Social Competence', *Journal of Speech and Hearing Disorders* 47(2), pp123–34, 1982.

Prutting CA & Kirchner DM, 'Applied Pragmatics', Gallagher TM & Prutting CA (eds), *Pragmatic Assessment and Intervention Issues in Language,* College-Hill, San Diego, 1983.

Prutting CA & Kirchner DM, 'A Clinical Appraisal of the Pragmatic Aspects of

Language', *Journal of Speech and Language Disorders* 52(2), pp105–19, 1987.

Pynte J, Girotto V & Baccino T, 'Children's Communicative Abilities Revisited: Verbal Versus Perceptual Disambiguating Strategies in Referential Communication', *Journal of Child Language* 18(1), pp191–213, 1991.

Rapin I & Allen D, 'Development Language Disorders: Nosologic Considerations', Kirk U (ed), *Neuropsychology of Language, Reading & Spelling,* Academic Press, New York, 1983.

Rapin I & Allen D, 'Developmental Dysphasia and Autism in Pre-School Children: Characteristics and Sub-Types', *Proceedings of the First International Symposium on Specific Speech and Language Disorders in Children,* University of Reading, AFASIC, London, 1987.

Ratner N & Bruner J, 'Games, Social Exchange and the Acquisition of Language', *Journal of Child Language* 5, pp391–402, 1978.

Redwood H & Bracher Y, 'Investigating Special Time', *Bulletin of the College of Speech and Language Therapists,* June, 1993.

Renfrew C, *Word Finding Vocabulary Test,* 4th edn, Winslow Press, Bicester, 1995.

Renfrew C, *The Bus Story,* 4th edn, Winslow Press, Bicester, 1997.

Retherford Stickler K & Cannon L, 'Variations in Children's Language Performance During Two Different Activities', Poster presented at the American Speech and Hearing conference, San Francisco, 1984.

Reynell J, *Reynell Development Language Scales,* NFER-Nelson, Windsor, 1977.

Rice ML, Sell MA & Hadley PA, 'The Social Interactive Coding System (SICS): An On-line, Clinically Relevant Descriptive Tool', *Language, Speech and Hearing Services in Schools* 21(1), pp2–14, 1990.

Richards BJ, *Language Development and Individual Differences: A Study of Auxiliary Verb Learning,* Cambridge University Press, Cambridge, 1990.

Richards BJ & Gallaway C, 'Input and Interaction in Child Language Acquisition', Asher RE & Simpson JMY (eds), *The Encyclopedia of Language and Linguistics,* Pergamon, Oxford, 1993.

Richards BJ & Robinson WP, 'Environmental Correlates of Child Copula Verb Growth', *Journal of Child Language* 20, pp343–62, 1993.

Richardson TM & Foster SL, 'Teacher Measures for Assessing Children's Social Skills', *Association for Child Psychology and Psychiatry Review and News Letter* 16(4), pp198–205, 1994.

Rinaldi W, *Social Use of Language Programme: Enhancing the Social Communication of Children and Teenagers with Special Needs,* NFER-Nelson, Windsor, 1992.

Ripich DN, 'Building Classroom Communication Competence: A Case for a Multiperspective Approach', *Seminars in Speech and Language* 10(3), pp231–40.

Ripich DN & Panagos JM, 'Accessing Children's Knowledge of Sociolinguistic Rules for Speech Therapy Lessons', *Journal of Speech and Hearing Disorders* 50, pp335–46, 1985.

Ripich DN & Spinelli FM, 'An Ethnographic Approach to Assessment and Intervention', Ripich DN & Spinelli FM (eds), *School Discourse Problems,* Taylor & Francis, London, 1985.

Robinson E & Robinson W, 'Children's Explanations of Communication Failure and the Inadequacy of the Misunderstood Message', *Developmental Psychology* 13, pp156–61, 1977.

Robinson E & Robinson W, 'Development of Understanding About Communication: Message Inadequacy and its Role in Causing Communication Failure', *Genetic Psychological Monographs* 98, pp233–79, 1978.

Robinson E & Robinson W, 'The Relationship Between Children's Explanations of Communication Failure and their Ability Deliberately to Give Bad Messages', *British Journal of Social and Clinical Psychology* 17, pp219–25, 1981.

Robinson EJ & Robinson WP, 'The Young Child's Understanding of Communication', *Development Psychology* 12(4), pp328–33, 1976.

Rochester S & Martin JR, *Crazy Talk: a Study of the Discourse of Schizophrenic Speakers,* Plenum Press, New York, 1979.

Rosenbeck J, La Pointe LL & Wertz R, *Aphasia: a Clinical Approach,* College-Hill, Boston, 1989.

Rosetti L, *The Rosetti Infant-Toddler Language Scale: A Measure of Communication and Interaction,* Lingui Systems, Illinois, 1990.

Roth F & Spekman N, 'Assessing the Pragmatic Abilities of Children Part 1: Organizational Framework and Assessment Parameters', *Journal of Speech & Hearing Disorders* 49(1), pp2–11, 1984a.

Roth F & Spekman N, 'Assessing the Pragmatic Abilities of Children. Part 2: Guidelines, Considerations and Specific Evaluation Procedures', *Journal of Speech and Hearing Disorders* 49(1), pp12–17, 1984b.

Row V, 'An Interactive Therapy Group', *Child Language Teaching and Therapy* 9(2), pp133–40, 1993.

Rustin L, *Assessment and Therapy Programme for Dysfluent Children,* NFER-Nelson, Windsor, 1987.

Rutter M, 'Social/Emotional Consequences of Day Care for Pre-School Children', *American Journal of Orthopsychiatry,* 1981.

Rutter M, 'Annotation: Child Psychiatric Disorders in ICD 10', *Journal of Child Psychology & Psychiatry* 30(4), pp499–513, 1989.

Rutter M, *Maternal Deprivation Reassessed,* Penguin, London, 1991.

Ryan T & Walker R, *Life Story Work*, British Agencies for Adoption and Fostering, London, 1993.

Sachs J, 'Children's Play and Communicative Development', Schiefelbusch RI & Pickar J (eds), *The Aquisition of Communicative Competence*, University Park Press, Baltimore, 1984.

Sachs J, Anselmi D & McCollam K, 'Young Children's Awareness of Presuppositions Based on Community Membership', paper presented at the 5th International Congress for the Study of Child Language, Budapest, Hungary, 1990.

Sacks H, Schegloff E & Jefferson G, 'A Simplest Systemics for the Organization of Turn-Taking in Conversation', *Language* 50, pp696–735, 1974.

Sahlén B & Nettelbladt U, 'Context and Comprehension: a Neurolinguistic and Interactional Approach to the Understanding of Semantic–Pragmatic Disorder', *European Journal of Disorders of Communication* 28(2), pp117–40, 1993.

Sarno MT, *The Functional Communication Profile,* Institute of Rehabilitation Medicine, New York University Medical Centre, 1969.

Schaffer HR, *Studies in Mother-Infant Interaction*, pp427–55, Academic Press, New York, 1977.

Schiefelbusch RL, 'Afterword. Assisting Children to Become Communicatively Competent', Schiefelbusch RL & Pickar J (eds), *The Acquisition of Communicative Competence*, University Park Press, Baltimore, 1984.

Schwartz S, 'Is There a Schizophrenic Language?', *Behavioral and Brain Sciences* 5, pp579–623, 1982.

Searle J, *Speech Acts: An Essay in the Philosophy of Language*, Cambridge University Press, Cambridge, 1969.

Searle J, 'A Taxonomy of Illocutionary Acts', Gunderson K (ed), *Language, Mind and Knowledge*, University of Minnesota Press, pp344-69, 1975a.

Searle J, 'Indirect Speech Acts', Cole P & Morgan J (eds), *Syntax and Semantics 3 Speech Acts*, pp59–82, Academic Press, New York, 1975b.

Seibert JM & Oller DK, 'Linguistic Pragmatics and Language Intervention Strategies', *Journal of Autism and Developmental Disorders* 11(1), 1981.

Semel E, Wiig E & Secord W, *Clinical Evaluation of Language Fundamentals,* Harcourt Brace, London, 1993.

Shatz M, 'Theory of Mind and the Development of Social Linguistic Intelligence in Early Childhood', Lewis C & Mitchell P (eds), *Children's Early Understanding of Mind: Origins and Development,* pp311–29, Lawrence Erlbaum Associates, Hove, 1994.

Shatz M & Gelman R, 'The Development of Communication Skills: Modifications in the Speech of Young Children as a Functioner of Listener', *Monographs of the Society for Research in Child Development* 38(5,152), pp1–37, 1973.

Shields J, 'Semantic–Pragmatic Disorder: A Right Hemisphere Syndrome?', *British Journal of Disorders of Communication* 26 (3), pp383–92, 1991.

Shulman BB, *Test of Pragmatic Skills*, Communication Skill Builders, Arizona, 1985.

Simon CS, *Communicative Competence: a Functional-Pragmatic Approach to Language Therapy*, Communication Skill Builders, Arizona, 1980.

Simon CS (ed), *Communication Skills and Classroom Success: Therapy Methodologies for Language–Learning Disabled Students*, Taylor & Francis, Basingstoke, 1985a.

Simon CS (ed), *Communication Skills and Classroom Success: Assessment of Language–Learning Disabled Students*, Taylor & Francis, Basingstoke, 1985b.

Simon CS, *Evaluating Communicative Competence: A Functional Pragmatic Procedure*, Communication Skill Builders, Arizona, 1986.

Sims A, *Symptoms in the Mind: An Introduction to Descriptive Psychopathology*, Ballière Tindall, London, 1988.

Skinner C, Wirz S, Thompson I & Davidson J, *Edinburgh Functional Communication Profile*, Winslow Press, Bicester, 1984, out of print.

Smedley M, 'Semantic–Pragmatic Language Disorder: a Description With Some Practical Suggestions for Teachers', *Child Language Teaching and Therapy* 5(2), pp174–90, 1989.

Smith BR, 'Pragmatics and Speech Pathology', Ball M (ed), *Theoretical Linguistics and Disordered Language*, Croom Helm, London, 1988.

Smith BR, 'Communication Therapy: The Application of Pragmatics and Discourse Analysis to the Work of Speech Pathologists', Grunwell P & James A (eds), *The Functional Evaluation of Language Disorders,* Croom Helm, London, 1989.

Smith BR & Leinonen E, *Clinical Pragmatics: Unravelling the Complexities of Communicative Failure*, Chapman & Hall, London, 1992.

Smith L, 'Communicative Activities of Dysphasic Adults: A Survey', *British Journal of Disorders of Communication* 20(1), pp31–44, 1985.

Smith MM, 'Speech by Any Other Name: The Role of Communication Aids in Interaction', *European Journal of Disorders of Communication* 29(3), pp225–40, 1994.

Snow CE, 'The Development of Conversation between Mothers and Babies', *Journal of Child Language* 4, pp1–22, 1977.

Snow CE, 'Conversations with Children', Fletcher P & Garman M (eds), *Language*

Snow CE, *Acquisition,* Cambridge University Press, Cambridge, 1979.

Snow CE, 'Parent–Child Interaction and the Development of Communicative Ability', Schiefelbusch RL & Pickar J (eds), *The Acquisition of Communicative Competence,* University Park Press, Baltimore, 1984.

Snow CE, 'Beginning from Baby Talk: Twenty Years of Research Input in Interaction', Gallaway C & Richards BJ (eds), *Input and Interaction in Language Acquisition,* Cambridge University Press, Cambridge, 1994.

Snow CE, 'Issues in the Study of Input: Fine Tuning, Universality, Individual and Developmental Differences and Necessary Courses', MacWhinney B & Fletcher P (eds), *Handbook of Child Language,* Blackwell, Oxford, 1995.

Snow CE & Fergusson C (eds), *Talking to Children: Language Input and Acquisition,* Cambridge University Press, Cambridge, 1977.

Snow CE, Midkif-Borunda S, Small A & Proctor A, 'Therapy as Social Interaction: Analysing the Context for Language Remediation', *Topics in Language Disorders* 4(4), pp72–85, 1984.

Snow CE, Perlmann RY, Gleason JB & Hooshyar N, 'Development Perspectives on Politeness: Sources of Children's Knowledge', *Journal of Pragmatics* 14, pp289–305, 1990.

Snyder LS & Sylverstein J, 'Pragmatics and Child Language Disorders', Schiefelbusch RL & Loyd LL (eds), *Language Perspectives: Acquisition, Retardation and Intervention,* Pro-Ed, Texas, 1988.

Sonnenschein S & Whitehurst GJ, 'The Effects of Redundant Communications on the Behaviour of Listeners: Does a Picture Need a Thousand Words?', *Journal of Psycholinguistic Research* 11(2), pp115–25, 1982.

Sparrevohn R & Howie PM, 'Theory of Mind in Children with Autistic Disorder: Evidence of Development Progression and the Role of Verbal Ability', *Journal of Child Psychology, Psychiatry and Allied Disciplines* 36(2), pp249–63, 1995.

Spence L, Fleetwood A, Geliot J, Wrench B, Earls L & Searby C, 'A Descriptive Study of a Sub-Group of Moor House Children with High Level Semantic Difficulties', Grunwell P & James A (eds), *The Functional Evaluation of Language Disorders,* Croom Helm, London, 1989.

Spence R & Hitchens A, 'Assessing the Pragmatic Skills of People with Learning Disabilities', *Human Communication* 1(3), pp18–20, 1992.

Starratt Myrers P (ed), 'Right Hemisphere Impairment', Holland AL, *Language Disorders in Adults: Recent Advances,* College-Hill, San Diego, 1984.

Steckol D, 'Are We Training Young Language Delayed Children for Future Academic Failure?', Winitz H (ed), *Treating Language Disorders: For Clinicians by Clinicians,* University Park Press, Baltimore, 1983.

Steel G, 'Life's a Beach: Running Groups for School Age Children with Semantic-Pragmatic Disorder', *Bulletin of the Royal College of Speech and Language Therapists* 519, pp12–13, 1995.

Stenhouse G, *Confident Children: Develop Your Child's Self-Esteem,* Oxford University Press, Oxford, 1994.

Stephens MI, 'Pragmatics', Nippold MA (ed), *Later Language Development Ages Nine through Nineteen,* Pro-Ed, Austin, Texas, 1988.

Stern DN, 'Mother and Infant at Play: The Dyadic Interaction Involving Family Behaviours', Lewis M & Rosenblum LA (eds), *The Effect of the Infant on its Carer,* Wiley, New York, 1974.

Stern DN, *The First Relationship: Infant and Mother,* Fontana Open Books, London, 1977.

Stern DN, 'The Development of Biologically Determined Signals of Readiness to Communicate which are Language "Resistant"', Stark R (ed), *Language Behaviour in Infancy and Early Childhood,* Elsevier/North Holland, New York, 1981.

Stern D, Jaffe J, Beebe B & Bennett SL, 'Vocalizing in Unison and in Alternation: Two Modes of Communication within the Mother-Infant Dyad', *Annals of the New York Academy of Sciences* 263, pp89–100, 1975.

Stott DA, *Studies of Troublesome Children,* Tavistock, London, 1966.

Strain PS, Shores RE & Timm MA, ' Effects of Peer Social Initiations on the Behaviour of Withdrawn Pre-school Children', *Journal of Applied Behaviour Analysis* 10(2), pp289–98, 1977.

Stubbs DR, *Assertiveness at Work: A Necessary Guide to an Essential Skill,* Pan Books, London, 1986.

Stubbs M, *Discourse Analysis: The Sociolinguistic Analysis of Natural Language,* Blackwell, Oxford, 1983.

Stutzman Graser N, *125 Ways to be a Better Listener, a Program for Listening Success,* Lingui Systems, Illinois, 1992.

Tannen D, 'Gender Differences in Topical Coherence: Creating Involvement in Best Friends Talk' (Special issue: Gender and conversational interaction), *Discourse Processes* 13(1), pp73–90, 1990.

Tannen D, *Gender and Conversational Interaction,* Oxford University Press, New York, 1993.

Tantum D, 'Asperger's Syndrome', *Journal of Child Psychology and Psychiatry,* 29(3) pp245–55, 1988.

Taylor B, 'A Pragmatic Approach to the Pre-School Child with Specific Language Impairment', *Human Communication* 1(3), pp15–16, 1992.

Terrell B, Schwartz R, Prelock P & Mesick C, 'Symbolic Play in Normal and Language-

Impaired Children', *Journal of Speech and Hearing Research* 27, pp424–30, 1984.

Tizard B & Hughes M, *Young Children Learning: Talking and Thinking at Home and at School*, Fontana, London, 1984.

Toomey M, *Teaching Kids of All Ages to Ask Questions,* Circuit Publications, Marblehead, Mass, 1994a.

Toomey M, *Telling a Story,* Circuit Publications, Marblehead, Mass, 1994b.

Tough J, *The Development of Meaning: A Study of Children's Use of Language*, Allen & Unwin, London, 1977a.

Tough J, *Talking & Learning: A Guide to Fostering Communication Skills in Nursery & Infant Schools*, Ward Lock, London, 1977b.

Trevarthen CT, 'Communication and Co-operation in Early Infancy: A Description of Primary Intersubjectivity', Bullowa M (ed), *Before Speech*: *The Beginning of Interpersonal Communication*, pp321–47, Cambridge University Press, Cambridge, 1979.

Ulatowska HK & Bond SA, 'Aphasia: Discourse Considerations', *Topics in Language Disorders* 3(4), pp21–48, 1983.

Van Hasselt VB, 'A Behavioural-Analytic Model for Assessing Social Skills in Blind Adolescents', *Behaviour Research and Therapy* 23(4), pp395–405, 1985.

Van der Gaag A, *CASP*, Speech Profiles Ltd, London, 1988.

Varni JW & Corwin DC, *Growing Up Great: Positive Solutions for Raising Confident, Self-Assured Children*, Berkley Books, New York, 1996.

Vygotsky LS, *Thought & Language*, The MIT Press, Cambridge, Mass, 1962.

Vygotsky LS, *Mind and Society*, Harvard University Press, Cambridge, Mass, 1978.

Walsh J, *Let's Make Friends*, Souvenir Press, London, 1986.

Warner J, Byers-Brown B & McCartney E, *Speech Therapy: A Clinical Companion*, Manchester University Press, Manchester, 1984.

Warren AR & McCloskey LA, 'Pragmatics: Language in Social Contexts', Berko-Gleason J (ed), *The Development of Language*, MacMillan, New York, 1993.

Warren SF & Rogers-Warren AK, *Teaching Functional Language: Generalization and Maintenance of Language Skills,* Pro-Ed, Austin, Texas, 1985.

Watt S, *Simply Silly About Sentences,* Mayer-Johnson, Solana Beach, California, 1994.

Weintraub S & Mesulam MM, 'Developmental Learning Disabilities of the Right Hemisphere: Emotional, Interpersonal and Cognitive Components', *Archives of Neurology* 40, pp463–8, 1983.

Weiss R, 'INREAL Intervention for Language Handicapped and Bilingual Children', *Journal of the Division of Early Childhood* 4, pp463–8, 1981.

Wells G, 'Adjustments in Adult–Child Conversation: Some Effects of Interaction', Giles H (ed), *Language: Social Psychological Perspectives*, Pergamon Press, London, 1980.

Wells G, *Learning through Interaction: the Study of Language Development*, Cambridge University Press, Cambridge, 1981.

Wells G, 'Language Development in the Pre-school Years', *Language at Home and at School* 2, Cambridge University Press, Cambridge, 1985.

Westby CE, van Dongen R & Maggart Z, 'Assessing Narrative Competence', *Seminars in Speech and Language* 10(1), pp63–76, 1989.

Wetherby AM & Prizant BM, 'The Expression of Communicative Intent: Assessment Guidelines', *Seminars in Speech and Language* 10(1), pp77–91, 1989.

Weybright G & Rosenthal Tanzer J, *Putting it into Words: An Introduction to Indirect Language Stimulation,* Communication Skill Builders, Tucson, Arizona, 1986.

Whitehurst GJ & Fischel JE, 'Early Developmental Language Delay: What, If Anything, Should the Clinician Do About It?', *Journal of Child Psychology and Psychiatry* 35(4), pp613–648, 1994.

Wiig EH & Secord W, 'Linguistic Competence in Early Adolescents with Learning Difficulties: Assessing and Developing Strategies for Learning and Socialization', Levine MD & McAnarney ER (eds), *Early Adolescent Transitions*, pp209–26, Lexington Books, Lexington, Mass, 1988.

Wiig EH & Semel E, *Language Assessment and Intervention*, 2nd edn, Merrill, Ohio, 1984.

Wilcox MJ & Webster EJ, 'Early Discourse Behaviour: An Analysis of Children's Responses to Listener Feedback', *Child Development* 51(4), pp1120–5, 1980.

Wilkinson J & Canter S, *Social Skills Training Manual*, Wiley, Chichester, 1982.

Williams D, *Nobody Nowhere,* Corgi, London, 1992.

Wing L, 'The Continuum of Autistic Characteristics', Schopler E & Mesibov GB (eds), *Diagnosis and Assessment in Autism*, Plenum, New York, 1988.

Winitz H (ed), *Treating Language Disorders: For Clinicians by Clinicians*, University Park Press, Baltimore, 1983.

Wirz S, 'The Pragmatics of Language and the Mentally Handicapped', Fraser W & Grieve R (eds), *Communicating with Normal and Retarded Children*, John Wright, Bristol, 1981.

Wolff S & McGuire RJ, 'Schizoid Personality in Girls: A Follow-up Study – What are the Links with Asperger's Syndrome?', *Journal of Child Psychology & Psychiatry* 36(5), pp793–818, 1995.

Wood D, Wood H, Griffiths A & Howarth I, *Teaching and Talking with Deaf Children*, Wiley & Sons, Chichester, 1986.

Index

A

Aarons and Gittens, literature review 135
Abbeduto and Rosenberg, literature review 135
abilities
   lack of demonstration of 39-40
   not being used 127
abuse 39, 128
   touching clients, clinical policies 78
accepting communication difficulty 73, 123-4
accountability 38, 65
actions, describing 81-2
activities
   effect on communication 33, 39, 40-1, 93
      type of, percentage use of communicative functions 17, *18*
   facilitating pragmatic development 92-106
      crafts, construction and home skills 93, 94, 103
      drama and role-play 94, 98-9
         see also role-play
      drawing 94, 101-2
      music 94, 100
      narrative 94, 98, 104-6
      play 93-4, 95-7
      symbolic 71-2, 93-4, 95, 96
Adams and Bishop, literature review 135
addition 82
adults
   assessment 44
      interviews 48-9
   contexts for working on pragmatics
      crafts, construction and home skills 103
      drama 99
      drawing 102
      musical activities 100
      narrative 106
      play 97
   dysphasia 127, 129
      assessments 45, 51
      functional communication 64
      modelled communicative acts 89
   interaction with infants 18, 19, 22
   pragmatic skills 24
   relationship building 77
advanced communication 92-3
      see also adults; older children
   communication facilitation techniques 83-4
amateur dramatics companies 99
appendices
   child information sheet 143
   client information sheet 144
   client-centred assessment questionnaire 141-2
   literature review 135-40
art therapy 102
articulatory problems 126
Asperger's syndrome 13, 34, 35
   literature reviews 135, 140
assertiveness
   communicatively impaired children 3
   training 65, 73, 107, 121-2, 131
      content 121-2
      teaching techniques 121
assessment 37-45
   definition of pragmatics 38
   depth of 41-2
   formal 38, 42-5, 48
      adults and older children 44, 48-9
      pre-linguistic clients up to school age 43-4
      school-age children within classroom 44
   informal 38, 47-61
   methods of 42
   multidisciplinary teams 67, 76
   problems in 38-42
   production 43-5
   reasons for 38
   variety of contexts 10
assessor, influence of 39
assistants, group work 112
Association for All Speech Impaired Children (AFASIC) 3
associative noises/gestures 81
attention
   control 64, 132
   difficulties 110
   disorders 132
   sharing 77-8, 81, 130
audio recordings 49, 84
auditory
   discrimination 64
   trainers 126
authority figures, addressing 41
autism 28, 34, 35, 129, 131
   discourse of empathy 13
   literature reviews 135, 136, 140
avoidance strategies 29

B

barrier referential communication games 122-3
baseline, establishing 38
behaviour
   appropriate, inconsistencies in 16-17, 39
   as communication 78
   assertive 122
   communicative partners 32-3
   components of 113
   directive 86, 87
   discouraging immature 124
   initiating and response 6, 135
      IREC completion 52
   observation of pragmatic, McTear assessment 43
   search 29
   unsuitable 89
      severely disruptive 110, 112, 130
The Behavioural Inventory of Speech Act Performances (BISAP) 44
behaviourist approaches 65-6
   advantages 65
   disadvantages 65-6
beliefs, assertive 122
Beveridge and Conti-Ramsden, literature review 136
bibliography 146-59
Bishop and Adams, literature review 136
Bishop, literature review 136
Blank and Marquis, school age assessment 44
board games 96
The Boehm Test of Basic Concepts 42
brain damage, literature review 137

brainstorming 113
Brinton and Fujiki 12
   assessment, adults and older children 45
      presuppositional forms 21
      topic skills 19
Bristol Language Development Scales 43
British Journal of Disorders of Communication 136
British Picture Vocabulary Scales (BPVS) 42
'broken record technique' 122
Browning, literature review 136
Brown's
   stage I-III, clarification and repair 19
   stage I-V, topic skills 19
   stage V, use of language 17, 18
Bryan, assessment of adult dysphasia 45
Bus Story Test 44
Byers-Brown and Edwards, literature review 136

C

cake icing activity, percentage use of communicative functions 17, *18*
caregivers 6, 38, 110
   see also parents; relatives
   client abuse or neglect 128
   as communicative partners, assessing 50-7, 59, *60-1*
      analysis of style 51
      methods of assessment 51
      guidance and training 67, 77-8, 84, 128
         briefing for contexts, pragmatic work 96-106
         general principles of interaction *80*
      pre-assessment questionnaires 40, 48
      viewpoint 40
categorization and sequencing 64
causes, pragmatic difficulty 32
chalk boards 113
characteristics, effective/poor communicators 24, *25*
Child Language Disorders conference, Norway, literature review 136
CHILDES computerized database 26
clarification and repair 12
   development of 19-20, 24
   low self-esteem 130
   pragmatic impairment 29, 35
client factors, pragmatic impairment 30, 128-33
clinicians
   interaction styles, modifying 67-8, 84
   role, social learning theory 6
co-operation 8
   in play, encouraging 96
   maxims, successful speech acts 9
Coggins and Carpenter 17
   pre-linguistic assessment 43
cognitive factors, pragmatic impairment 30, 33, 131-2
   see also comprehension
   presupposition 21
coherence 10-11
   weak inner 131
cohesion 11-12
communication
   aids 8
   as feedback loop 78
   breakdowns 35
   facilitation techniques (CFTs) 80-4, 89
      complex language stage 83-4
      linguistic stage 82
      pre-linguistic stage 81-2

   on client's own terms 129
   strategies, compensatory 29, 35, 39, 123
Communication Assessment Profile (CASP) 45
communicative
   behaviour *see* behaviour
   confidence 3, 31, 33, 36, 72, 129-30
      examining 32
      story work 94
   functions 7
      Dore's 9, *10*, 17
   partners
      analyzing 53
      assessing 48, 49, 50-7
      behaviour 32-3
      communicative partner profile (CPP) 60-1
      knowledge of 41
Communicative Appropriateness 45
Communicative Effectiveness Index (CETI) 45
community drama classes 99
compensatory communication strategies 29, 35, 39
   validating 123
complex
   language stage *see* advanced communication skills, pragmatic rating scale 59
components
   of behaviour 113
   speech acts 7
comprehension
   see also cognitive factors, pragmatic impairment; interpretation, speech acts
   infants 22
      progression of 23
   inferential, literature review 136
   pragmatic
      assessment 42-3
      impairment 29-30
   semantic, assessment 42
computer work 131
concealment strategies, literature review 139
concept boundaries, rigidity of 132
concepts in pragmatics, difficulty in defining 16
confidence *see* communicative confidence
confirmation/agreement 82
conjunction 11
consent, informed 49, 50
construction tasks 93, 94, 103
contexts for working on pragmatic skills 93-106
contextual influence 9-10, 33, 39, 40-1, 50
Conti-Ramsden and Gunn, literature review 137
Conti-Ramsden, literature review 136
contingent responding 86-7, 88, 89
controlling
   covert approaches 70
   negative approach 70-1
   positive approach 68
conversation
   balance of dominance 6-7, 39
   initiating 31, 115, 124
   interactional approaches 6
   literature reviews 136, 137
   management of 9-13, 18-22
      joining in 116
      pragmatic impairment 29
      pragmatic rating scale 58
      saying the right amount 116
   managers *10*
conversational data analysis, Coggins and Carpenter 43
Coupe *et al*, assessment, learning difficulties 45

craftwork 94, 103
criticising client 11
cultural factors 17, 33, 39, 40

D

Damico, assessment, adults and older children 44
data
   collection, observational 49-59
   interview 48-9
   shortage of normative 28, 39
databases, CHILDES 26
defensiveness 131
deficits, specific 129-33
defining pragmatic concepts, difficulty in 16
deixis 11, 29
delayed and disordered speech development 126
demonstrative pronouns 21
development, pragmatic skills 15-26
   describing 17
   facilitating through activities 92-106
   future information on development 26
   normal 16-17, 17-22, 39
      adults 24
      by nine years 24
      four to five years 24
      one to two years 23
      seven to eight years 24
      six to seven years 24
      three to four years 23
      two to three years 23
      up to one year 22-3
developmental
   language disorder (DLD), subcategories
      literature review 138-9
   progression, importance of pragmatics 2
   status 92-3
      accepting and validating 124
      advanced communication level 92-3
      early communication level 92
      immaturity 128-9
      linguistic communication level 92
      treatment approaches 93
Dewart and Summers
   pre-linguistic assessment 43
   school-age assessment 44
diagnosis 32-4, 38
   accurate, educational purposes, literature
      review 135
   labels used 33-4
   misdiagnosis 12, 34
direct instruction 73, 122-3, 133
directive behaviour 86, 87
discourse tracking difficulty 133
disruption, social/emotional/family life 34-5
disruptive behaviour 110, 112
   low self-esteem 130
dolls 96, 98, 99
dominance, balance of 6-7
Donahue, literature review 137
Dore's communicative functions 9, *10*, 17, 43
drama 94, 98-9
   therapy 99
drawing 94, 101-2
dressing-up 98
drills 72-3, 122
dyadic interaction 8
dysfluency 51, 127
   non-verbal communication 64
dysphasia 127, 129

assessments 45, 51
functional communication 64
modelled communicative acts 89

E

early communication level 92, 129
   see also infants; pre-linguistic stage
   intentional communication 17
   treatment approaches 93
echolalia 29, 35, 39
Ecoscale 43
Edinburgh Functional Communication Profile 45
educational
   difficulties *see* learning difficulties
   performance, later on 3
   plans, preparation 44, 67
effect, of utterance 7
effective
   communicator, characteristics 24, *25*
   pragmatic functioning, knowledge and skills 31
effectiveness of treatment 2-3
ellipsis 11
emotion
   expressing, young children 19
   sharing 81
emotional
   disruption 34
   factors, pragmatic impairment 129-31
      and comprehension 43
empathy 13, 21
   lack of 29, 35, 132-3
'empty terms' 21, 24, 29
environment 128
   exploring 88
   optimal social 86
   positive and supportive learning 110-11
   problems within 33, 39
      doubt about safety 128
essays, incoherent 35
ethologists 26
European Journal of Disorders of
   Communication 137
expansion 82
expectancies 78
   conforming to 89
expressive pragmatic abilities 31

F

facial expression, difficulty in interpreting 13, 30, 133
facilitation and teaching 91-124
family values 17
fantasy, discussing 97
feedback
   enhancing self-esteem 130
   loop 78
   pragmatic skills training 110-11, 113, 114
   visual, difficulty in interpreting 133
felicity conditions 8, 44, 89
   development of awareness of 23
Fey and Leonard, literature review 137
figurative meanings, teaching 108
file/tape number, IREC 52
focus
   intervention, IREC use 52
   positive 35-6
formal
   assessment 38, 42-5, 48
   speech acts 7

free play, percentage use of communicative functions 17, *18*
frequency of difficulties 35
Friel-Patti and Conti-Ramsden, literature review 137
friends
   imaginary 96
   keeping 119-20
   making new 115-18
functional communication *see* intentional communication
Functional Communication Profile (FCP) 45
Functional Pragmatic Procedure 44
functions of communication 7

G

Gallagher
   clarification and repair 19-20
   literature review 137
games 96, 97
   board 96
   charades 99
   chasing 98
   interactive 78, *79*
   object-permanence 95
   referential communication 73, 122-3
   relationship building 77
   rescue 96
gender differences, politeness forms 21-2
generalization of skills
   behaviourist approaches 65
   group setting 110
   importance of pragmatics 2-3
Gentle Teaching approach 88
gestures 81
   young children 19
giving praise 130
goals
   setting through special activities 92
   social learning approaches 6
Gravell and France, literature review 137
Grice, maxims, successful speech acts 9, 20
gross motor play 95
group work
   behaviourist approaches 66
   contexts facilitating pragmatic development 92-106
     crafts, construction and home skills 103
     drama and role-play 98-9
     drawing 101, 102
     musical activities 100
     narrative 104, 105, 106
     play 96, 97
   creating compatible groups 34
   interaction styles 84
   making diagnosis during 33
   pragmatic skills training 109-14
     content of session 113-14
     group rules 112
     structure of training 111-14
'Guess Who' game 123
Gutfreund, pre-linguistic assessment 43

H

Halliday, pre-linguistic assessment 43
Hanen Program 71, 87-8
Hassibi and Breuer, literature review 137
hearing-impaired children 84
help, offering/asking for 118

Heublein and Bate, INREAL 44
high level language disorder 33, 35
   literature reviews 138, 139
Holland, assessment of adult dysphasia 45
home crafts 94, 103
   cake icing activity, percentage use of communicative functions 17, *18*
homework, pragmatic skills training 114
humour 28, 30, 33
   sharing 77
Hyde-Wright and Cray, literature review 137

I

idiomatic expressions 42
illocutionary force 7
imaginary friends 96
imagination, use of 72
   discussing fantasy 97
   symbolic activities 71-2, 93-4, 95, 96
   weak ability 132
imitation 65, 80, 81, 98
   group work 112
   infants 22
importance of pragmatics 2-3
incidental learning 103
indirect speech acts 8-9
inductive reasoning, pragmatic impairment 30, 33
infants, communicative interaction 6, 22, 77
   topic skills 19
   turn taking 18
inferences 42-3
inferential
   comprehension, literature review 136
   context 41
informal
   assessment 38, 47-61
   speech acts 7
information
   child information sheet 144
   client information sheet 145
   dissemination of, prevention work 76
   group preparation 111
   processing, cognitive maturity 21
   providing honest 131
   sharing 34, 38
informativeness 13, 21, 29
informed consent 49, 50
initiating behaviour 6, 31, 115, 124, 135
   IREC completion 52
   literature review 135
inner language 94
INREAL (Interactive Learning) 44, 51, 87
insight 35
institutionalization 32, 35, 39, 40
instructions, giving/following 122-3
integration of knowledge 8
   and behaviourist approaches 66
   development of 23
   literature review 135
   weak ability 31, 131
intensive interactive therapy 13
intentional communication 7-9
   communication facilitation techniques 82
   development of 17-18
     infants 19, 22
   facilitating speech act development 92-3
   naturalistic therapy 87-9
   pragmatic

impairment 8-9, 29
    rating scale 58
    speech act type, IREC completion 52
Interaction Record (IREC) 51
    benefits of using 51
    completing 52-3
    methods of using 52
    modifying clinician's interaction style 84
    specimens 54
        completed 55-7
interactionist approaches 6-7, 66
interactions
    facilitating, communicative partner profile 60
    general prinicples of 78, *80*
    implications for, responsive parent behaviour 79
    monitoring 12
    style of
        clinicians 67-71, 84
        pragmatic impairment 29
interactive games 78, *79*
interdisciplinary awareness, understanding origins of cohesive difficulties 12
interpretation, speech acts 8, 9, 10, 30, 42
    see also comprehension
    pragmatic impairment 30
interpretative function 17, *18*
interruption skills
    development of 18, 20
        at two to three years 23
intervention 75-89
    clarification and repair 12
    effectiveness of 2-3
    facilitation and teaching 91-124
        direct instruction 72-3, 122-3, 133
            metapragmatic awareness training 65, 72-3, 107-22
        special activities 92-106
    negotiating meanings of words 13
    past approaches 64
    performing speech acts 8
    planning and prioritizing treatment 34, 38
    principles of 63-73
        behaviourist approaches 65-6
        interactionist approaches 6-7, 66
        linguistic approaches 64-5, 93
        pragmatic intervention 66-73
        social learning approaches 6, 66
    topic handling 11
    training others and ourselves 77-85
    treatment suggestions
        specific client groups 126-7
        specific pragmatic difficulties 127-33
interview data 48-9
introductions 115
irony 33

J

Joanette and Brownell, literature review 137
Johnson, literature review 137
Johnson, Weinrich and Johnston, pre-linguistic assessment 43
Johnston, literature review 137
Journal of the Association for Child Psychology and Psychiatry 132

K

Keenan and Klein, topic skills 19
Kiernan and Reid, pre-linguistic assessment 43

knowledge
    base, pragmatic impairment 29-30
    deficits 133
    integration of 8
        and behaviourist approaches 66
        and skill, pragmatic 31, 40, 133
        development of 23
        literature review 135
        weak ability 31, 131

L

language stimulation techniques *see* communication: facilitation techniques (CFTs)
language use, teaching 105
language-delayed children 35
    Brown's stage V, use of language 17, 18
    literature review 136
learning difficulties 35, 129
    asking for clarification 12
    assessment 44, 45, 50, 51
    literature review 136-7
    modelled communicative acts 89
    social skills training 109-10
lesson plan preparation 44, 67
lexical
    cohesion 11
    knowledge and skills 42
lexical-syntactic deficit syndrome 139
linguistic
    approaches 64-5, 93
    context 41
    deficit 132
    knowledge 133
    processing, slow 131
linguistic stage 92, 93
    communication facilitation techniques 82
    contexts, working on pragmatics
        crafts, construction and home skills 103
        drama and role play 99
        drawing 102
        musical activities 100
        narrative 105
        play 96
listener needs, awareness of, pragmatic rating scale 59
listening 130
    skills 24, 26
    to music 100
    to others, making friends 117
literacy, progression from oral language 107
literal meanings 108
literature review 135-40
location
    group work 111-12
    IREC 52
locutionary aspect 7
Lomas, assessment of adult's dysphasia 45
loss of speech 127
    see also dysphasia
low involvement with others/tasks 129
Lucas
    assessment
        learning difficulties 45
        school age children 44
        literature review 137-8
Lucas Arwood, literature review 138

M

MacDonald and Gillette, pre-linguistic assessment 43
McLean and Snyder-McLean, pre-linguistic assessment 43
McTear
   literature review 138
   pre-linguistic assessment 43
McTear and Conti-Ramsden, literature review 138
'making sense', process of 7
manner, maxim of 9
maxims, successful speech acts 9, 20
meanings 12, 13
   beyond the words 7
   contextual influence 9
   implicit 33
   negotiating 13, 42
   teaching figurative and literal 108
media, using to disseminate information 76
memory 21
   problems, pragmatic impairment 30, 42, 133
      cohesive difficulties 12
mental illness 51
metapragmatic awareness 24, 107
   training 65, 72-3, 107-22
      assertiveness training 65, 72, 107, 121-2
      pragmatic skills training 72, 107, 109-20
      teaching metapragmatic awareness 72-3, 107-9
      mild pragmatic difficulties 35
misdiagnosis 12, 34
misinterpretation
   facial expression 13, 30, 133
   speech acts 9
modelled communicative acts
   client observation 89
   pragmatic skills training 95, 113
moderate pragmatic difficulties 35
modesty, making friends 117
Mogford-Bevan and Sadler, literature review 138
monitoring
   individual progress, groups 110
   interactions 12
Morris-Smith, literature review 138
motivation 32, 38
music and music therapy 94, 100

N

narrative 94, 98, 104-6
National Society for the Prevention of Cruelty to Children (NSPCC) 69, 130
naturalistic approaches 72
   aims 85-6
   benefits 86
   during pragmatic skills training 111
   facilitating speech acts 87-9
   goals 88-9
negative
   co-operative approach 71
   controlling approach 70
neurological disorders 32, 128
noises/gestures 81
non-communication in childhood 126
non-directive play therapy 96
non-facilitative strategies, communicative partner profile 60
non-symbolic activities 72
non-verbal
   behaviour 31
      as speech act 8
      IREC completion 53
   communication
      pragmatic impairment 29, 30
      pragmatic rating scale 59
normal
   development
      pattern, cohesive devices 12
      pragmatic skills 16-17, 17-26, 39
   pragmatic functioning 28
normative data, shortage of 28, 39

O

object-permanence games 95
objects
   describing 82
   encouraging functional use 95
observation 89
   data collection 49-59
      recording 49-50
   identifying feelings by 87
   Social Interactive Coding System (SICS) 43-4
   subjectivity of 39
observer, IREC completion 52
obsessions, intense 96
older children
   advanced communication 92, 93
   assessment 44
      interviews 48
   clarification 20
   development of pragmatics 24
   interaction styles, caregivers and clinicians 84
   politeness forms 22
   topic skills 19
one-way windows 50
organizations, supporting 76
orthographic transcription 53
outcomes, predicting 34
   retelling simple narratives 94
overassessment 40
'ownership of skills' 69

P

page number, IREC 52
painting and drawing 94, 101-2
paraphasia 29
parents
   see also caregivers; relatives
   educating 76
   guidance 78, 80-4
      general principles of interaction *80*
   interactive games 78, *79*
   responsiveness 78
participants, IREC completion 52
party games 96
passivity 132
pauses and silence 84
Peabody Picture Vocabulary Test (PPVT) 42
peers
   addressing 41
   keeping friends 119-20
   making new friends 115-18
pen and paper recording 49
Penn, assessment of adult dysphasia 45
performance of speech acts, reducing complexity 8
performatives *10*
perlocutionary forces 7-8

permissive approach *see* negative: co-operative approach
perseveration 29
personal
   characteristics, pragmatic impairment 30, 129
   contributions *85*
   pronouns 21
   relationships 9
      see also relationships
perspective, imagining partner's 12, 13
phatics *85*
phonetic transcription 52
phonological delay and disorder 126
photographs, use of 101
physical closeness 78
picture books 93
planning and prioritizing treatment 34, 38
play 93-4, 95-7
   percentage use, communicative functions 17, *18*
   therapy
      non-directive 96
      texts 88
playing in parallel 96
Polaroid camera, use of 101
politeness forms 17
   cultural influences 40
   knowledge and use of 21-2, 23, 33, 40
   requesting use of 93
   teaching through metapragmatic awareness 107-8
poor communicator, characteristics 24, *25*
positive
   co-operative approach 69-70
   controlling approach 68-9
post-school education and employment survey 3
Powell and Jordan, literature review 135
pragmatic
   comprehension assessment 42-3
   development *see* development, pragmatic skills
   dysfunction 8-9, 26, 27-36
      causes of difficulty 32
      concept definition 16
      contributing factors 30
      defining characteristics 28-30
      diagnosis 32-4
      difference from other communication disorders 31
      severity rating 34-6
   intervention 7, 66-73
      see also intervention
   rating scale 53, 58-9
   skills training 73, 107, 109-20
      key components 110-11
      problems 114
      specific skill format 114-20
      structure 111-14
Pragmatic Profile of Communication Skills in Childhood 44
pragmatics
   definition 2
   as field of study 16
   importance of 2-3
Pragmatics Observation List 43
The Pragmatics Profile of Early Communication Skills 43
Pragmatics Protocol 43
Pragmatics Screening Test 44
praising clients 130
pre-assessment questionnaires 40, 48

pre-linguistic stage
   assessment, clients up to school age 43-4
   communication facilitation techniques 81-2
   contexts, working on pragmatics
      crafts, construction and home skills 103
      drama and role play 98
      drawing 101
      musical activities 100
      narrative 104
      play 95
   pragmatic rating scale 58
pre-school children
   Dore's communicative functions 9, *10*
   presuppositional knowledge 20-1
Pre-verbal Communication Schedule 43
presupposition 12-13
   general assumptions 20-1
   pragmatic impairment 29
pretend friends 96
pretending 72, 93-4, 96, 98, 132
prevention 38, 67, 76-7, 89
previous conversations, reference to 11
primitive communicative acts 89
Prinz and Weiner, school-age assessment 44
production, assessment 43-5
professionals
   education and training 67, 76
   sharing information 34
Profile in Semantics (PRISM) 42
projective function, free play/cake icing activity 17, *18*
pronouns
   overuse 29
   use of 21, 35
prosody, abnormal 29
prosopagnosia 13, 30, 133
proto-words 22-3
proxemics 6
Prutting and Kirchner
   literature review 138-9
   pre-linguistic assessment 43
psychiatric
   disorders 34, 35, 121, 128
      see also autism
      psychosis 34, 35, 137
      schizoid personality 140
      schizophrenia 121
   literature, pragmatic dysfunction 28
puppets 99
   teaching metapragmatic awareness 107-8

Q

quality and quantity, maxims of 9
questionnaires
   assessment 42, 48
      alternative 143
      client-centred 141-3
   pre-assessment 40, 48
The Pragmatics Profile of Early Communication Skills 43
questions 39, 124, 132
   excessive use of
      caregiver's 52
      client's 132
   forced alternative 83
   group work 84
   rhetorical 83
   two-choice *85*
   wh- questions 83, *85*

R

range of difficulties 35
Rapin and Allen, literature review 139
rationales, pragmatic skills training 111
reality testing 97
receptive pragmatic abilities 31
recording observational data 49-50
reference
    development, appropriate use of 21, 24
    pragmatic impairment 28, 30
    to previous conversations 11
referential communication games 73, 122-3
reformulation
    complex language stage 83
    linguistic stage 82
reinforcement schedules, behaviourist approaches 65
relation, maxim of 9
relational function *18*
relationships 9, 41
    and ability to empathize 133
    building 77, 110, 129
    facilitating, communicative partner profile 60
relatives
    see also caregivers; parents
    correcting client's speech 36
    sharing information 34
    viewpoint 40
relevance 10-11
    pragmatic impairment 29
Renfrew, assessment
    school-age children 44
    semantic 42
The Renfrew Word Finding Vocabulary Test 42
repair and clarification *see* clarification and repair
repetitions 29, 82
    enforced *85*
requests *10*, 17
    development of 19-20, 23
research, field of pragmatics 16
responding, contingent 86-7, 88, 89
response
    behaviour 6
        IREC completion 52
    of others to pragmatic difficulties 36
    sensitive 11
    types of, pre-school children *10*
response/initiation (R/I) behaviour 6
    IREC completion 52
responsibility
    attributing for pragmatic difficulty 32
    client 111, 131
responsiveness 78, *79*
rhetorical questions 83
rhymes 95, 100
Rice, pre-linguistic assessment 43
right cerebral hemisphere dysfunction 32, 34, 35, 51
    literature reviews 137, 140
Right Hemisphere Language Battery 45
rigidity of thought 132
Robinson and Robinson, requesting clarification 20
role relationships, interaction 22, 41
role-play 93-4, 96, 98-9
    assertiveness training 122
    pragmatic skills training 111, 114
Roth and Spekman 7, 17
    assessment, adults and older children 44
Royal College of Speech and Language Therapists 135
rules, group work 112

S

Sahlén and Nettelbladt, literature review 139
sand play 95
Sarno, assessment of adult dysphasia 45
'scaffolding' 19
schizoid personality, literature review 140
schizophrenic clients, assertiveness training 121
school-age children
    assessment 44
    functional communication *16*, 17, 24
    literature reviews 136, 137
schools
    children at special, literature reviews 139
    failure in later educational performance 3
screening for pragmatic difficulties 38, 41
search behaviours, pragmatic impairment 29
seating arrangements, group work 112
secrets, keeping 120
self
    factors in 131
    perception of 43
    pragmatic impairment 30
self-esteem
    enhancing 51, 92, 130-1
        story work 94
    low 3, 130
semantic
    comprehension assessment 42
    impairment 2, 29, 32, 34, 94, 132
semantic-pragmatic disorder 13, 33, 35
    literature reviews 135, 136, 137, 139, 140
sequencing and categorization 64
severe pragmatic difficulties 35
severity rating 34-6
    advantages 34
    definition 34
    procedure for 34-5
Shulman, school-age assessment 44
shyness 31, 110
sign-language 8
Simon, school-age assessment 44
single word use 19
situations
    effect on communication 33, 39, 40
    interactive, observations 50
skill mixes, group work 111
Skinner, assessment of adult dysphasia 45
Smedley, literature review 139
Smith and Leinonen 17
    assessment 43
    literature review 139
social
    development, importance of pragmatics 2
    disruption 34
    environment, optimal 86
    factors 30, 32, 33, 129-31
        knowledge of roles 22, 41
        lack of knowledge 133
    learning theory approaches 6, 66
    rituals 31
    skills training 72, 109-14
    styles, teaching appropriate 108-9
Social Interactive Coding System (SICS) 43-4
sound mirrors 126

spatial awareness, pragmatic impairment 30
speaker's intention *see* illocutionary force
'Special Times' 88
speech acts *see* intentional communication
Spence *et al*, literature review 139-40
statements *10*, 83-4
states of mind, describing 81
stories 94, 104-6
stress of assessment 40
substitution 11
suggestions, making 83
support groups 131
survey, post-school education and employment 3
symbolic activities 72, 93-4, 95, 96
syntactic delays and disorders 126-7
syntax 12, 13, 41, 42

T

tactfulness 28
tangential remarks 10-11
   developmental delay 19
   pragmatic impairment 29
Teacher Ratings Scale 44
teachers 40
   behavioural principles 65
teaching
   assertiveness training 121
   metapragmatic awareness 72, 107-9
      background 107
      method 107
      politeness and friendliness rules 107-8
      using puppets 107
teasing 110, 111
television 98, 99
terminology, pragmatic impairment 33-4
Test of Communicative Abilities in Daily Living (CADL) 45
Test of Pragmatic Skills 44
Test for the Reception of Grammar (TROG) 42
theoretical approaches 5-13
   'theory of mind' 13, 23
   weak or absent 132
time allocation 128
topic 41
   handling 11, 35
      pragmatic impairment 29
   skills, development of 19
touching clients, clinical policies 78
Tough
   classification functional communication 17, *18*
   school-age assessment 44
toys 95, 96, 98
training 67-71, 77-85

metapragmatic awareness 72-3, 107-22
   other professionals 67
transcription
   sample length 51
   use of IREC 52, 53
   video recordings 49
transcripts, databank of child 26
trust, lack of 129
turn number, IREC 52
turn taking
   development of 18-19, 22, 23
   pragmatic impairment 29
'Twenty Questions' game 123

U

uterrance number, IREC 52
utterances 7

V

Van der Gaag, assessment of learning difficulties 45
verbal communication, IREC completion 52-3
video recordings 49, 84, 99, 111, 132
   communicative partner assessment 51
video-relaying facilities 50
visual
   approaches 126
   awareness, encouraging 101
   feedback, difficulty in interpreting 133
visually handicapped, assertiveness training 121
voice problems 127
   volumes 108
Vygotsky, social learning 6

W

water play 93, 95
Weatherby and Prizant, pre-linguistic assessment 43
Weintraub and Mesulam, literature review 140
Weiss, INREAL 44
welcoming clients, group work 113
wide-angled lenses 49
Wiig and Semel, assessments, older children and adults 45
Wilcox and Webster, clarification and repair 20
wipe boards 113
Wirz, assessment learning difficulties 45
Wolff and McGuire, literature review 140
word-finding difficulty 29, 133, 138, 139

Z

'zone of proximal development' (ZPD) 6

Working with... the Complete Series

In dealing with day-to-day management of clients, the Speechmark Working with... series has established an enviable reputation as the essential resource for every speech and language professional. The following titles are available:

Working with Adults with a Learning Disability
Alex Kelly

This comprehensive and practical resource covers all aspects of working with adults with a learning disability. Topics covered include: assessment of clients and their environment; profound and multiple disability; challenging behaviour; augmentative and alternative communication; social skills and dysphagia. In addition the author addresses staff training, group therapy, accessing the criminal justice system and working within a multidisciplinary team. A revised version of the author's popular *Personal Communication Plan* is included.

Working with Children's Language
Jackie Cooke & Diana Williams

Containing a wealth of ideas and a wide range of activities, the practical approach to language teaching has helped establish this book as a leading manual in its field. Games, activities and ideas suitable for developing specific language skills make this handbook a valuable resource for everyone working with children.

Working with Children's Phonology
Gwen Lancaster & Lesley Pope

Successfully bridging the gap between theory and practice, this book provides a wealth of creative ideas for lively and entertaining activities for therapy. This thoroughly practical manual also examines recent advances in the analysis and description of phonological disorders and describes their management within the clinic.

Working with Dysarthrics
Sandra Robertson & Fay Thomson

This is a unique source of ideas for individual and group speech therapy with patients who have dysarthria as a result of acquired neurological damage.

Current theory on the problems of dysarthria and assessment procedures as well as the principles, goals and efficacy of treatment are discussed. These are linked with practical activities and large print exercises to improve all aspects of motor speech.

Working with Dysfluent Children
Trudy Stewart & Jackie Turnbull

This essential manual analyses dysfluency in children and provides the reader with practical ways of handling these difficulties in collaboration with the child, parents and carers.

Complete with case studies, key summaries, notes on teaching the easy onset technique, lists of therapy resources and a comprehensive index, this text will be an essential reference for all those involved in working with dysfluent children.

Working with Dyspraxics
Susan Huskins

This informative working manual brings together current findings on dyspraxia of speech in adults and presents a meaningful approach to its assessment, diagnosis and treatment.

The author deals lucidly with a wide range of topics – from differential diagnosis to specific therapy procedures and alternative methods of communication.

Articulatory diagrams are included; these are arranged phonetically for ease of access and may be photocopied.

Working with Oral Cancer
Julia Appleton & Jane Machin

This addition to the series presents clinicians with a practical working knowledge of swallowing and speech disorders arising as a result of surgery for carcinoma of the oral cavity.

With very little written matter presently available on this specialist subject area, this title will be invaluable to therapists and students who wish to develop new skills or would like to build on existing knowledge.

Working with Pragmatics
Lucie Andersen-Wood & Benita Rae Smith

Covering the principles and practice of pragmatics and firmly grounded in theory, this title contains practical teaching activities to help develop communication skills. Assessment and diagnostic measures are also provided. The appendices contain a useful literature review and a list of the characteristics of pragmatic dysfunction. There are also photocopiable materials including a client-centred assessment form and child and client information sheets. A comprehensive bibliography and index complete this excellent resource. A ground-breaking title written by speech & language therapists who have also worked together as senior lecturers on this topic.

Working with Swallowing Disorders
Judith Langley

This practical book examines in detail the structures and processes involved in eating and drinking. Every aspect is considered, from the senses of taste and smell and the value of oral hygiene to the neural organisation of chewing and swallowing, as well as the significance of breakdowns in any of the functions involved.

The reader will find a wealth of sound advice and helpful suggestions for developing individual swallowing rehabilitation programmes in addition to thorough assessment procedures.

Working with Voice Disorders
Stephanie Martin & Myra Lockhart

This new title provides an essential resource for clinicians of varying levels of experience from student to specialist. It follows the client's journey along the health continuum from disorder back to health, providing practical insights and direction in all aspects of patient management. The authors provide a sound theoretical framework to this specialism and offer a rich variety of photocopiable, practical resource material.

The multi-dimensional structure of the book allows the clinician to examine specific aspects of patient management, as well as issues of clinical effectiveness, clinical governance and service management. The clinician-friendly, patient-centred approach makes this an essential resource.

These are just a few of the many therapy resources available from Winslow. A free catalogue will be sent on request. For further information please contact:

**Telford Road • Bicester
Oxon • OX26 4LQ • UK
Tel: (01869) 244644
Fax: (01869) 320040
www.speechmark.net**

Related Resources

Children's Phonology Sourcebook by Lesley Flynn & Gwen Lancaster;
Dysarthria Sourcebook by Sandra Robertson, Barbara Tanner & Fay Young;
Dysfluency Resource Book by Jackie Turnbull & Trudy Stewart;
The Voice Sourcebook by Stephanie Martin & Lyn Darnley.